VITAL SIGNS

1996

VITAL SIGNS 1996

The Trends That Are Shaping Our Future

with

Janet N. Abramovitz   Anne E. Platt

Anjali Acharya   Michael Renner

Hilary F. French   David M. Roodman

Gary Gardner   Aaron Sachs

Nicholas Lenssen   Odil Tunali

Toni Nelson

Lester R. Brown
Christopher Flavin
Hal Kane

Editor: Linda Starke

W.W. Norton & Company

New York   London

VITAL SIGNS and WORLDWATCH INSTITUTE trademarks are registered in the U.S. Patent
and Trademark Office.

The views expressed are those of the authors and do not necessarily represent those of
the Worldwatch Institute; of its directors, officers, or staff; or of its funders.

The text of this book is composed in Garth Graphic
with the display set in Industria Alternate.

Composition by Worldwatch Institute; manufacturing by the Haddon Craftsmen, Inc.
Book design by Charlotte Staub.

ISBN 0-393-03928-5
ISBN 0-393-31426-X (pbk)

W.W. Norton & Company, Inc.
500 Fifth Avenue, New York, N.Y. 10110
W.W. Norton & Company Ltd.
10 Coptic Street, London WC1A 1PU

1 2 3 4 5 6 7 8 9 0

This book is printed on recycled paper

CONTENTS

Part One: KEY INDICATORS

Part Two: SPECIAL FEATURES

ACKNOWLEDGMENTS

A work that covers the wide-ranging subject matter found in *Vital Signs* can only be accomplished with the generous help and support of many people. The research and writing of *Vital Signs* is funded by three organizations. The Surdna Foundation helped launch the series in 1992. The W. Alton Jones Foundation and the U.N. Population Fund both provided financial support for this volume.

Vital Signs grows out of the Institute's entire research program and its extensive information-gathering system. So we would also like to thank those funders that make all our research possible. They include the Carolyn, Cummings, Geraldine R. Dodge, Energy, Ford, George Gund, William and Flora Hewlett, John D. and Catherine T. MacArthur, Andrew W. Mellon, Curtis and Edith Munson, Edward John Noble, Turner, Wallace Genetic, Weeden, and Winslow foundations; The Pew Memorial Trusts; the Lynn R. and Karl E. Prickett Fund; the Rockefeller Brothers Fund; and Rockefeller Financial Services.

As she has for every edition of *Vital Signs*, and for every edition of *State of the World*, independent editor Linda Starke has anchored the project with her always careful attention to detail and her endless memory of what was written in earlier editions. For research assistance, we would like to thank Tonje Vetleseter, who worked ably with a wider range of subject matter and a larger number of researchers than anyone should have to deal with. Reah Janise Kauffman assisted the senior author with his contribution of individual indicators and with the overview chapter, while Toni Nelson provided research support. And for production support, we would like to thank Lori Baldwin, Suzanne Clift, and Laura Malinowski.

This year a special welcoming acknowledgment goes to Jennifer Seher, who produced *Vital Signs* in-house, on our own computer, for the first time. This let us make changes to the text at a later stage in the production process, it has simplified production, and, perhaps most important, it will reduce publishing costs substantially over the years.

Many experts, professors, professionals, statisticians, and others have provided information and reviewed early drafts. We would like to thank Nils Borg, Pete Burr, John R. Christy, Jane Dignon, Peter du Pont, Paul Epstein, Sharon Getamal, Paul Gipe, James Hansen, Carl Haub, Lori Heise, Paul Hunt, Peter Johnson, John Lawson, Stuart Levy, Birger Madsen, Sandra Marquardt, Paul Maycock, Jens Peter Molly, Stephen Morse, Steve Nadel, Maurizio Perotti, Carl Smith, Daniel Tarantola, Timothy Whorf, and Dana Younger.

At W.W. Norton & Company, we are grateful to Iva Ashner, Amy Cherry, Patricia Anthonyson, and their colleagues for their uncommon efficiency and good humor throughout the production process.

Lester R. Brown
Christopher Flavin
Hal Kane

FOREWORD

This fifth edition of *Vital Signs: The Trends That Are Shaping Our Future* will, we believe, be more useful than ever in allowing policymakers, journalists, and academic researchers to chart and understand the major ecological, economic, and social forces affecting the world. In 1996, we have included 33 key indicators, most of which present data from 1950 through 1995, and an additional 12 special features.

This year's report, produced by 14 contributing researchers, includes most of the basic indicators we have been charting since 1992, such as world population, grain production, and carbon emissions. But it also incorporates 10 entirely new vital signs, all of them in Part 2. In this section, we continue to seek out new, less noticed, trends, many of which are not regularly charted by the world's national and international statistical agencies.

Among the disturbing trends described in these features are a resurgence of infectious diseases, including many that the world's health authorities thought were under control and gradually diminishing; growing threats to aquatic ecosystems, which have extinguished or endangered one fifth of all fish species; and the laying of 110 million landmines across 64 countries, which maim thousands of people each year, many of them children.

One of the trends covered for the first time in *Vital Signs 1996* is the rising insurance claims for weather-related disasters, which went from $16 billion for the decade of the eighties to $48 billion for just the first half of the nineties. Although this trend cannot be definitively linked to human-induced global climate change, the risk is high enough that many insurance companies are now reviewing their exposure to weather-related losses. Other new trends covered this year include bans on pesticide use, green taxes, and violence against women.

Despite the bleakness of many of these trends, *Vital Signs* continues to report on a number of encouraging developments. Markets for some of the technologies needed to create a sustainable global economy reached new highs in 1995, including a 15-percent rise in sales of the highly efficient compact fluorescent light bulbs, a 17-percent increase in shipments of photovoltaic cells, and a 33-percent increase in the installation of wind turbines. If such double-digit growth rates continue for a few more years, they will help curtail the emissions of sulfur dioxide, nitrogen oxides, and carbon dioxide that are documented elsewhere in the report.

Readers around the world continue to tell us about a range of new uses they are finding for *Vital Signs* statistics. For example, several major newspapers regularly download *Vital Signs* data from our Database Disk to create their own graphic representations of global trends. Many top government and industry officials say that they rely on *Vital Signs* for information in their policy deliberations.

It is not often that a work of reference excites people, but *Vital Signs* frequently does just that. Those coming across it for the first time are taken by its simplicity, historical perspective, and the expert commentary accompanying and explaining every trend. Rowland Morgan, reviewing *Vital Signs* in *The Guardian* in London, said, "Its cool appraisal of our planet makes all other works of reference look trivial."

So far, *Vital Signs* has been published in 17 languages, a market that we plan to continue expanding in the years ahead. We were pleased to add a Vietnamese edition of *Vital Signs 1995* and have signed a contract for a Chinese edition of this year's volume with the Institute of Scientific and Technical Information in Beijing.

Sales of the Institute's Database Disk, which includes all the data in *Vital Signs* plus those appearing in all other Worldwatch publications, reached a new high of 1,365 in 1995, up 57 percent from the year before.

Expanding our reach still further, the Institute launched a site on the World Wide Web this spring, which includes a press release, table of contents, two sample indicators from *Vital Signs 1996,* and full ordering information, including an on-line order form. You can reach us at http://www.worldwatch.org.

We continue to welcome your suggestions on how we can improve *Vital Signs,* and would also like to hear how you use the material contained in it.

Lester R. Brown
Christopher Flavin
Hal Kane
March 1996

Worldwatch Institute
1776 Massachusetts Ave., N.W.
Washington, D.C. 20036

VITAL SIGNS 1996

OVERVIEW

A Record-Setting Year

Lester R. Brown

The year 1995 brought new records for several of the most basic indicators affecting human welfare. For climate—the most pervasive indicator of all—it was the warmest year since recordkeeping began some 130 years ago. As temperatures were climbing, the world grain harvest was shrinking, making it the smallest since 1988. As a result, carryover stocks of grain dropped to 48 days of consumption, the lowest level ever.

The world economy grew by nearly 4 percent in 1995, pushing the output of goods and services to some $21 trillion and lifting income per person to $3,600, both new highs. China completed its fourth consecutive year of double-digit economic growth. International trade, responding to the liberalization of both trade and investment, also soared to a record high.

On the energy front, wide differences in the growth of various energy sources hinted at a restructuring of the world energy economy. The production of oil, coal, and natural gas each expanded by roughly 1 percent in 1995, but even this small gain was enough to push carbon emissions from fossil fuel burning to a new high. Nuclear power generation also expanded by nearly 1 percent.

In contrast, the harnessing of renewable energy was growing by leaps and bounds. Wind electric generation expanded by a phenomenal 33 percent and shipments of photovoltaic cells grew by 17 percent. While the 1,290 megawatts of new wind generating capacity in 1995 is still below the 2,000 megawatts of new nuclear capacity, the gap has narrowed dramatically. And it is likely that the growth in wind will eclipse that of nuclear power before the end of this decade.

Social trends in 1995 were not particularly encouraging. During the year, the world's population grew by 87 million, with more than 80 million added in developing countries, many of which already face shortages of cropland, water, and firewood. HIV infections jumped by a record 4.7 million, as the epicenter of the disease shifted from Africa to Asia. On the bright side, the campaign by the World Health Organization to eradicate polio, patterned after its successful effort to eradicate smallpox, has eliminated this crippling disease in 145 countries.

EARTH GETTING WARMER

The average global temperature in 1995 reached 15.39 degrees Celsius, breaking the previous mark of 15.38 degrees in 1990. (See pages 66–67.) Perhaps more important than this single-year record was the additional evi-

---

Units of measure throughout this book are metric unless common usage dictates otherwise. Historical population data used in per capita calculations are from the Center for International Research at the U.S. Bureau of the Census. Data in *Vital Signs* are updated each year, incorporating any revisions in series done by originating organizations.

dence it offered of a trend of rising temperatures since the late seventies. The 10 warmest years in the last 130 have all occurred in the eighties and nineties. And within these 10, the three warmest years were in the nineties. (See Figure 1.)

With atmospheric concentrations of heat-trapping carbon dioxide moving to a new high each year, continuing rises in temperature are likely. In 1995, carbon emissions from the burning of fossil fuels reached nearly 6.1 billion tons, breaking the previous record of just over 6.0 billion tons set in 1991. (See pages 64–65.) Among other things, this indicates that most governments of industrial societies are failing to meet the goal of limiting carbon emissions that was established by the Framework Convention on Climate Change signed at the 1992 Earth Summit. In 1995, the burning of oil, coal, and natural gas all edged upward, each contributing to the rise in carbon emissions. (See pages 48–53.)

Global climate models show that as temperatures rise, warmer oceans release more energy into the atmosphere, leading to more intense and violent storms. Illustrative of the new breed of more intense storms was a cyclone (hurricane) with winds of 270 kilometers per hour that hit Bangladesh in 1991, destroying more than a million homes and claiming 139,000 lives. When Hurricane Andrew hit Florida in August 1992, with winds of 235 kilometers per hour, it flattened 85,000 homes and left almost 300,000 people homeless. With $25 billion worth of damage, it was the most destructive storm in history. During the nineties, Europe has also faced storms of record intensity and destructiveness.

Worldwide, insurance industry payouts for weather-related damage have climbed from $16 billion during the eighties to $48 billion thus far during the nineties. (See pages 118–19.) The insurance industry, one of the world's largest, is reeling from this dramatic

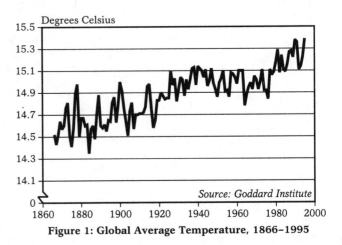

Figure 1: Global Average Temperature, 1866–1995

surge in claims. Voicing the fears of many in the industry, Franklin Nutter, president of the Reinsurance Association of America, says, "The insurance business is first in line to be affected by climate change...it could bankrupt the industry." As a result, industry leaders are now joining atmospheric scientists and environmentalists in urging governments to reduce dependence on fossil fuels and arrest the buildup in the atmospheric concentration of greenhouse gases.

FOOD BECOMING SCARCE

The insurance industry is not the only one affected by rising temperatures. Crop-withering heat waves in the summer of 1995 helped reduce the world grain harvest well below consumption, contributing to a steep drawdown in world grain stocks. (See pages 36–37.) In response, prices of wheat, rice, and other grains rose by nearly half during 1995.

The intense mid-summer heat wave that hit Chicago, with temperatures reaching daily highs of 101–06 degrees Fahrenheit, claimed some 660 lives and adversely affected agriculture. Each day the temperatures topped 100 in Chicago, on the northern edge of the Corn Belt, the U.S. corn harvest shrank a bit more. At harvest time, it was clear that this record-setting heat wave, along with high temperatures later in the summer, had sharply reduced the corn harvest. As the summer progressed, the U.S. Department of Agriculture lowered its estimate for the grain harvest across the northern tier of industrial countries—the United States, the European Union, the Ukraine, and Russia. The principal reason was crop-withering heat waves.

Although the world demand for food, driven by the annual addition of 87 million people and by record rises in affluence in Asia, is increasing by unprecedented amounts in the nineties, the world's farmers are no longer getting any help from fishers in expanding the food supply. In addition to contending with the highest prices for wheat, rice, and corn in many years, the world's consumers are faced with a rise in seafood prices that has been under way for many years.

Even as world grain supplies tightened, the demand for meat, a grain-intensive food, surged to record levels in many countries in Asia, led by China. (See pages 28–29.) Consumption of pork in China jumped by a phenomenal 14 percent in 1995, accounting for half of the growth in world meat consumption. This higher pork intake, combined with greater use of beef, further reinforces China's new position as the world's leading consumer of red meat. Total red meat consumption is now nearly double that of the United States.

GLOBAL ECONOMY EXPANDING

In 1995, the global economy grew by an estimated 3.7 percent, slightly more than the 3.6-percent gain in 1994 and the largest since the 4.6 percent growth of 1988. (See pages 74–75.) Although this impressive expansion raised the global output of goods and services per person by more than 2 percent, it also increased the unsustainable demands on the earth's natural systems and resources—croplands, aquifers, fisheries, rangelands, and forests.

Helping drive this growth in economic output was the liberalization of both investment and trade, two steps that greatly increased the flow of private capital into developing countries (see pages 116–17), most notably

into the larger nations in Asia, such as China, India, and Indonesia. Closely related to the growth in investment was an increase in trade as multinational corporations located manufacturing facilities in developing countries to take advantage of low wages and to gain access to their markets. (See pages 76–77.)

Economic growth in the developing countries averaged some 6 percent in 1995, more than double the 2.5 percent of the industrial regions. Within the developing regions, Asia, excluding Japan, expanded by 8.7 percent, marking the third consecutive year of growth in excess of 8 percent. The most rapid growth in the region occurred in China, which completed its fourth consecutive year of double-digit economic growth, expanding its economy by an astounding 57 percent in four years. This put it well ahead of the official goal of quadrupling its 1980 economy by the end of the century.

Within the former Eastern bloc, the economies that were among the first to reestablish growth following the shock of economic reform, such as Poland, the Czech Republic, Romania, and the Baltic States, continued to expand their economies. In contrast, the two major economies in the former Soviet Union—Russia and the Ukraine—continued to decline.

DISPARATE ENERGY TRENDS

The widely varying growth rates of various energy sources in 1995 provided further evidence of the expanding role of renewable energy resources and the movement toward a solar/hydrogen economy. Production of coal, oil, natural gas, and nuclear power each expanded by a meager 1 percent or so. (See pages 48–55.)

The dramatic energy output gains came in wind electric generation capacity, which expanded by 33 percent, and in the sales of photovoltaic (solar) cells, which climbed by 17 percent. (See pages 58–59.) Growth in wind generation capacity, which was once concentrated in the United States and Denmark, has now spread to other major economies, such as Germany and India. Germany led the world in new capacity in 1995 with 505 megawatts, closely followed by India with 375 megawatts.

With the World Bank now beginning to invest in renewable energy resources, and particularly in solar cells in those Third World villages not connected to power grids, this use of solar energy is also likely to multiply rapidly in the years ahead. As concern about the effects of global warming on food security and the insurance industry escalates, the pressure to shift to energy sources that do not disrupt climate seems certain to intensify. More and more international development agencies and national governments are beginning to support this shift.

The production of automobiles, the use of which accounts for much of the growth in oil production, increased by 1 percent in 1995, almost regaining the 1990 historical high of just over 36 million. (See pages 84–85.) As recently as 1969, when 23 million cars and 25 million bicycles were produced, the output of automobiles appeared ready to overtake that of bikes. But then came Earth Day 1970, with its rising environmental awareness, followed by the oil price hikes of the seventies. While automobile manufacture was climbing to 36 million, that of bicycles reached a staggering 114 million in 1995. (See pages 82–83 and Figure 2.)

The boom in bicycle manufacturing provided encouraging evidence of the growing demand for this energy-efficient transport vehicle. This growth, continuing a trend under way since 1969, reflects the bicycle's continuing popularity as an inexpensive and reliable form of transportation. China remains the world's leading manufacturer of bicycles, but India is now also emerging as a competitive producer and exporter. Mounting concern about air pollution, traffic congestion, carbon emissions, and land scarcity all augur well for the bicycle's future.

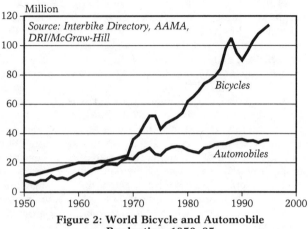

Figure 2: World Bicycle and Automobile Production, 1950–95

Another encouraging development on the energy efficiency front is the growth in sales of highly efficient compact fluorescent lamps to 240 million in 1995, an expansion of 15 percent. (See pages 60–61.) These lights, which use only one fourth as much electricity as traditional bulbs and last 10 times as long, are a key technology for reducing carbon emissions. Replacing one 75-watt incandescent bulb, which draws its electricity from a coal-fired power plant, with an 18-watt compact fluorescent will avoid more than a quarter of a ton of carbon emissions over the light bulb's lifetime. Much of the growth in the manufacturing of these bulbs in 1995 was concentrated in China, which has eclipsed the United States to become the world leader.

THE EARTH'S DETERIORATING PHYSICAL CONDITION

Key indicators show that the physical condition of the earth is deteriorating. The deforestation of the planet continues unabated, reducing the capacity of soils and vegetation to absorb and store water. The result is more rainfall runoff and soil erosion. The number of plant and animal species, perhaps the best single indicator of the earth's health, is diminishing.

One of the most distressing environmental

trends of the late twentieth century is the accelerating loss of freshwater fish species. (See pages 124–25.) An estimated 37 percent of the fish species that inhabit the lakes and streams of North America are either in jeopardy or extinct. Ten North American freshwater fish species have disappeared during the last decade. The situation may be even worse in Europe, where some 80 species of freshwater fish out of a total of 193 are threatened, endangered, or of special concern. Two thirds of the 94 fish species in South Africa need special protection to avoid extinction. Worldwide, the principal causes of this loss are habitat degradation in the form of pollution and the growing human demand for the water in freshwater ecosystems.

Forests, too, are disappearing. (See pages 122–23.) The forests that once blanketed more than 40 percent of the earth's land surface now cover only 27 percent of it. Most of the loss has occurred since 1950. Beginning at mid-century, much of the disappearance of the world's forest cover was concentrated in the tropical and subtropical regions as a result of the clearance of forestland for farming, the logging of tropical hardwoods, and firewood gathering. But now heavy damage is occurring in the northern temperate zone as well. Canada may now be losing a million hectares of forest cover annually. Even worse destruction is occurring in Siberia, which may now be losing 4 million hectares a year.

One of the threats to both freshwater fish and forests is the acid rain that is associated with emissions of sulfur and nitrous oxides from the burning of fossil fuels. While these emissions are falling in Eastern Europe and the former Soviet Union as the economic depression lowers coal use there, they are rising in China and India, where prosperity is boosting coal use. (See pages 70–71.) Overall, emissions of sulfur and nitrous oxides in 1993 (the most recent year for which data are available) are estimated at 70 and 27 million tons, respectively, roughly the same as in 1992.

KEY SOCIAL TRENDS

In 1995, the world added an estimated 87 million people to its population, as many people as live in the United Kingdom, Belgium, Denmark, Norway, and Sweden. (See pages 88–89.) And the overwhelming majority were added in developing countries—where forests are shrinking, soils are eroding, and aquifers are being depleted.

Within this larger trend of massive growth, there were some encouraging reductions. For example, in India, the annual increment fell from 17 million in 1993 to 15.6 million in 1995. The average number of children born to a woman in her lifetime in India dropped from 3.9 in 1993 to 3.4 in 1995.

In some countries, population growth is slowing, but for the wrong reasons. In Russia, the combination of economic deterioration and environmental pollution has raised death rates, while a loss of hope in the future has lowered birth rates. Together, they reduced Russia's population, excluding migration, by 0.6 percent in 1995. This is the most rapid decline on record for a country not at war. The net effect in Russia of this excess of deaths over births is an annual loss of roughly 880,000 people.

In Zimbabwe, births still exceed deaths, but by much less than a few years ago because AIDS-related deaths are increasing. (See pages 88–89.) As recently as 1992, Zimbabwe added an estimated 250,000 people, an annual growth of roughly 2.2 percent. In 1995, only 100,000 people were added, dropping population growth to only 0.9 percent.

Another important health indicator—the number of cigarettes produced per person in the world—declined, dropping from 972 in 1994 to 966 in 1995. (See pages 90–91.) Despite this encouraging per capita decline, the number of cigarettes produced in the world increased, with the growth being particularly dramatic in the Third World. As cigarette-related mortality begins to increase in developing countries, the worldwide death toll from smoking is rising. The World Health Organization (WHO) now estimates worldwide smoking-related deaths at roughly 3 million people a year, up from earlier estimates of 2 million.

While cigarette deaths are climbing, a combination of growing resistance to antibiotics, a decline in public health services, and increased growth in urban populations is leading to a resurgence of traditional infectious diseases such as tuberculosis and malaria. (See pages 130–31.) In 1993, the latest year for which data are available, tuberculosis took 2.7 million lives and malaria, 2 million. Exacting an even greater toll were acute respiratory infections, which claimed 4.1 million lives, and diarrheal diseases, which killed 3 million people, mainly children. Among major infectious diseases, AIDS is growing most rapidly and is likely within a matter of years to move to the top of the list. (See pages 92–93.)

Another newer toll of human health is 20,000 annual pesticide-related deaths, according to WHO. In response to these deaths and to other possible adverse health effects of pesticides on farm workers, efforts to ban the most destructive pest control agents have gained momentum over the last decade. (See pages 108–09.) In 1983, there were 53 national bans on one or another of 18 of the world's most hazardous pesticides. By 1995, this had increased to 689.

KEEPING THE PEACE

There was good news and bad news about international peacekeeping in 1995. The good news was that the war in Bosnia came to an end late in the year. Also in this category, the U.N. Security Council is functioning much more as it was intended to. Since the end of the cold war and the ideological conflict that divided this body into rival camps, the use of the veto has dropped to a near negligible level, enabling the United Nations to respond to various conflicts and other crises in a more unified way. The bad news is that many U.N. members failed to pay their share of peace-keeping expenses. (See pages 102–03.) In August 1995, they were behind in their assessments by a record $2.95 billion—close

to a full year's expenditures. This forced the U.N. Secretary General to do an extraordinary juggling of U.N. accounts just to keep food supplies flowing to the peacekeeping troops in the field.

Despite growing opposition to the use of landmines, the number of these instruments of terror in place around the world increased again in 1995. (See pages 132–33.) An estimated 110 million landmines are now scattered throughout the countryside in 64 countries. In some of the most severely affected countries, 20-60 mines are found per square kilometer. The tragedy of this situation was summed up by a question posed in the European Parliament: "What crop costs a hundred times more to reap than to plant and has no market value when harvested?"

One consequence of conflict, including the placement of millions of landmines, is displaced people. Last year, the number of refugees eligible for U.N. assistance jumped by a record 4.4 million—from 23.0 million in 1994 to 27.4 million in 1995. (See pages 96–97.) For this indicator of social stress, the trend in recent years has been all too strongly upward.

One last bit of good news is worth noting: nuclear arsenals continue to decline. Not only did the number of nuclear weapons decline from 44,500 in 1994 to 40,640 in 1995—a drop of one tenth—but serious efforts are under way to phase these weapons of total destruction out entirely. (See pages 100–01.) In December 1995, the Australian government announced formation of the Canberra Commission on the Elimination of Nuclear Weapons, a bold initiative designed to free the world of all nuclear weapons.

Part

Key Indicators

Food
Trends

World Grain Production Falls

Lester R. Brown

The 1995 world grain harvest of 1,680 million tons, the smallest in seven years, was down 67 million tons from the 1994 harvest of 1,745 million tons, a drop of nearly 4 percent.[1] (See Figure 1.) Of more concern, it was down exactly 100 million tons from the bumper harvest of 1990 that launched the decade.[2]

The steady growth in the world grain harvest from 1950 to 1990 has stalled during the nineties. With population continuing to grow by nearly 90 million per year, the amount of grain produced per person is falling.[3] (See Figure 2.) The 1995 harvest of 293 kilograms per person—the lowest since 1965—is down 5 percent from the 309 kilograms in 1994.[4] And it is 15 percent below the historic peak of 346 kilograms in 1984.[5]

After rising more than 1 percent a year from 1950 to 1984, the grain harvest per person declined by more than 1 percent a year during the following 11 years, indicating a new trend--one that may be difficult to reverse.[6]

The widening gap between the growing world demand for grain and static production over the last five years has been partially offset by drawing down stocks. Between 1991 and 1996, carryover stocks of grain, the amount of grain in the bin when the new harvest begins, dropped from 342 million tons to 229 million tons.[7] This average decline of some 22 million tons per year helped compensate for the lack of growth in production since 1990. But now that stocks are down to little more than pipeline supplies, supply and demand are being balanced by rising prices.

There are several reasons for the decline in the 1995 grain harvest, but among these, weather stands out. The two countries most affected by adverse growing conditions in 1995 were the United States and Russia. A cold, wet spring in the U.S. Corn Belt delayed planting beyond the point where maximum yields could be expected. Crop-withering summer heat waves reduced both the U.S. and the Russian grain harvest.

The levelling off of world grain production since 1990 is due largely to the decline in world fertilizer use since 1989.[8] From 1950

until 1989, the steady rise in fertilizer use was one of the most predictable of all global economic trends. Since then, fertilizer use has dropped sharply. Much of the actual decline has occurred in the former Soviet Union as a result of the economic reforms launched in 1988.[9] Shifting from heavily subsidized fertilizer prices to world market prices led to a precipitous fall in Soviet fertilizer use. Meanwhile, fertilizer use was levelling off or declining slightly in other major food-producing regions, such as North America and Europe.[10] U.S. farmers are using somewhat less fertilizer in the mid-nineties than they did in the early eighties.[11]

Over the last half-century, farmers have relied on expanding irrigation, expanding fertilizer use, and the adoption of ever higher yielding varieties to raise output. But this potent combination is no longer bringing the rapid sustained growth that dominated the period from 1950 until roughly 1990.

In a world where fertilizer use is no longer steadily rising, raising land productivity is difficult. The negative forces that affect production, such as soil erosion, the conversion of grainland to nonfarm uses, and spreading water scarcity, now loom much larger. The cumulative effects of soil erosion may be more visible in years when fertilizer use is no longer rising. With world grainland area shrinking, with the amount of irrigation water declining in many areas, and with a slow decline in the amount of topsoil available to produce food, it is much more difficult for farmers to satisfy the needs of 90 million additional people each year.[12]

In the fall of 1995, the U.S. Department of Agriculture announced that it would be releasing for production in 1996 the modest amount of remaining commodity set-aside land.[13] The European Union disclosed that it would reduce the grainland being held out of production from 12 percent in 1995 to 10 percent in 1996.[14] But given the gap that is unfolding between growing world demand for grain and its production, even returning all the European cropland to production is not likely to be enough both to satisfy expanding world demand and to rebuild stocks.

WORLD GRAIN PRODUCTION, 1950–95

YEAR	TOTAL (mill. tons)	PER CAPITA (kilograms)
1950	631	247
1955	759	273
1960	847	279
1965	917	274
1966	1,005	294
1967	1,029	295
1968	1,069	301
1969	1,078	297
1970	1,096	296
1971	1,194	316
1972	1,156	299
1973	1,272	323
1974	1,220	304
1975	1,250	306
1976	1,363	328
1977	1,337	316
1978	1,467	341
1979	1,428	326
1980	1,447	325
1981	1,499	331
1982	1,550	336
1983	1,486	317
1984	1,649	346
1985	1,664	343
1986	1,683	341
1987	1,612	321
1988	1,564	306
1989	1,685	324
1990	1,780	336
1991	1,696	315
1992	1,776	316
1993	1,703	307
1994	1,745	309
1995 (prel)	1,680	293

SOURCES: USDA, *World Grain Database* (unpublished printouts), 1991; USDA, "Production, Supply, and Demand View" (electronic database), January 1996; USDA, "World Agricultural Supply and Demand Estimates," January 1996; USDA, *Grain: World Markets and Trade*, January 1996.

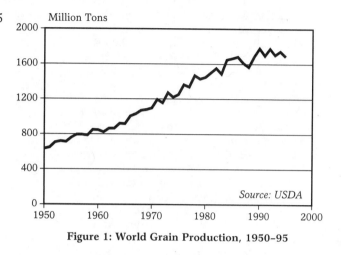

Figure 1: World Grain Production, 1950–95

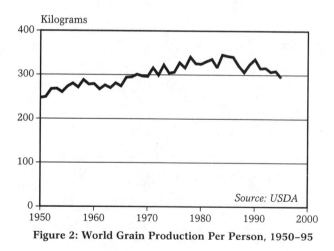

Figure 2: World Grain Production Per Person, 1950–95

Soybean Production Drops
Lester R. Brown

The 1995 world soybean harvest of 125 million tons was down 8 percent from the all-time record of 136 million tons in 1994.[1] (See Figure 1.) Worldwide, the per capita soybean supply dropped from just over 24 kilograms to just under 22, a decline of nearly one tenth.[2] (See Figure 2.)

Most of the drop in the harvest came in the United States, where adverse weather took a toll on the crop in all phases—at planting time, during the growing season, and near the harvest. The year began with a cold, wet spring in the U.S. Midwest that delayed planting, diminishing the prospects for high yields. Blistering heat waves during the summer also hurt the crop. And then in the fall, early frosts in some midwestern states further reduced the harvest.

Despite weather setbacks, U.S. farmers brought in nearly 60 millon tons of beans, just under half the total.[3] Brazil, China, and Argentina accounted for most of the remainder.[4] Together, these four countries produce 88 percent of the world harvest.[5]

In yield per hectare, the United States, Brazil, and Argentina are remarkably close, with the United States having a slight edge at 2.4 tons per hectare and Brazil and Argentina at 2.1 and 2.2 tons per hectare, respectively.[6] Farmers in China, where the soybean originated, average only 1.6 tons per hectare.[7]

Soybeans continue to dominate the world oilseed economy, accounting for half of the 253-million-ton harvest of all oilseeds, which includes peanuts, sunflower, rapeseed, cottonseed, coconuts, and palm kernels.[8]

In each major producing country, the lion's share of the harvest is crushed, converting it into oil and oilseed meal. The meal, accounting for more than four fifths of the soybean by weight, is the more valuable product.[9] The world livestock, poultry, and aquacultural industries depend on soybean meal for perhaps 60 percent of the protein meal they use to supplement the vast quantities of grain that they feed.[10] In effect, soybean meal is a near-universal protein supplement used by farmers throughout the world to upgrade their feed supplies, increasing the efficiency with which grain is converted into animal protein.

Soybeans figure prominently in world agricultural trade. The United States is expected to export nearly 22 million tons (more than one third) of its 1995 harvest as whole beans.[11] Brazil, with just under 4 million tons, ranks second as an exporter of beans.[12] Together, these two countries totally dominate world soybean exports.

Exports of whole beans go largely to the European Union and East Asia. The former takes 15 million tons, compared with just under 5 million tons for Japan.[13] Other principal importers are Taiwan (2.6 million tons) and South Korea (1.3 million tons).[14]

In many countries, producers rotate soybeans with cereal crops. In the United States, land use in the Corn Belt is dominated by the corn/soybean rotation. By planting soybeans, a legume, in alternate years, farmers build up the nitrogen supply that is so important for corn. In some situations, farmers plant wheat as a winter crop and soybeans in the summer.

In the United States, the soybean harvest has eclipsed the wheat harvest in value. It now trails only the corn crop in total worth.[15]

As incomes rise in Asia, where more than half the world's people live, the demand for vegetable oils for cooking is rising rapidly. This can be seen in both China and India, which together contain 2.1 billion people.[16] China actually has a surplus of soybean meal, which it exports, while it is a major net importer of vegetable oil.[17] If its demand for livestock products continues to climb, however, the exportable surplus of soybean meal may soon disappear. India sells even more soybean meal abroad, some 2.3 million tons, while importing soybean oil.[18]

World carryover stocks of soybeans in 1996 are projected at 17.5 million tons, down from 25.8 million tons the year before.[19] This is not an all-time low, but it is well below the long-term average. The reduced 1995 harvest in the United States, and to a lesser degree in Brazil, dropped world soybean production well below consumption in 1995/96.[20]

WORLD SOYBEAN PRODUCTION, 1950–95

YEAR	TOTAL (mill. tons)	PER CAPITA (kilograms)
1950	17	6
1955	19	7
1960	25	8
1965	32	9
1966	36	11
1967	38	11
1968	42	12
1969	42	12
1970	44	12
1971	47	12
1972	49	13
1973	62	16
1974	55	14
1975	66	16
1976	59	14
1977	72	17
1978	78	18
1979	94	21
1980	81	18
1981	86	19
1982	94	20
1983	83	18
1984	93	20
1985	97	20
1986	98	20
1987	103	21
1988	95	19
1989	106	21
1990	103	20
1991	106	20
1992	116	21
1993	117	21
1994	136	24
1995 (prel)	125	22

SOURCES: USDA, "Production, Supply, and Demand View" (electronic database), January 1996; USDA, "Oilseeds: World Markets and Trade," October 1995.

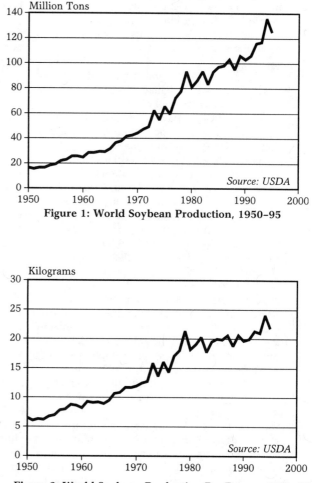

Figure 1: World Soybean Production, 1950–95

Figure 2: World Soybean Production Per Person, 1950–95

Meat Production Climbs Sharply Lester R. Brown

In 1995, world meat production climbed some 4 percent, going from 184 million tons in 1994 to nearly 192 million tons.[1] (See Figure 1.) Meat production per person climbed from 32.7 kilograms per person in 1994 to a record 33.4 kilograms in 1995.[2] (See Figure 2.)

World meat production is responding to the rapid growth in demand, especially in East Asia. Four years of double-digit economic growth in China have led to record meat production gains.[3] Its poultry meat output has doubled over the last four years.[4]

As economic expansion accelerates in the Indian subcontinent, consumption of livestock products is rising. Although starting from very low levels, the production of all livestock products, including poultry, eggs, milk, and even beef, is on the rise. India's broiler industry, for example, which had roughly 30 million birds in 1980, climbed to 300 million in 1995.[5] India's production of beef and veal in 1995 totalled 1.1 million tons, up from 920,000 tons in 1991—a rise of 12 percent.[6] The demand for meat is also rising in several smaller Asian countries, reflecting their rapid economic gains. The demand for beef in South Korea, for example, went up by an estimated 10 percent in 1995.[7]

While consumption of livestock products was climbing in Asia, it was actually declining in Europe. In Eastern Europe, the drop was largely the result of economic reforms and the associated economic disruption. In Russia, for instance, per capita consumption of beef has dropped from nearly 37 kilograms in 1990 to 21 kilograms in 1995, a fall of 40 percent.[8] In Germany, meanwhile, beef consumption per person has dropped from 19 kilograms in 1990 to less than 17 kilograms in 1995—a decline of one tenth—largely because of worries about the possible presence of growth hormones in beef and concerns about fat intake.[9] German pork consumption dropped even more during the same period.[10]

In the United States, by contrast, per capita consumption of all major meats has increased during the nineties. Between 1990 and 1995, beef consumption per person increased by 1 percent, pork by 6 percent, and poultry by more than 10 percent.[11]

The worldwide growth in meat consumption in 1995 was led by pork, which climbed by more than 6 percent.[12] (See Figure 3.) China accounted for almost all this increase, boosting its pork intake by a phenomenal 14 percent.[13]

Beef production grew for a second consecutive year, expanding by more than 2 percent.[14] Over half the worldwide growth was accounted for by China, which has raised its beef consumption per person from 1.0 kilograms in 1990 to 3.6 kilograms in 1995.[15]

After many years of leading the other meats in growth, poultry production grew by only 2.9 percent in 1995, down from 7.2 percent in 1994.[16] In China, poultry output went up by only 1 percent in 1995 as farmers were squeezed by the steep rise in feed prices.[17]

After years of little or no gains in world mutton production, output jumped by 3 percent in 1995, largely because wool prices are recovering from their collapse in the mid-eighties.[18] China's production expanded by roughly 25 percent in 1995 and is projected to grow by a comparable amount in 1996.[19]

World pork production is dominated by China, which produced 37 million tons in 1995—nearly half the world total of just under 80 million tons.[20] The United States, a distant second, produced only 8 million tons.[21]

With beef, the United States leads, accounting for roughly one fifth of world production with 11.5 million tons.[22] The European Union is second with 8 million tons, followed by Brazil with 4.6 million tons.[23]

The United States also leads the world in poultry production, accounting for nearly 14 million tons out of the global total of 50 million.[24] China is now second, with 7.5 million tons, followed by Brazil and France.[25]

The surge in world meat production in the last two years reflects a robust growth in the world economy, with much of the increase concentrated in lower- and middle-income countries in Asia. With world feedgrain prices up by more than a third during 1995, however, it remains to be seen whether the steady rise in production will continue through 1996.[26]

WORLD MEAT PRODUCTION, 1950–95

YEAR	TOTAL (mill. tons)	PER CAPITA (kilograms)
1950	44	17.2
1955	58	20.7
1960	64	21.0
1965	81	24.2
1966	84	24.5
1967	86	24.5
1968	88	24.8
1969	92	25.5
1970	97	26.2
1971	101	26.7
1972	106	27.4
1973	105	26.8
1974	107	26.6
1975	109	26.7
1976	112	26.9
1977	117	27.6
1978	121	28.2
1979	126	28.8
1980	130	29.1
1981	132	29.2
1982	134	29.0
1983	138	29.4
1984	142	29.7
1985	146	30.1
1986	152	30.8
1987	157	31.2
1988	164	32.1
1989	166	31.9
1990	171	32.4
1991	173	32.1
1992	175	31.9
1993	177	31.9
1994	184	32.7
1995 (prel)	192	33.4

SOURCES: FAO, *1948-1985 World Crop and Livestock Statistics* (1987); FAO, *FAO Production Yearbooks 1988-1991*; USDA, *Livestock and Poultry: World Markets and Trade*, October 1995.

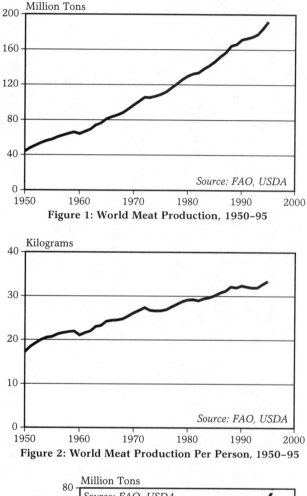

Figure 1: World Meat Production, 1950–95

Figure 2: World Meat Production Per Person, 1950–95

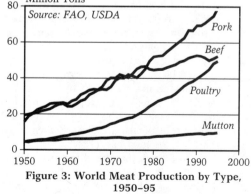

Figure 3: World Meat Production by Type, 1950–95

World Fish Harvest Hits New High
Anne E. Platt

The total fish harvest, which includes both the fish catch and fish farming output, climbed to 109 million tons in 1994, up from 102 million tons in 1993.[1] (See Figure 1.) This 7-percent increase in production came primarily from expanding aquaculture and larger catches in China, Peru, and Chile.[2] These countries accounted for 37 percent of the world catch; Japan, the United States, India, and the former Soviet Union contributed 20 percent.[3]

The world fish catch climbed to 91.1 million tons in 1994, up 5.8 percent from 86.1 million tons in 1993, and 2.7 percent above the peak catch of 88.7 million tons in 1989. Of the total catch, an estimated 6.6 million tons were caught in inland waters, while 84.5 million tons were caught in marine areas in 1994.[4] The per capita fish harvest reached 19.3 kilograms in 1994, up from the previous year but slightly below the peak of 19.4 kilograms in 1988.[5] (See Figure 2.)

Despite the growth in total harvest, supplies cannot keep pace with increasing population. To meet growing demand for fish, tough choices are required. To increase aquacultural output, grain stocks and water supplies must be diverted from direct human consumption to fish production. To boost fish catch, countries must reduce fishing effort and allow marine stocks to rebuild. Otherwise, there will be a grim future for the more than 20 million people whose livelihoods depend on fishing and the 1 billion people in developing countries for whom fish is the primary source of protein.[6]

Reducing bycatch is one way to allow stocks to rebound. In the Gulf of Mexico shrimp fishery, for example, 80 percent of all fish caught—an estimated 450,000 tons annually—is discarded in the process, damaged, or killed.[7] This is creating a growing deficit of juvenile and mature stocks of key commercial species, threatening the long-term health of the Gulf fishery. Globally, an estimated 27 million tons of fish are discarded each year, a fourth of the total harvest.[8]

Even though the global harvest is at an all-time high, many species have been overfished, forcing a switch to lower-value, less preferred ones.[9] Groundfish such as cod, haddock, and flounder used to be plentiful in the Northwest Atlantic, for instance, but squid, dogfish, and skate now dominate there.[10] Bluefin, skipjack, and yellowfin tuna stocks have been devastated in parts of the Atlantic and South Pacific, due to increasing pressure from fleets far from their home ports.[11] Changes in composition and abundance of species can hurt both the health of marine ecosystems and the economies based on fisheries.[12]

Protests, disputes, and even violence plagued the fishing industry in 1995. Canadian patrol boats seized Spanish trawlers in international waters off Newfoundland, while Iceland and Norway battled for fishing rights in the Barents Sea and Arctic waters.[13] More than 7.5 million Indian fishers went on strike to protest joint ventures with foreign fleets.[14] In southeast Asia, several countries used their navies and security forces to detain vessels and capture illegal fishers.[15] And on the Galápagos Islands, displaced Ecuadoran fishers took up arms and held hostages.[16]

Worldwide, quota reductions, fishery closures, job layoffs, and ships lying idle at port signal the need for a fundamental overhaul of fisheries management and conservation principles.

On paper, 1995 was a very good year for marine fisheries. The United Nations Conference on Straddling Fish Stocks and Highly Migratory Fish Stocks adopted a binding international treaty late in the year.[17] Although specifics are conspicuously lacking, these principles have been accepted as official supplements to the globally recognized Law of the Sea.[18] And members of the U.N. Food and Agriculture Organization moved closer to passing a voluntary Code of Conduct for Responsible Fisheries that calls for more selective fishing gear to reduce bycatch.[19]

Implementing global agreements quickly will lay a solid foundation for improving fisheries management. Without the political will to further reduce fishing effort in the short term, however, and without the cooperation of fishers themselves, conflicts will continue and fish supplies for human consumption will decline.

WORLD FISH HARVEST, 1950–94

YEAR	TOTAL (mill. tons)	PER CAPITA (kilograms)
1950	21	8.6
1955	29	10.4
1960	40	12.5
1965	54	16.1
1966	57	16.7
1967	61	17.2
1968	64	18.0
1969	63	17.4
1970	66	17.8
1971	66	17.5
1972	62	16.1
1973	63	16.0
1974	67	16.7
1975	66	16.2
1976	69	16.6
1977	68	16.1
1978	70	16.3
1979	71	16.2
1980	72	16.2
1981	75	16.6
1982	77	16.7
1983	78	16.4
1984	84	17.6
1985	86	17.7
1986	93	18.8
1987	95	18.9
1988	99	19.4
1989	100	19.2
1990	98	18.5
1991	98	18.2
1992	99	18.1
1993	102	18.4
1994	109	19.3

SOURCES: FAO, *Yearbook of Fishery Statistics: Catches and Landings* (various years); 1994 data, FAO, Rome, private communication, January 25, 1996.

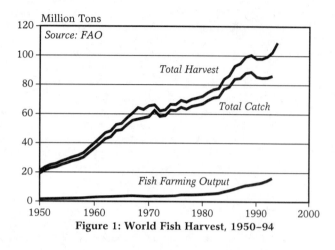

Figure 1: World Fish Harvest, 1950–94

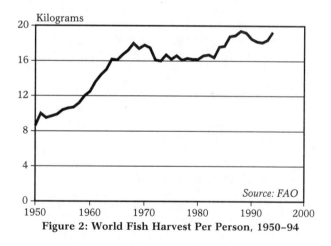

Figure 2: World Fish Harvest Per Person, 1950–94

Aquaculture Production Rises Anjali Acharya

Fish farming, or aquaculture, produced 16.3 million tons of fish in 1993, the latest year for which data are available—more than double the 6.9 million tons produced in 1984.[1] (See Figure 1.) Global aquaculture production expanded during those nine years at an average annual rate of 10 percent by quantity and almost 14 percent by value.[2]

Aquaculture produces three commodities (excluding plants): about two thirds is finfish such as tilapia, salmon, and flounders; one fourth is mollusks such as oysters and mussels; and the remainder is crustaceans such as shrimps and prawns.[3] Inland rivers, lakes, ponds, and artificial tanks account for two thirds of the output.[4] The rest is coastal mariculture—grown in bays or the open ocean.[5]

In 1993, aquaculture accounted for two thirds of the world's supply of freshwater finfish, 43 percent of the mollusks, and almost 90 percent of the mussels.[6] More than a third of all salmon and a quarter of shrimps and prawns are raised by fish farmers.[7] By contrast, aquaculture produces under 1 percent of the world's supply of marine fish.[8]

Asia dominates world fish farming—with 86 percent of global production in 1993.[9] (See Figure 2.) China, the traditional home of fish farming, contributes 63 percent of Asia's production and more than half the total world output.[10] In India—the second largest producer—aquaculture provides almost a third of its total catch.[11] Other major producers include Japan, at 900,000 tons; Indonesia, at 600,000 tons; and the Philippines, Thailand, and the United States, with about 400,000 tons each.[12]

Aquaculture output is now valued at almost $30 billion—three times the figure in 1984.[13] Individual species vary widely in value, ranging from those used for fishmeal, at less than $100 a ton, to luxury species such as lobsters, at more than $10,000.[14] The production of high-priced shrimp has dominated the high end of aquaculture. Boosted by market demand, short-term gain, and export potential, shrimp farming rose by more than 350 percent between 1984 and 1993.[15] With a global value of more than $5 billion in 1993, shrimp culture is booming.[16]

Fish farming is more efficient than produc-ing pork, chicken, or beef. Fish need only 2 kilograms or less of feed per kilogram of live weight gain, compared with 2.2 kilograms for chicken, 4 for pork, and 7 for beef.[17]

Yet fish farming shares many of the problems of the livestock and poultry industries. Diseases among fish kept in close quarters have emerged as a major constraint to the sustainable growth of aquaculture in Asia and the shrimp culture industry in Latin America.[18] In addition, organic wastes from intensive aquaculture lead to increased eutrophication and consequent deaths of fish stocks and other aquatic life. Fish farmers also use a wide range of chemicals as vaccines and disinfectants, some of which are ingested by scavenging fish.[19]

Exotic and genetically modified species have played a crucial role in the development of aquaculture. But cultured fish often escape and can displace or interbreed with local stocks, causing genetic degradation and destruction of natural habitat.[20]

While making demands on land and water resources, expanding shrimp farms and other aquaculture activities have often resulted in fragile wetland ecosystems, such as mangroves, being cleared—resulting in losses of tens of thousands of hectares per year.[21] Clearing mangrove forests for aquaculture destroys the sanctuary and breeding grounds for countless terrestrial and aquatic fauna.[22]

Funding for aquaculture projects is increasing. Aid to aquaculture in 1988–93 represented 34 percent of the total committed to fisheries and aquaculture.[23] More than 440 aquaculture projects were started during that period—with more than $910 million in grants and loans.[24]

Thirteen of the world's 15 major fishing areas are in serious decline, causing the world fish catch to level off at 85–90 million tons.[25] Aquaculture is taking up the slack, increasing its contribution to world food fish supply from 12 percent in 1984 to 22 percent in 1993.[26] According to a recent report, aquaculture could meet up to 40 percent of the world demand for fish within 15 years.[27]

Aquaculture Production Rises

Aquaculture Production, 1984–93[1]

YEAR	WORLD (mill. tons)
1984	6.9
1985	7.7
1986	8.8
1987	10.1
1988	11.2
1989	11.7
1990	12.4
1991	13.1
1992	14.4
1993	16.3
YEAR	CHINA
1984	2.45
1985	2.82
1986	3.56
1987	4.38
1988	5.08
1989	5.43
1990	5.80
1991	6.13
1992	7.21
1993	8.88
YEAR	INDIA
1984	0.51
1985	0.64
1986	0.69
1987	0.79
1988	0.89
1989	1.00
1990	1.01
1991	1.22
1992	1.39
1993	1.44
YEAR	JAPAN
1984	0.77
1985	0.72
1986	0.76
1987	0.81
1988	0.79
1989	0.85
1990	0.87
1991	0.87
1992	0.89
1993	0.91

[1]Excludes aquatic plants.

Source: FAO, "Aquaculture Production Statistics 1984–1993," Fisheries Circular No. 815, Revision 7, Rome, 1995.

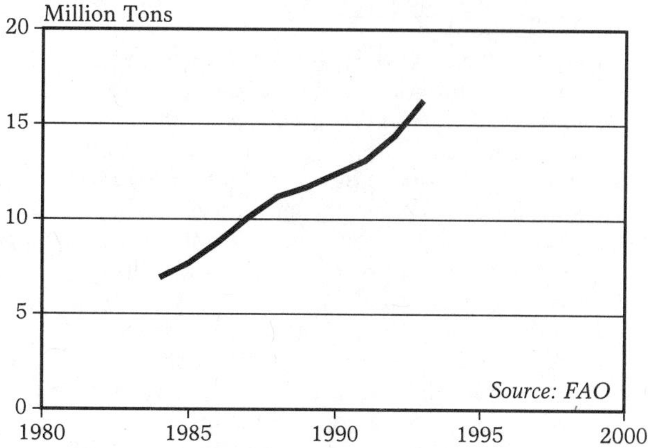

Figure 1: Global Aquaculture Production, 1950–93

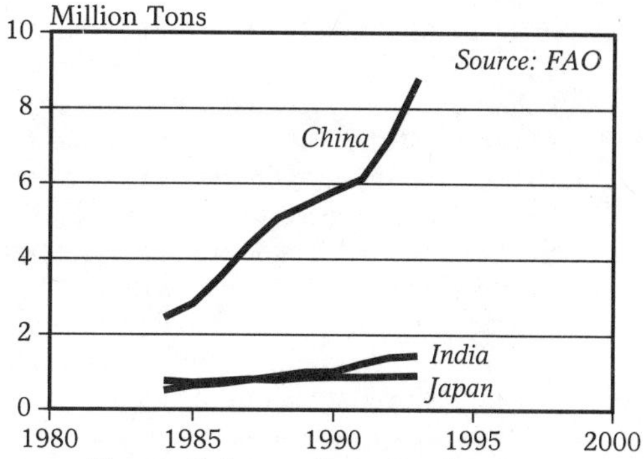

Figure 2: Aquaculture Production in China, India and Japan, 1984–93

Worldwide Feedgrain Use Drops   Lester R. Brown

The grain used to feed livestock, poultry, and fish around the world in 1995 totalled 644 million tons, down from 671 million tons in 1994.[1] (See Figures 1 and 2.) Fully one third of this 27-million-ton drop was due to a continuing decline in feedgrain use in the former Soviet Union. The remainder was due to the rise in grain prices during 1995 that led farmers elsewhere to cut feedgrain use.

At 644 million tons, feedgrain use accounted for 37 percent of total grain consumption, the lowest recorded since 1965.[2] Since then, the share of grain used as feed has ranged consistently between 38 and 40 percent.[3]

Without the rise in grain prices, feedgrain use would undoubtedly have climbed in 1995, given the near 4 percent rate of global economic growth.[4] A similar projected growth in the world economy for 1996 will keep pressure on feedgrain supplies.

The largest user of feedgrains, not surprisingly, is the United States, which fed roughly 153 million tons to cattle, pigs, poultry, and fish in 1995.[5] Other major users of feed are members of the European Union and China. China's rapidly growing use of grain for feed reached 95 million tons in 1995 even though the price of corn, its dominant feedgrain, had risen well above world market levels.[6] Four consecutive years of double-digit economic growth are driving up the demand for livestock products at an unprecedented rate.

Projected feedgrain carryover stocks in 1996, measured in days of consumption, are at their lowest level since records were first kept in 1961. As a share of consumption, the carryover stocks of corn and other feedgrains, such as barley and sorghum, amounted to 10.7 percent of estimated 1996 consumption.[7] This compares with the previous low of 12.2 percent in 1973.[8]

One consequence of such a low level of stocks has been higher prices as importing countries compete for scarce exportable supplies. The U.S. corn export price climbed by more than a third in 1995.[9]

Corn is by far the world's dominant source of feed. Although corn is a food staple in some countries in Africa and Latin America, the bulk of the global harvest of more than

500 million tons—roughly the same as that of wheat—is fed to livestock and poultry.[10]

In Europe and the former Soviet Union, large amounts of wheat are also used as feed. In Europe, 45 percent of the wheat used is consumed as feed.[11] In the former Soviet Union, it is 37 percent of the total.[12] For Eastern Europe, it is 35 percent.[13]

The United States accounts for some 40 percent of the world corn harvest—roughly 200 million tons out of a world harvest of 500 million.[14] It supplies an even larger share of corn entering international trade channels: as China and Thailand have faded from the scene as corn exporters, the U.S. share of world corn exports has climbed to roughly four fifths of the total.[15]

The leading importers of corn are in East Asia. Three traditionally dominant importers are Japan, bringing in roughly 16 million tons; South Korea, 9 million tons; and Taiwan, 6 million tons.[16] Together these three countries account for nearly half of world corn imports.

The region with the most rapidly growing use of feed is Asia. The number of mills that mix feedstuffs into rations for poultry, pigs, cattle, and fish is increasing almost daily. China is the leader, but the market is also growing rapidly in Indonesia, whose 200 million people are developing strong appetites for poultry and eggs.[17] As recently as the beginning of this decade, Indonesia was a small exporter of corn. In 1995, it imported 2 million tons.[18] Feedgrain use is now rising in India as well, as the poultry industry grows by leaps and bounds.

Late-1995 prices in China are well above the world market rate. In the corn-deficit provinces, corn may now cost $200 per ton, compared with the U.S. export price of roughly $150 per ton.[19] Without a bumper corn harvest in the United States in 1996, high feedgrain prices are likely to continue through 1996 and well into 1997.

WORLD GRAIN USE, 1960–95

YEAR	TOTAL GRAIN USE (mill. tons)	GRAIN USED FOR FEED	
		TOTAL (mill. tons)	SHARE (percent)
1960	822	294	36
1961	823	294	36
1962	845	295	35
1963	851	292	34
1964	908	315	35
1965	940	348	37
1966	958	361	38
1967	991	376	38
1968	1,022	397	39
1969	1,079	422	39
1970	1,113	432	39
1971	1,153	467	41
1972	1,178	483	41
1973	1,241	496	40
1974	1,196	453	38
1975	1,216	459	38
1976	1,283	488	38
1977	1,321	511	39
1978	1,396	556	40
1979	1,423	571	40
1980	1,456	560	38
1981	1,461	574	39
1982	1,484	592	40
1983	1,519	583	38
1984	1,569	610	39
1985	1,576	620	39
1986	1,633	652	40
1987	1,652	661	40
1988	1,637	628	38
1989	1,683	649	39
1990	1,719	666	39
1991	1,721	657	38
1992	1,731	665	38
1993	1,751	658	38
1994	1,762	671	38
1995 (prel)	1,750	644	37

SOURCES: USDA, "Production, Supply, and Demand View" (electronic database), January 1996; USDA, "World Agricultural Supply and Demand Estimates," January 1996; USDA, *Grain: World Markets and Trade*, January 1996.

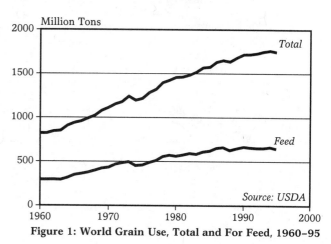

Figure 1: World Grain Use, Total and For Feed, 1960–95

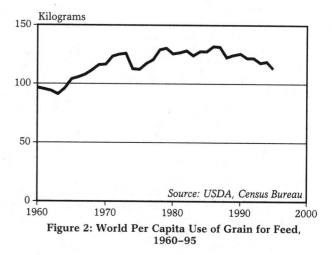

Figure 2: World Per Capita Use of Grain for Feed, 1960–95

Grain Stocks Drop to All-Time Low — Lester R. Brown

World carryover stocks of grain for 1996 are projected to drop to 229 million tons, down from 296 million tons in 1995.[1] (See Figure 1.) This decline will reduce stocks to only 48 days of world consumption, the lowest level on record.[2] (See Figure 2.)

When grain stocks reached the previous record low of 55 days of consumption in 1973, grain prices doubled, driving food prices up everywhere.[3] This experience showed that when grain carryover stocks--the amount in the bin when the new harvest begins—fall below 60 days of consumption, markets can become highly volatile, easily influenced by weather.

The markets started to become nervous in 1995 when carryover stocks dropped to 61 days of consumption. When cold, wet weather reduced the area planted to spring wheat in the northern Great Plains of the United States and Canada and delayed corn planting in the U.S. Midwest to well past the period when peak yields could be expected, prices began to rise across the board.[4] Those of wheat and rice, the world's food staples, rose by close to half during 1995.[5] Prices of corn, the leading feedgrain, were up by at least a third.[6]

Although the wet weather was the triggering event that escalated grain futures prices, the stage for this rise was set by the lack of growth in the world grain harvest since 1990.[7] The levelling off during the nineties, even while world population continues to grow by nearly 90 million per year, is leading to stock drawdowns.[8] Merely maintaining world per capita grain consumption requires an additional 28 million tons of grain output per year, or 78,000 tons per day.

With world grain production dropping in 1995, consumption exceeded production for the third consecutive year, further reducing grain stocks.[9] Thus between 1993 and 1996, world grain stocks dropped from 351 million tons to 229 million tons.[10] Unfortunately, with stocks now down to little more than pipeline supplies, similar shortfalls in the future will likely translate into sharply higher food prices.

Another reason for the stock drawdown is the extraordinary growth in demand for food in China, where incomes for 1.2 billion people rose by half from 1991 to 1995.[11] Much of this additional income translates into demand for livestock products, which in turn requires additional grain. In 1994, China had net grain exports of 9 million tons.[12] In 1995, rising internal grain prices led to the import of 16 million tons, making China the world's second largest grain importer, trailing only Japan.[13]

Rebuilding world grain stocks to a more secure level will not be easy. After stocks fell in 1973, it took three years of fencerow-to-fencerow planting to rebuild stocks by 10 days of world consumption. In the late nineties, rebuilding could be even more difficult, since the annual addition to world population is now nearly 90 million, compared with 74 million in the mid-seventies.[14] In addition, water scarcity and the declining yield response of crops to additional fertilizer in so much of the world make it more difficult to expand production.

As prices climb, a politics of food scarcity is beginning to emerge. Within China, some provinces have banned grain exports to other provinces to prevent runaway rises in prices.[15] In early May 1995, Vietnam (the world's third ranking rice exporter) restricted rice exports in order to control domestic rice prices.[16]

In December 1995, the European Union—a leading exporter of grain—imposed an export tax on wheat of $32 per ton in an effort to discourage exports and to arrest the rise in bread prices.[17] It followed this in early January 1996 with an export tax on barley, the principal feedgrain, because of a similar fear of rising prices of meat, milk, eggs, and cheese.[18] Although this helps Europe control food prices internally, it means that prices will rise even higher in the rest of the world.

The tightening of the market now under way could mark the conversion of the buyer's market of the last half-century to a seller's market. Competition among exporting countries for markets that never seemed large enough may be replaced by competition among importers for exportable supplies that never seem adequate.

WORLD GRAIN CARRYOVER STOCKS, 1961–96[1]

YEAR	STOCKS (mill. tons)	(days use)
1961	203	90
1962	182	81
1963	190	81
1964	193	82
1965	194	77
1966	159	61
1967	190	71
1968	213	77
1969	244	86
1970	228	76
1971	193	62
1972	217	68
1973	180	55
1974	192	56
1975	200	60
1976	220	65
1977	280	78
1978	278	77
1979	328	84
1980	315	81
1981	288	71
1982	309	77
1983	357	87
1984	304	72
1985	366	85
1986	434	100
1987	465	104
1988	409	90
1989	316	70
1990	301	65
1991	342	73
1992	317	69
1993	351	76
1994	313	65
1995	296	61
1996 (prel)	229	48

[1]Data are for year when new harvest begins.
SOURCES: USDA, *Grain: World Markets and Trade*, January 1996; USDA, "Production, Supply, and Demand View" (electronic database), January 1996.

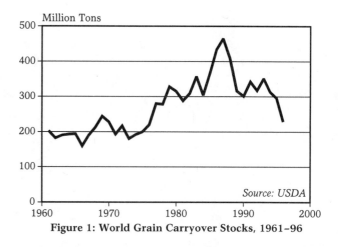

Source: USDA

Figure 1: World Grain Carryover Stocks, 1961–96

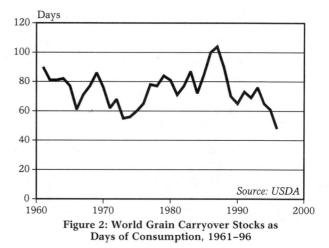

Source: USDA

Figure 2: World Grain Carryover Stocks as Days of Consumption, 1961–96

Agricultural Resource

Trends

Decline in Fertilizer Use Halts

Lester R. Brown

World fertilizer use increased slightly to 122 million tons in 1995, up from 121 million tons in 1994.[1] (See Figures 1 and 2.) This upturn ended a string of five consecutive annual declines that dropped world fertilizer use from its historic peak of 146 million tons in 1989 to 121 million tons in 1994—a fall of 17 percent.[2]

The decline after 1989 was not widely anticipated. After multiplying tenfold from 14 million tons in 1950 to 146 million tons in 1989, fertilizer use was generally expected to continue increasing.[3] Indeed, for four decades the rise in world fertilizer use was one of the most predictable of all global economic trends.

Yet from 1989 to 1995, per capita use fell from a high of 28 kilograms to 21 kilograms, a drop of one fourth.[4] It is no accident that this decline was accompanied by one in grain production per person, which fell from 324 kilograms to 293 kilograms—a drop of some 8 percent.[5]

Not all the decline in fertilizer use translated into a decline in production, however. Much of the drop between 1989 and 1994 occurred in the former Soviet Union, a country that was using far more fertilizer than was economically justified by world prices. After the economic reforms in the Soviet agricultural sector in 1988, prices of fertilizer moved upward to world market levels. This, combined with a decline in domestic grain prices, led to a precipitous drop of fertilizer use of more than two thirds.[6]

During the period when world fertilizer use was declining, the cultivated area remained essentially unchanged. As a result, the hectare rate of fertilizer use dropped from 110 kilograms in 1989 to 94 kilograms in 1995, a decline of more than 14 percent.[7]

Sixty percent of all fertilizer used in the world is applied to grain: wheat, corn, rice, barley, sorghum, millet, oats, and rye.[8] Other major uses include aiding the production of oilseeds and of fodder for cattle, including pasture. These three uses account for roughly three fourths of all farm fertilizer use.[9] Most of the remaining one fourth is applied to pulses (beans and peas), vegetables and fruits, tubers, sugarcane, and fibers, such as cotton.

Of all the major geographic regions, the Indian subcontinent—covering India, Bangladesh, and Pakistan, countries that collectively contain nearly 1.2 billion people—recorded the most consistent gains in 1995.[10] India achieved the largest gain of all, going from using just under 12.4 million tons of fertilizer to more than 13.5 million tons, a 9-percent jump.[11] Pakistan and Bangladesh each raised their fertilizer use by 2 percent in 1995.[12] All three countries are expected to increase their fertilizer use further in 1996.

The U.S. Department of Agriculture's decision to remove all limits on land set aside under commodity programs should lead to a small increase in U.S. grain planted area in 1996.[13] The European Union similarly is reducing the grainland held out of production from roughly 12 percent to 10 percent of the total.[14] In both cases, this should lead to at least modest increases in fertilizer use.

At the same time, the extraordinarily steep decline in fertilizer use in the former Soviet Union is believed to have bottomed out in 1995. Industry officials expect use there to increase at least slightly in 1996.[15] Other countries where fertilizer use is expected to increase in 1996 include those of central Europe, such as Poland, Bulgaria, and Czechoslovakia.[16] Within Latin America, the largest increase is projected for Argentina.[17] Higher export prices have encouraged Argentine farmers, who use relatively little fertilizer, to step up their applications.

With prices of grain and other major commodities such as oilseeds and cotton climbing during 1995 to record and near-record highs, fertilizer use is expected to expand in 1996. The International Fertilizer Industry Association estimates that 1996 consumption could reach 126 million tons, which would represent an annual gain of more than 3 percent.[18]

WORLD FERTILIZER USE, 1950-95

YEAR	TOTAL (mill. tons)	PER CAPITA (kilograms)
1950	14	5.5
1955	18	6.5
1960	27	8.9
1965	40	12.0
1966	45	13.2
1967	51	14.6
1968	56	15.8
1969	60	16.5
1970	66	17.8
1971	69	18.2
1972	73	18.9
1973	79	20.1
1974	85	21.2
1975	82	20.1
1976	90	21.6
1977	95	22.5
1978	100	23.2
1979	111	25.3
1980	112	25.1
1981	117	25.8
1982	115	25.0
1983	115	24.5
1984	126	26.4
1985	131	27.0
1986	129	26.1
1987	132	26.3
1988	140	27.4
1989	146	28.0
1990	143	27.0
1991	138	25.7
1992	134	24.5
1993	126	22.7
1994	121	21.6
1995 (prel)	122	21.3

SOURCES: FAO, *Fertilizer Yearbook* (various years);
International Fertilizer Industry Association,
62nd Annual Conference, May 9, 1994;
Worldwatch Institute.

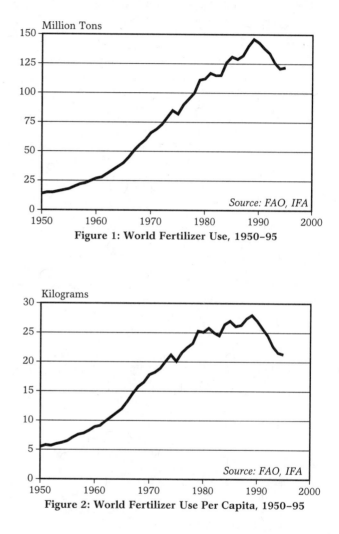

Source: FAO, IFA

Figure 1: World Fertilizer Use, 1950–95

Source: FAO, IFA

Figure 2: World Fertilizer Use Per Capita, 1950–95

In 1995, the world grain harvested area totalled 666 million hectares, down from 675 million hectares the year before.[1] (See Figure 1.) This decline of 9 million hectares—just over 1 percent of the total—reflected the loss of cropland to nonfarm uses in Asia, a slight increase in commodity set-aside land in the United States, and another sharp decline in grain harvested area in Russia, the Ukraine, and Kazakstan because of heat- and drought-induced crop failure.[2]

After increasing rather steadily from 587 million hectares in 1950 to 732 million hectares in 1981, the world grain area has declined in most of the 14 years since then, dropping some 9 percent from the historical peak.[3] In per capita terms, the grain harvested area per person has shrunk from 0.23 hectares in 1950 to 0.12 hectares in 1995.[4] (See Figure 2.)

Some increase in the grain harvested area can be gained by returning to production cropland that is idled under commodity set-aside programs designed to control supply. In the United States, the announcement by the Department of Agriculture that all corn set-aside land would be released for production in 1996 means a likely gain of 2 million hectares in the grain harvested area.[5] The European Union will also be returning an estimated 2 million hectares of the grainland set aside under its supply management program.[6] If it decided to bring all its land back, it could increase the harvested grain area by perhaps an additional 6 million hectares.[7]

Additional cropland could also come from the Conservation Reserve Program (CRP) in the United States, where some 14 million hectares of highly erodible cropland has been retired under 10-year contracts.[8] Beginning in 1996, the earliest of these contracts expires. The lion's share of this 14 million hectares is wheatland, most of it highly vulnerable to wind erosion.[9] Perhaps half of this could be farmed sustainably with the appropriate cultural practices. This would add 7 million hectares to the harvested cropland area over the next five years as the CRP contracts expire.

One influence on grainland area is the amount of water available for irrigation. In some parts of the world, such as Saudi Arabia or Arizona in the United States, when aquifers are depleted or water is diverted to urban uses, natural rainfall is so low that land must simply go back to desert.

As industrialization has accelerated in Asia, spreading beyond Japan to other countries, it has begun to consume large amounts of cropland. China, for example, has experienced a steady loss of riceland over the last several years in the southern coastal provinces. A combination of rapid industrialization and conversion of cropland to other nonfarm uses, such as recreation, has taken such a heavy toll on riceland that it entirely offset gains in rice yield per hectare, preventing any growth in the harvest.[10]

As China industrializes, farmland is being claimed not only by factories, housing, and roads, but also by shopping centers, tennis courts, golf courses, and private villas. In rapidly industrializing Guangdong Province, an estimated 40 golf courses have been built in the newly affluent Pearl River delta region alone.[11] Concern about this wholesale loss of cropland has led the Guangdong Land Bureau to cancel the construction of all golf courses planned but not yet completed.[12]

Other countries are now facing heavy losses. Each year, Indonesia loses an estimated 20,000 hectares of cropland on Java alone, which is enough to supply rice to 378,000 people.[13] In Vietnam, Prime Minister Vo Van Kiet banned the building of factories in rice paddies in the spring of 1995 in order to preserve cropland.[14] Just four months later he changed his mind—allowing the Ford Motor Company and other firms to build on 6,310 hectares of farmland near Hanoi.[15]

The trends since 1981 make it clear that maintaining the current grain harvested area will be difficult. Even if further declines are somehow avoided, the addition of some 90 million people a year to the world's population will steadily shrink grainland area per person.[16]

WORLD GRAIN HARVESTED AREA, 1950–95

YEAR	TOTAL (mill. hectares)	PER CAPITA (hectares)
1950	587	0.23
1955	639	0.23
1960	639	0.21
1965	653	0.20
1966	655	0.19
1967	665	0.19
1968	670	0.19
1969	672	0.19
1970	663	0.18
1971	672	0.18
1972	661	0.17
1973	688	0.17
1974	691	0.17
1975	708	0.17
1976	717	0.17
1977	714	0.17
1978	713	0.17
1979	711	0.16
1980	722	0.16
1981	732	0.16
1982	716	0.16
1983	706	0.15
1984	710	0.15
1985	715	0.15
1986	709	0.14
1987	685	0.14
1988	686	0.13
1989	694	0.13
1990	693	0.13
1991	687	0.13
1992	688	0.13
1993	677	0.12
1994	675	0.12
1995 (prel)	666	0.12

SOURCES: USDA, ERS, "Production, Supply, and Demand View" (electronic database), January 1996; USDA, *Grain: World Markets and Trade*, January 1996.

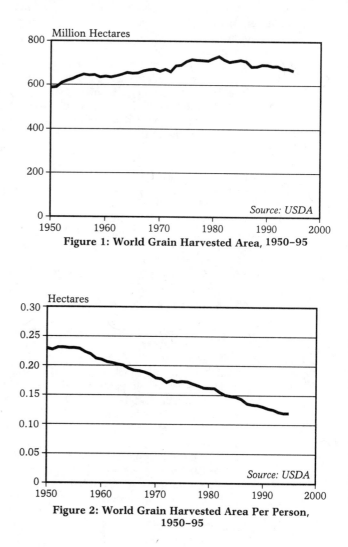

Figure 1: World Grain Harvested Area, 1950–95

Figure 2: World Grain Harvested Area Per Person, 1950–95

Irrigated Area Dips Slightly   Gary Gardner

World irrigated area decreased by more than 0.5 percent in 1993, the last year for which global data are available.[1] (See Figures 1 and 2.) Some of the decline appears to represent downward corrections to earlier irrigation estimates, especially for Indonesia and possibly for the former Soviet Union.[2] Eight republics of the former Soviet Union accounted for more than half the net global decline in irrigated area, with more than 800,000 hectares of irrigated land taken off the books between 1992 and 1993.[3]

The former Soviet Union is one of five nations that together claim more than two thirds of the world's irrigated area.[4] China, India, Pakistan, and the United States are the other giants; the three Asian nations alone hold nearly half of the world's irrigated area.[5] By contrast, Latin America and Africa accounted for 7 and 5 percent of global irrigated area, respectively, in 1993.[6]

By providing water in a timely and consistent manner, irrigation raises yields and allows land in some regions to produce two or even three crops each year. The result is higher agricultural productivity: irrigated land, while only 17 percent of global agricultural area, produces perhaps 40 percent of the world's food.[7] Given increasingly tight global food supplies—grain reserves have fallen in each of the past three years—the importance of irrigation has never been greater.[8]

Prospects for expansion are quite limited.[9] Irrigated area has grown at less than 1 percent annually in the nineties—not even half the rate of growth of the mid-seventies.[10] Because the most easily constructed major irrigation projects are already built, future projects will likely be more expensive.[11] This, combined with low food prices and increased citizen opposition to large-scale dams, has dampened interest in expansion of irrigation; funding for such projects has fallen some 25-33 percent since the mid-seventies.[12]

Expansion is also constrained by competition for investment funds. Rehabilitation and upgrading of old irrigation systems can claim a large share of the financing available for irrigation—more than half of all World Bank spending on irrigation, for example.[13]

Environmental remediation—to correct waterlogging and salt buildups created by inadequate drainage—also demands sizable investments. Ten percent of world irrigated area is estimated to suffer from salinization serious enough to lower crop yields; the problem is spreading at a rate of 2 million hectares annually, offsetting a good portion of the gains achieved by irrigation expansion.[14]

In some regions, irrigated area could contract because overpumped aquifers face depletion or pollution. An estimated 10 percent of China's cultivated area, for instance, and 33 percent of Iran's depend on overdrafted groundwater.[15] In the Indian states of Maharashtra, Gujarat, and Haryana, wells are severely overdrawn or flooded with encroaching ocean salt water, rendering many unfit for use in agriculture.[16] Overconsumption in Texas has pulled thousands of hectares of irrigated land from active production or converted them to less productive rain-fed farmland.[17] And on the Arabian peninsula, irrigated agriculture is largely unsustainable: 75 percent of water for crops comes from deep, "fossil" aquifers that are not replenished by rainfall.[18]

Moreover, farmers face increasing competition from cities for water supplies. Industrial and domestic water demand, which together account for roughly a third of total demand today, is projected to reach 45-50 percent by 2025.[19] In parts of India, Indonesia, and Malaysia, the supply of irrigation water will fall 15-30 percent short of projected requirements in coming decades if urban needs are fully met.[20] Cities typically can outbid farmers for water; in the southwestern United States, cities commonly purchase water rights from farmers, or pay them not to cultivate during drought years.[21]

The constraints on irrigation make substantial expansion of the sector unlikely on a global scale. If 1995 crop price increases herald a new era of food scarcity, investment in irrigation projects could be stimulated in some areas. But economic and environmental pressures to limit expansion are real, and many nations will be doing well just to preserve existing irrigated area.

WORLD IRRIGATED AREA, 1961–93

YEAR	TOTAL (mill. hectares)	PER CAPITA (hectares per thousand population)
1961	139	45.3
1962	142	45.2
1963	145	45.2
1964	148	45.1
1965	151	45.1
1966	154	45.2
1967	157	45.1
1968	160	45.2
1969	165	45.5
1970	169	45.5
1971	172	45.5
1972	176	45.5
1973	182	46.1
1974	185	46.2
1975	190	46.6
1976	196	47.0
1977	201	47.4
1978	204	47.5
1979	209	47.8
1980	211	47.4
1981	214	47.3
1982	217	47.1
1983	216	46.2
1984	222	46.6
1985	226	46.5
1986	227	46.0
1987	232	46.2
1988	231	45.3
1989	235	45.1
1990	239	45.1
1991	243	45.1
1992	249	45.5
1993	248	44.4

SOURCES: Worldwatch Institute, based on FAO, *Production Yearbook* (various years), and Bill Quinby, ERS, USDA, personal communication, January 24, 1996.

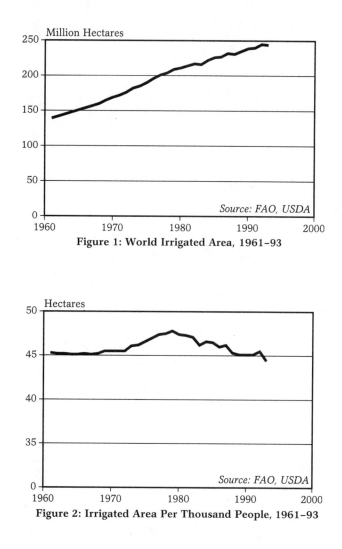

Source: FAO, USDA

Figure 1: World Irrigated Area, 1961–93

Source: FAO, USDA

Figure 2: Irrigated Area Per Thousand People, 1961–93

Energy
Trends

Oil Production Rises   Christopher Flavin

World oil production rose 1.5 percent in 1995, to 3,031 million tons (60.5 million barrels a day), according to preliminary estimates.[1] (See Figure 1.) This is the largest annual rise since 1990. Oil production continues to climb in scores of countries that are not members of the Organization of Petroleum-Exporting Countries (OPEC); oil shortages appear unlikely during the next five years, and production is likely to surpass the all-time record set in 1979.[2] Meanwhile, prices rose slightly in 1995 to just over $17 per barrel, spurred by rising demand in developing countries. (See Figure 2.)

In 1995, oil production rose 1.8 percent in Africa, 2.8 percent in Asia, and 2.9 percent in Western Europe.[3] Most increases occurred outside the major oil-exporting countries, in developing nations that are now encouraging multinational oil companies to explore for and develop their oil reserves. The higher output from such countries has cut OPEC's share of world oil production from 55 percent in 1973 to 43 percent in 1995.[4]

Saudi Arabia, the world's largest producer, now depends economically on the 2 million barrels per day of Iraq's production quota it has claimed since the international embargo was imposed on Iraq prior to the Gulf War.[5] If, as expected, Iraq returns to the oil market in 1996 or 1997, it will put additional downward pressure on prices. OPEC members will then have to rethink their production quotas, which they were already exceeding by about 1 million barrels a day in 1995.[6]

After falling for five consecutive years, oil production in Russia nearly levelled off in 1995 at about 6 million barrels per day—half the peak levels of the late eighties.[7] A slow, gradual rebound in Russian oil production is likely in the next few years as liberalized investment laws bring western capital and technology into Russia's abused oil fields. This will likely be offset by rising consumption, however, as the Russian economy begins to expand and more Russians are able to buy automobiles.[8]

In the new republics of Central Asia, an oil boom got under way in 1995 as the region's extensive reserves were tapped by multinational joint ventures.[9] But the complex physical and political geography presents major challenges for those who want to get oil to market.[10]

One surprise in 1995 was the slowing rate of decline in U.S. oil production, which was down by just 1.8 percent.[11] Advancing technology has allowed U.S. oil companies to locate and exploit remaining small oil reserves that would have been uneconomical a few years ago.[12] Also, U.S. offshore oil production is again expanding, thanks to new deep-water technology.[13]

Even as production rose in 1995, however, the industry was nursing its worst self-inflicted wounds since the Exxon Valdez ran aground in Prince William Sound. In the spring, Royal Dutch Shell shocked many Europeans when it announced plans to dump the Brent Spar, a worn-out oil rig containing toxic chemicals, in the North Sea.[14] Greenpeace campaigned against the move; soon, outraged citizens in the Netherlands and Germany were boycotting Shell gas stations, and their leaders pleaded with British Prime Minister John Major to force Shell to dispose of the platform on shore.[15] Shell finally backed down, but not before its reputation had been tarnished.[16]

Shell ran into more serious trouble in Nigeria's Ogoniland, where it had worked with the nation's military rulers to suppress protests by local people against the extensive environmental damage caused by Shell's oil fields.[17] After violent protests erupted in Ogoniland, the Nigerian military regime arrested and then executed Ogoni leader Ken Saro-Wiwa and eight of his followers in late 1995.[18] Although Shell had earlier turned its Ogoni oil fields over to local operators, it was widely criticized for encouraging the government crackdown and failing to urge the Nigerian government to spare the Ogoni leaders.[19]

These tragic events are symbolic of the Faustian nature of the world's dependence on petroleum. This gooey liquid on which more than 1 billion people depend for transportation and other vital tasks is poisoning the atmosphere, waterways, and even the political fabric of some countries.

WORLD OIL PRODUCTION, 1950–95

YEAR	PRODUCTION (mill. tons)
1950	518
1955	767
1960	1,049
1965	1,509
1966	1,638
1967	1,743
1968	1,937
1969	2,050
1970	2,281
1971	2,410
1972	2,547
1973	2,779
1974	2,803
1975	2,659
1976	2,901
1977	2,988
1978	3,023
1979	3,122
1980	2,976
1981	2,779
1982	2,644
1983	2,619
1984	2,701
1985	2,659
1986	2,774
1987	2,754
1988	2,881
1989	2,918
1990	2,956
1991	2,928
1992	2,999
1993	2,956
1994	2,986
1995 (prel)	3,031

SOURCES: API, *Basic Petroleum Data Book* (Washington, D.C.: 1994); Worldwatch estimates based on BP and *Oil & Gas Journal*.

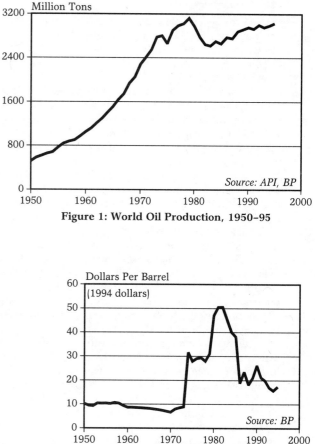

Figure 1: World Oil Production, 1950–95

Figure 2: Price of Oil, 1950–95

Natural Gas Production Edges Up   Christopher Flavin

World production of natural gas crept up to an estimated 2,114 million tons of oil equivalent in 1995.[1] The 0.5-percent increase marked the second slow year in a row for the gas industry. (See Figure 1.) The global figure was again depressed by a decline of roughly 3.5 percent in oil production in the former Soviet Union.[2]

If not for the continuing retraction of the economies of Russia and the other new republics, which produce one third of the world's gas, global production would have risen more sharply in 1995.[3] Throughout the world, gas is now the preferred fossil fuel since it produces far less pollution than the others. Despite rising oil prices in 1995, gas prices continued to fall in response to growing competition.[4] (See Figure 2.)

Russia's huge gas resource is controlled by the world's largest monopoly—the privately owned Gazprom—which owns most of its gas fields as well as a huge network of pipelines.[5] Gazprom's facilities are deteriorating, yet its political base has grown since Victor Chernomyrdin, the former Gazprom chief, became Prime Minister. Gazprom lacks the incentive to expand markets or attract the foreign capital and expertise it needs. Although impressive schemes have been drawn up to pipe Russia's gas to the Far East and to expand European markets, progress will be slow until the industry is reformed.[6]

The fastest growth in gas production and use is in the scores of developing countries just beginning to tap their gas reserves and build the pipelines and processing plants needed to bring them to market, which frequently means crossing high mountains or fording deep seas. Still, the high initial cost of such projects—often in the billions of dollars—has constrained the pace of gas development in the mid-nineties.

One region in which gas is likely to play an important role is southern Africa, where most people lack both gas and electricity and where coal is still the principal fuel for factories and power plants. Large gas reserves were found in Mozambique in the sixties, but not until the end of apartheid and the opening of regional energy markets did business

leaders start developing the gas fields and building the pipelines needed to make natural gas a more important part of southern Africa's energy mix.[7]

In South America, ambitious plans to tap the resources of Argentina and Bolivia and move the gas to markets in Brazil, Chile, and elsewhere continued to gather momentum in 1995.[8] In Mexico, government leaders are now promising to open the gas industry to foreign investment, which might finally bring it to life.[9] In Asia, long-term, multibillion-dollar investments in offshore gas development are under way near China, Indonesia, Myanmar, and Vietnam.[10]

Natural gas has long been preferred for home heating and many industrial processes, but an important milestone was crossed in the early nineties when gas suddenly displaced nuclear power and coal to become the most popular fuel for new power plants.[11] New gas-turbine-based plants have efficiencies of more than 50 percent.[12] And compared with even the most advanced new coal-fired models, they can cut carbon emissions by half, nitrogen oxide emissions by 90 percent, and sulfur dioxide emissions by 99 percent.[13] Gas-fired plants cost only about half as much to build as coal plants do.[14] Gas-fired generators need not be large, and are often used for the combined production of heat and power in factories or district heating plants—which further boosts efficiency.

A device called a fuel cell will soon offer an even more versatile and efficient way to convert natural gas to electricity. Fuel cells are electrochemical devices with hardly any moving parts that turn the energy in a fuel such as natural gas into electricity without actually burning it. They are highly efficient and relatively nonpolluting, and in the future will be economical even at a very small scale, offering the possibility of generating electricity inside buildings and using waste heat for water and space heating.[15]

In 1995, manufacturers announced plans to boost fuel-cell performance and scale up production.[16] Production costs are likely to follow the same steep downward path blazed by cellular phones and personal computers.

Natural Gas Production Edges Up

World Natural Gas Production, 1950–95[1]

YEAR	PRODUCTION (mill. tons of oil equivalent)
1950	187
1955	297
1960	458
1965	664
1966	716
1967	770
1968	851
1969	929
1970	1,026
1971	1,106
1972	1,170
1973	1,241
1974	1,261
1975	1,267
1976	1,320
1977	1,354
1978	1,394
1979	1,495
1980	1,455
1981	1,492
1982	1,482
1983	1,489
1984	1,625
1985	1,693
1986	1,732
1987	1,813
1988	1,900
1989	1,962
1990	2,010
1991	2,045
1992	2,045
1993	2,091
1994	2,103
1995 (prel)	2,114

[1]Includes natural gas liquids production.
Sources: BP, *BP Statistical Review of World Energy* (1995); DOE, *Monthly Energy Review January 1996*; Worldwatch estimates based on DOE, BP, UN, and government sources.

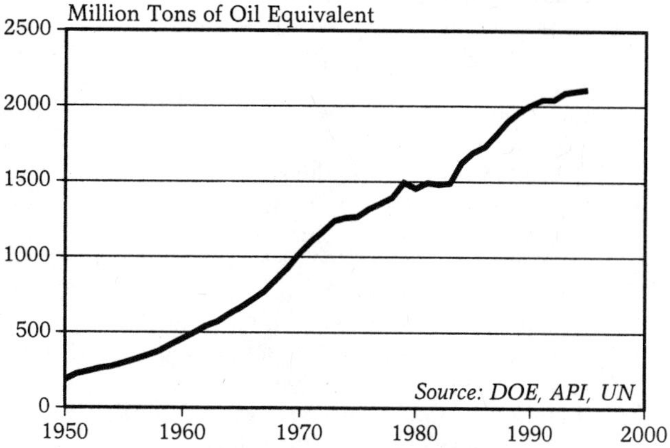

Figure 1: World Natural Gas Production, 1950–95

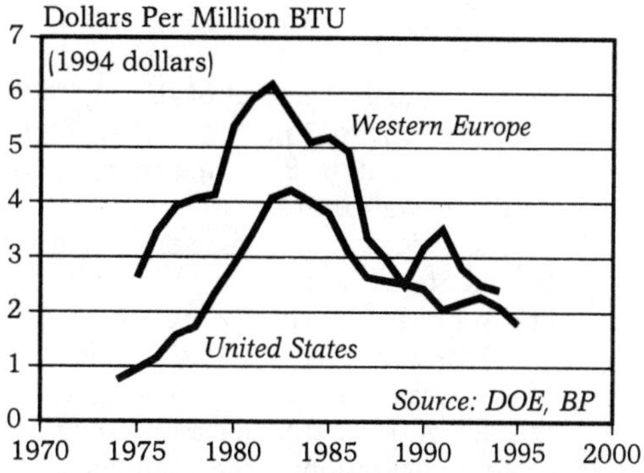

Figure 2: Price of Natural Gas in the United States and Western Europe, 1974–95

Coal Use Up Slightly   Hal Kane

World coal use rose slightly in 1995, to 2,109 million tons of oil eqivalent, an increase of 0.7 percent over 1994, according to preliminary estimates.[1] (See Figure 1.) Coal use remains below the 1989 peak of 2,189 million tons, continuing the slow-growth pattern of recent years.[2]

Economic growth in developing countries accounted for most of the 1995 increase. (See Figure 2.) Coal use in China during the first six months of 1995 was 5 percent higher than in the first half of 1994.[3] Since China's use accounts for more than one quarter of the world total, this affects the global trend a great deal.[4] Reliance on coal has been rising elsewhere in the Third World as well, but all the other developing countries together still use only about half as much coal as China does.[5]

Offsetting these trends, coal use in the former Soviet Union plummeted. Based on figures for nine months of 1995, coal use fell by about 12 percent.[6] It is now only slightly more than half the level of use in 1987 and accounts for just 8 percent of the world total.[7] Use of coal fell in Eastern Europe as well, though not as dramatically.[8]

The second largest burner of coal is the United States, which accounted for about 23 percent of the world total in 1995.[9] U.S. consumption grew little in 1995, in part because of an increase in nuclear power generation in the central United States and strong hydroelectric generation in the Pacific states, but it has tended to rise over the last decade by an average of more than 1 percent a year.[10]

Western Europe's use of coal has fallen by about 18 percent during the nineties as subsidies were reduced in the United Kingdom.[11] The region now accounts for about 12 percent of the world total.[12]

The next largest consumers—India, Japan, South Africa, and Poland—account for 5.6, 4, 3.5, and 3.3 percent of world use respectively last year.[13] The only one whose coal use is growing consistently is India, while Poland's usage has been falling substantially.[14]

Coal is becoming increasingly marginal to the world energy system. Its heyday was in the nineteenth century when it fueled the Industrial Revolution, replacing wood as the principal energy source. Although coal was once burned directly to heat homes and power the steam engines in trains and machinery, most of those markets have since been taken by oil, natural gas, or electricity.

In advanced industrial countries, only two major uses of coal remain: smelting iron ore and running electric power plants. In the United States, nearly 90 percent of coal goes to electric utilities, up from just 17 percent in 1949.[15] Of the few remaining countries to use coal directly to heat homes or power trains, China is the only one large enough to affect the world trend significantly.

Coal is often said to be the least expensive source of energy. But it is only the least expensive source to find and extract; it may be the most expensive to use. Burning coal releases more pollutants than burning oil or natural gas does, and far more pollutants than most renewable sources of energy.[16] When coal's pollutants cause respiratory diseases in people and harm forests and lakes, the costs of burning coal are passed on to others. Thus many of the costs of using coal are not paid by those who buy it to burn, but by those who pay for medical care and environmental cleanups, and who suffer the lost productivity that accompanies illness or reduced harvests of forest and agricultural products.

And because coal contains 80 percent more carbon per unit of energy than natural gas and 30 percent more than oil, burning it contributes 36 percent of the world's annual emissions of carbon dioxide, the main greenhouse gas that is warming the earth's atmosphere.[17]

By one estimate, air pollution costs China $95 billion, almost 7 percent of its national yearly output, and will require more than $20 billion in pollution control over the next decade to stop the problem from getting worse.[18] It will be hard for China to move away from coal, however, because it is used there for everything from home heating and cooking to fueling factories, running railroads, and generating electricity, accounting for more than three quarters of China's commercial energy supply.[19]

WORLD COAL USE, 1950–95

YEAR	COAL USE (mill. tons of oil equivalent)
1950	884
1955	1,045
1960	1,271
1965	1,299
1966	1,321
1967	1,255
1968	1,317
1969	1,357
1970	1,359
1971	1,355
1972	1,355
1973	1,413
1974	1,434
1975	1,450
1976	1,525
1977	1,581
1978	1,615
1979	1,681
1980	1,708
1981	1,732
1982	1,751
1983	1,804
1984	1,877
1985	1,980
1986	2,001
1987	2,062
1988	2,183
1989	2,189
1990	2,109
1991	2,074
1992	2,098
1993	2,085
1994	2,095
1995 (prel)	2,109

SOURCES: UN, *World Energy Supplies, Yearbook of World Statistics,* and *Energy Statistics Yearbook*; 1992 figures except for former East Germany are based on UN and BP; 1991–92 former East Germany based on UN and *European Energy Report*, January 1994; 1995 is Worldwatch estimate based on UN, BP, and private communications.

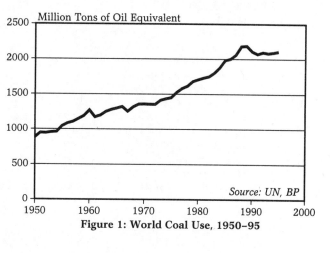

Figure 1: World Coal Use, 1950–95

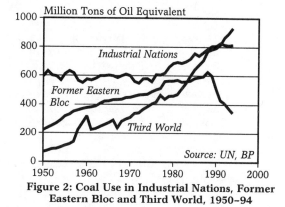

Figure 2: Coal Use in Industrial Nations, Former Eastern Bloc and Third World, 1950–94

Nuclear Power Virtually Steady

Nicholas Lenssen

Global nuclear power generating capacity reached 340,000 megawatts in 1995, according to preliminary estimates, up from 338,000 megawatts in 1994.[1] (See Figure 1.) The small climb came as reactor closures in Canada and Germany were offset by new units in India, Japan, South Korea, Ukraine, and the United Kingdom.[2] An additional reactor in Armenia, closed by the Soviet Union in 1989 after a devastating earthquake, was reopened in 1995 by Armenia's now independent government despite a western boycott of the project.[3]

In 1995, no government began construction on a new reactor project.[4] (See Figure 2.) Overall, just 34 reactors, representing 27,000 megawatts, remained under construction—the fewest in nearly 30 years.[5] Only France, Japan, India, and South Korea were actively constructing more than two reactors each.[6]

The two reactors that closed in 1995 raised the global total of retired plants to 84, representing 21,000 megawatts.[7] (See Figure 3.) The retired facilities operated an average of 17 years.[8]

By the end of 1995, just three reactors were under construction in the Americas: one each in Argentina, Brazil, and the United States.[9] With competition increasing in the U.S. electric power industry, some reactors are likely to be phased out early. The New York investment house of Shearson Lehman Brothers predicted that 25 U.S. reactors will close prematurely by 2003 because of high costs and accelerated aging.[10]

In Western Europe, nuclear expansion has stopped everywhere except in France, where four reactors remain under construction and are due to be completed by 1998.[11] But elsewhere the debate has shifted to when, not whether, to close existing reactors. In 1994, the Dutch parliament rejected industry requests to extend to 2007 the operating license of the country's only large nuclear plant, which is now expected to close no later than 2003.[12] Sweden's government, elected in 1994, has pledged to close one reactor by the end of 1998.[13]

The soon-to-be privatized British Energy, plc., declared in late 1995 that it would not build any more nuclear plants—a move designed to gain investors' confidence and capital.[14] Meanwhile, Germany dismantled a reactor in Bavaria at a cost of some $35 million more in real terms than it cost to build in 1972.[15]

Japan also has four plants under construction.[16] The Monju fast breeder reactor suffered a serious accident in December 1995 during testing: it leaked two to three tons of explosive sodium from its secondary cooling system—the largest leak ever recorded at a breeder reactor.[17] The plant's operator made matters worse by admitting that it took one-and-a-half hours to shut the reactor down because the accident did not occur in a way described in the plant's operating manual.[18]

So intense is opposition to nuclear power in Japan that the industry has obtained only two new sites for reactors since the 1979 Three Mile Island accident.[19] Opposition is now growing at existing sites; Kyushu Power cancelled plans to add a third reactor to its Kushima site due to public hostility in December 1995.[20]

With orders nonexistent in traditional nuclear markets, vendors continue to ply their wares in Asia. Sales, though, are few and far between. An expected order in Taiwan fell through in April 1995 when the state-owned utility rejected international bids for two new reactors, saying they were priced more than 20 percent too high.[21] The likelihood of building new reactors in Taiwan is now uncertain.[22]

The two confirmed orders for new plants in 1995 came from China, which signed up for two French-designed reactors, and from South Korea. The Chinese deal came with subsidies from the French government.[23] Yet China's two earlier reactors constructed with French help have been plagued with technical problems.[24] The South Korean order, meanwhile, is in jeopardy as local government officials, facing strong local opposition, in early 1996 revoked permission for the country's state-owned utility to build the plants.[25]

WORLD NET INSTALLED
ELECTRICAL GENERATING CAPACITY
OF NUCLEAR POWER PLANTS,
1960–95

YEAR	CAPACITY (gigawatts)
1960	1
1961	1
1962	2
1963	2
1964	0
1965	5
1966	6
1967	8
1968	9
1969	13
1970	16
1971	24
1972	32
1973	45
1974	61
1975	71
1976	85
1977	99
1978	114
1979	121
1980	135
1981	155
1982	170
1983	189
1984	219
1985	250
1986	276
1987	297
1988	310
1989	320
1990	328
1991	325
1992	327
1993	336
1994	338
1995 (prel)	340

SOURCE: Worldwatch Institute
database, compiled from the
IAEA and press reports.

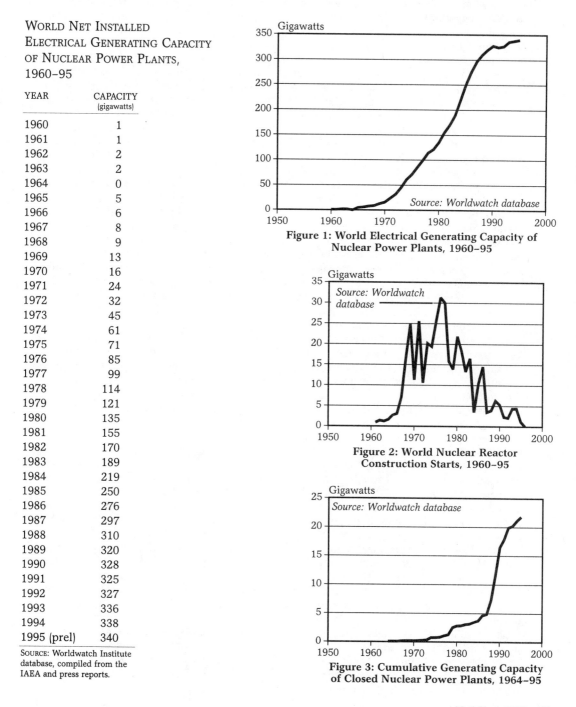

Figure 1: World Electrical Generating Capacity of
Nuclear Power Plants, 1960–95

Figure 2: World Nuclear Reactor
Construction Starts, 1960–95

Figure 3: Cumulative Generating Capacity
of Closed Nuclear Power Plants, 1964–95

Wind Power Growth Accelerates   Christopher Flavin

Global wind power generating capacity rose to 4,880 megawatts at the end of 1995, according to preliminary estimates, up 33 percent from 3,680 megawatts a year earlier.[1] (See Figure 1.) If all these turbines were spinning simultaneously, they could light 122 million 40-watt light bulbs. Although it still provides less than 1 percent of the world's electricity, wind power is now the world's fastest growing energy source.[2]

The United States led the world with total installed capacity of 1,650 megawatts at the end of 1995, but Germany was closing in fast with 1,130 megawatts, Denmark was third with 610 megawatts, and India fourth at 580 megawatts.[3] Altogether, Europe had 2,500 megawatts of wind power capacity at the end of 1995, up nearly threefold from 860 megawatts in 1992.[4] (See Figure 2.) In North America, by contrast, total capacity has not increased since 1991.[5]

The 1,290 megawatts of wind generating capacity added in 1995 was almost double the capacity added a year earlier, and up sixfold from the 1990 figure.[6] (See Figure 3.) In 1995, the country with the most new wind capacity was again Germany, which added 505 megawatts, the most any country has ever installed in a single year.[7] India added 375 megawatts to easily take the number two position.[8] Next in line was Denmark with 98 new megawatts, followed by the Netherlands with 95 and Spain with 58.[9]

Europe's continued domination of wind power development stems largely from the financial incentives and high purchase prices established for renewable energy in response to concern about the atmospheric pollution caused by fossil-fuel-fired power plants. Wind energy is now advancing rapidly in Finland, Greece, Sweden, and the United Kingdom, which is expected to add more than 100 megawatts in 1996.[10] And in France, despite the opposition of the nuclear industry, the government announced a new program aimed at adding 250–450 megawatts of wind power over the next decade.[11]

Europe is now home to most of the world's leading wind power companies, which are introducing larger and more cost-effective models. In Germany, the average turbine installed in 1995 had a capacity of 480 megawatts, up from 370 kilowatts in 1994 and 180 kilowatts in 1992.[12] Several manufacturers will soon introduce machines that can generate between 1,000 and 1,500 kilowatts.[13]

Unlike the United States, where most wind power development has consisted of large groups of 20–100 turbines, called "wind farms," Denmark and Germany have pursued a decentralized approach to wind power development. Most of their wind machines are installed one or two at a time, across the rural landscape. This has made them popular with local communities, which benefit from the revenues and jobs that result.[14]

In Germany, this approach has allowed determined investors and environmental advocates to beat back efforts by the electric utilities to reverse the 1991 "electricity in-feed law," which provides a generous price of about 11¢ per kilowatt-hour to electricity generators relying on solar, wind, and biomass energy. In a landmark vote in 1995, the Bundestag decided to uphold the law, though it remains under review by the courts.[15]

India is now the first developing country with a real commercial market for wind power. Countries such as Brazil, China, Egypt, and Mexico are installing a few machines for demonstration purposes, but only India has enough sustained business to encourage foreign companies to set up joint venture manufacturing. In the windy southern state of Tamil Nadu, hundreds of jobs have been created as a result.[16]

The biggest setback in 1995 was the near collapse of the U.S. wind industry, which is being hurt by uncertainty about the future structure of the electricity industry. Several large wind projects were cancelled in 1995, which drove the leading U.S. company's stock price down by 95 percent.[17] The country that led the world into wind power in the eighties actually saw a net decline of 8 megawatts in its installed capacity in 1995.[18] Some 50 megawatts were added—mainly in Texas—but 58 megawatts of old turbines were torn down in California.[19]

Wind Power Growth Accelerates

WORLD WIND ENERGY GENERATING CAPACITY, 1980–95

YEAR	CAPACITY (megawatts)
1980	10
1981	25
1982	90
1983	210
1984	600
1985	1,020
1986	1,270
1987	1,450
1988	1,580
1989	1,730
1990	1,930
1991	2,170
1992	2,510
1993	2,990
1994	3,680
1995 (prel)	4,880

NET ANNUAL ADDITIONS TO WORLD WIND GENERATING CAPACITY, 1980–95

YEAR	CAPACITY (megawatts)
1980	5
1981	15
1982	65
1983	120
1984	390
1985	420
1986	250
1987	180
1988	130
1989	150
1990	200
1991	240
1992	340
1993	480
1994	720
1995 (prel)	1,290

SOURCES: Birger Madsen, BTM Consult, Denmark, private communication, February 1996; Paul Gipe and Associates, Tehachapi, Calif., private communication, March 1, 1996.

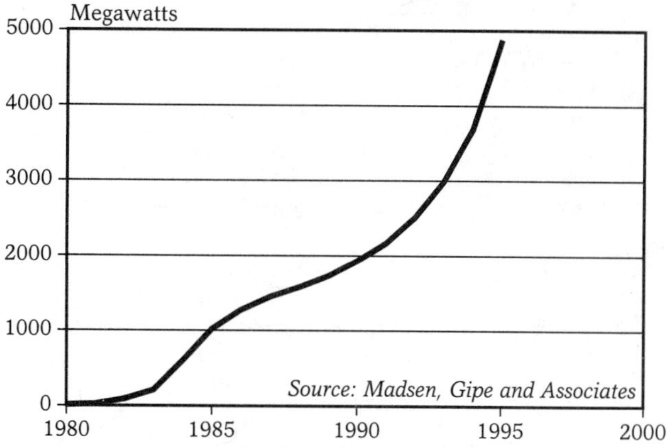

Figure 1: World Wind Energy Generating Capacity, 1980–95

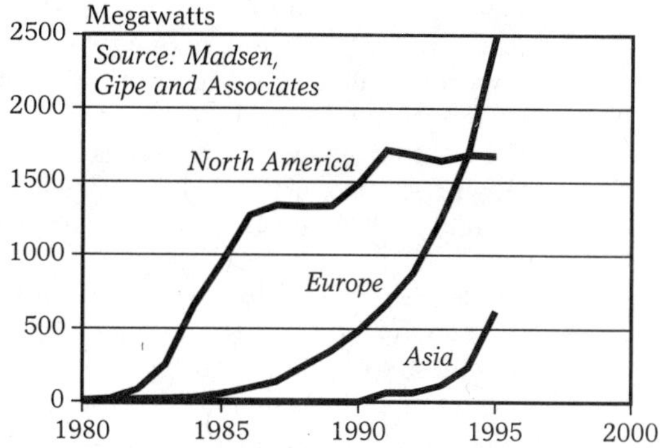

Figure 2: Wind Generating Capacity by Region, 1980–95

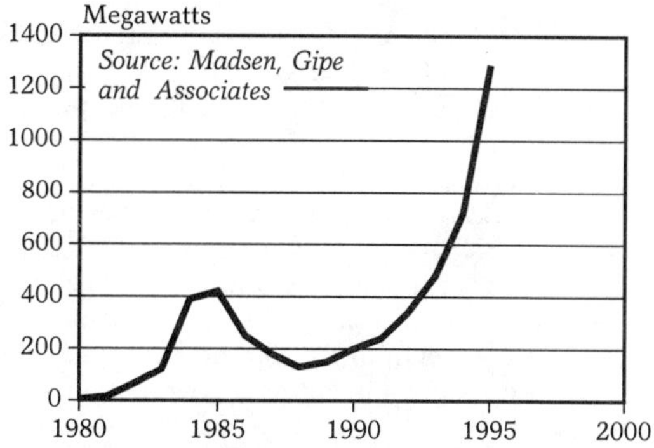

Figure 3: Net Annual Additions to World Wind Energy Generating Capacity, 1980–95

Solar Cell Shipments Jump   Odil Tunali

World shipments of photovoltaic (PV) cells—the thin silicon wafers that convert sunlight directly into electricity—jumped by 17 percent in 1995, to top 81 megawatts.[1] (See Figure 1.) This is the largest percentage increase in 10 years, and the second consecutive year of double-digit growth, signaling a solid recovery in the solar power industry after a slowdown in shipments in the early nineties.

The 1995 rise in shipments brought the global cumulative output of PV cells to just under 600 megawatts.[2] (See Figure 2.) The PV industry was operating at almost full capacity in 1995, keeping pace with growing demand, so the price of cells stayed at 1994 levels—around $4 per watt for wholesale factory prices.[3] (See Figure 3.)

The increase in global shipments was led by a 36-percent rise in the United States.[4] At 35 megawatts in 1995, this nation was again the largest producer of PV cells in the world, with government-assisted projects and exports boosting output.[5] Domestic purchases grew 25 percent in 1995, claiming 10 megawatts of the total output, while exports rose nearly 40 percent.[6]

Japanese shipments followed those of the United States with 19 megawatts—a 16-percent increase over 1994, and the second best year in Japan's PV history.[7] The growth in Japanese output was spurred mainly by the domestic market: the government's 70,000 Roofs project, an ambitious commercialization effort to install home rooftop units, accounted for all the nearly 4-megawatt increase in 1995.[8]

On the other hand, in Europe shipments fell slightly, to 21 megawatts.[9] This is mostly because European companies such as ASE GmbH and Siemens Solar Industries have been shifting production to their U.S. plants.[10] High production costs and reduced government incentive programs also contributed to the slowdown in PV shipments from Europe.[11] For example, the German government's 2000 Roofs program, which subsidized solar cell production, ended in 1995, leading to a production decline.[12]

Shipments from the rest of the world, including India, China, and Brazil, continued to grow, surpassing 6 megawatts for the first time.[13] Despite a 13-percent growth in 1995, these shipments accounted for less than one tenth of the world market for solar cells.[14] Reduced import tariffs in countries such as India have made it harder for small domestic producers to compete with foreign companies that have larger, automated plants.[15]

Developing countries such as India, China, Brazil, Morocco, Malaysia, and South Africa were among the hottest spots in the global PV market.[16] Apart from supplying power to a central electricity grid, the crucial advantage of PV cells is their rural applicability. For nearly 2 billion people, most of them in developing countries and far from a central power supply, PVs can provide essential electric services such as lighting, communications, and refrigeration for much less than adding power lines to the main grid would cost.[17]

Multilateral development institutions recently put solar power on their agenda as a way of meeting developing countries' energy needs. The World Bank, for example, has pledged $400 million to finance PVs and other renewable energy projects in developing countries.[18] And the Global Environment Facility has developed a PV Green Carrot program that will provide financial incentives to the utility industry and independent power producers to bring PV technology to developing countries.[19]

Despite the enormous potential of solar power, high costs are still a hurdle. But the quest to reduce costs continues. In Australia, for example, a team at the University of New South Wales has come up with a design breakthrough that will boost the efficiency of thin silicon solar cells to 21.5 percent, which could cut costs by almost 80 percent, making solar power competitive with coal-fired electricity.[20] The team is working with the electricity utility of New South Wales to make this technology commercially available in five to seven years.[21]

Solar Cell Shipments Jump

World Photovoltaic Shipments, 1971–95

YEAR	SHIPMENTS (megawatts)
1971	0.1
1975	1.8
1976	2.0
1977	2.2
1978	2.5
1979	4.0
1980	6.5
1981	7.8
1982	9.1
1983	17.2
1984	21.5
1985	22.8
1986	26.0
1987	29.2
1988	33.8
1989	40.2
1990	46.5
1991	55.4
1992	57.9
1993	60.1
1994	69.4
1995 (prel)	81.4

Sources: Paul Maycock, *PV News*.

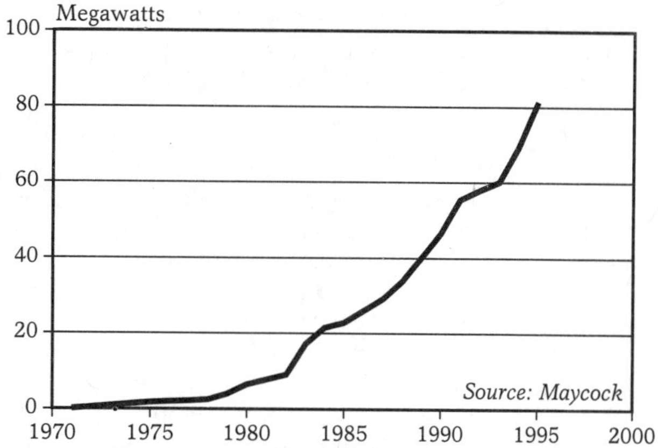

Figure 1: World Photovoltaic Shipments, 1971–95

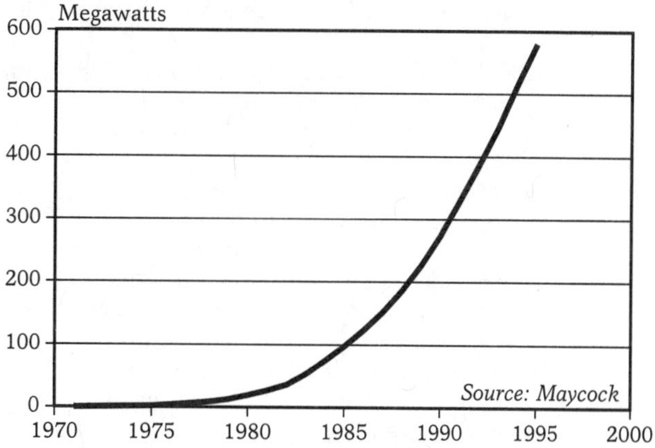

Figure 2: World Photovoltaic Shipments, Cumulative, 1971–95

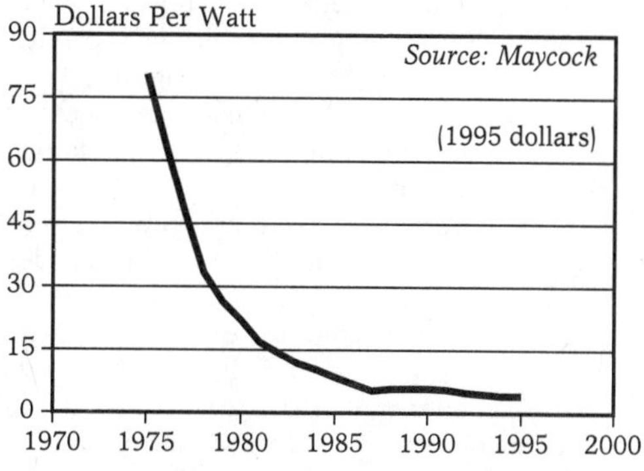

Figure 3: Average Factory Price for Photovoltaic Modules, 1975–95

Global sales of compact fluorescent lamps (CFLs) rose to 240 million in 1995, continuing the strong growth that has characterized this energy-saving technology since 1988.[1] (See Figure 1.) Sales in 1995 were 15 percent above those in 1994.[2]

North America and Western Europe continue to account for more than half of global CFL sales.[3] (See Figure 2.) U.S. sales increased by 10 percent in 1995, while those in Europe grew by 8.5 percent.[4] However, CFLs are rapidly gaining popularity in the former Soviet Union and developing countries, where sales growth rates are significantly higher than in the established markets. In 1995, sales increased by half in Eastern Europe and 31 percent in developing countries.[5] Latin America and the Asia Pacific region now account for 17 percent of global CFL sales.[6]

As CFL sales increase, new manufacturing facilities are appearing around the world. In 1992, the American Council for an Energy-Efficient Economy found production limited to the United States, Western Europe, Brazil, Mexico, Japan, Taiwan, South Korea, China, and Sri Lanka.[7] Since then, manufacturing plants have also opened in India, Thailand, Indonesia, Hungary, Poland, Russia, Ukraine, and Kyrgyzstan.[8]

Due in part to lower labor costs, production is shifting from industrial countries to developing ones and to former Soviet republics.[9] China has now overtaken the United States as the world's single largest CFL producer.[10] In 1994, China produced some 60 million CFLs, while U.S. production was only 34 million.[11] (See Figure 3.)

Government demand-side management (DSM) efforts, designed to reduce energy use and save money through energy efficiency and conservation, are responsible in part for the rapid growth of CFL use in many developing countries. China's five-year economic plan for 1996–2000, for example, identifies lighting in general and CFLs specifically as crucial elements of the government's energy efficiency efforts.[12] In Indonesia, the state-owned utility plans to install some 200,000 CFLs in residences around the country between 1995 and 1997.[13]

Thailand has an even more ambitious CFL plan: their Charge on the Bill program, in which customers pay for CFL purchases through incremental charges on their utility bills, will distribute some 1.5 million units, with an additional several hundred thousand targeted for low-income households.[14] Other pilot utility DSM programs to disseminate CFLs are under way in the Czech Republic, Hungary, and Honduras, among others.[15]

As more homes around the world become electrified, demand for lighting will increase. Currently, some 2 billion people around the world lack access to electricity.[16] Demand in developing countries is expected to rise by 7 percent annually through the nineties.[17] Some countries, such as India, project annual growth rates of at least 10 percent over the next decade.[18] Yet the economic and environmental costs of generating additional electricity are prohibitively high.[19]

Energy-efficient technologies such as CFLs offer an appealing alternative to construction of expensive new power plants. A typical 18-watt CFL provides the same light output as a 75-watt incandescent light bulb and lasts about 10 times as long, ultimately saving $33 in electricity and lamp replacement costs over its lifetime.[20] Replacing a 75-watt incandescent with an 18-watt CFL will also keep 267 kilograms of carbon from being produced at coal plants and approximately 7.5 kilograms of sulfur dioxide out of the atmosphere over the life of the lamp.[21]

As more countries begin to recognize the benefits of CFLs and as international development institutions begin to promote their use in the Third World, strong growth in global sales can be expected to continue. The World Bank and International Finance Corporation, with initial funding from the Global Environment Facility (GEF), currently manage energy-efficient lighting projects focused on CFL dissemination in Mexico and Poland.[22] The Bank is also considering expanding the pilot projects to additional countries in the near future using either GEF or conventional financing techniques.[23]

WORLD SALES OF COMPACT FLUORESCENT BULBS, 1988–95

YEAR	SALES (million)
1988	45
1989	59
1990	80
1991	115
1992	139
1993	180
1994	210
1995	240

SOURCES: Evan Mills, Lawrence Berkeley Labratory, private communication, February 3, 1993; Nils Borg, "Global CFL Sales," *International Association for Energy-Efficient Lighting Newsletter*, Vol. 4/94; Nils Borg, National Board for Industrial and Technical Development, Sweden, private communication, February 5, 1996.

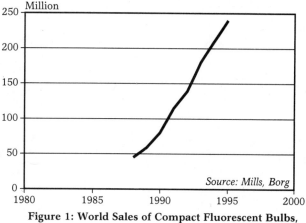

Figure 1: World Sales of Compact Fluorescent Bulbs, 1988–95

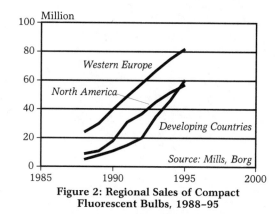

Figure 2: Regional Sales of Compact Fluorescent Bulbs, 1988–95

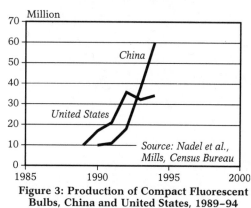

Figure 3: Production of Compact Fluorescent Bulbs, China and United States, 1989–94

Atmospheric Trends

Carbon Emissions Hit All-Time High Odil Tunali

Global emissions of carbon from fossil fuel burning broke a new record at 6.06 billion tons in 1995, surpassing the previous record set in 1991.[1] (See Figure 1.) Although this represents only a slight increase from 1994, it is enough to demonstrate that most nations are failing to meet the goal of the Framework Convention on Climate Change, which is to limit emissions.[2]

Carbon dioxide (CO_2) is the primary greenhouse gas that contributes to climate change by accumulating in the atmosphere and trapping the sun's heat. Although CO_2 is also released by natural systems, including forests, the scientific community is now virtually unanimous in its conclusions that the recent rise in carbon accumulation in the atmosphere is not due to natural causes.[3]

Of the roughly 6 billion tons of carbon emitted each year from the burning of fossil fuels, about 3 billion tons is absorbed by oceans and forests combined.[4] But emissions have been occurring at a faster rate than these natural systems can take up, leading to an increase in the amount that remains in the atmosphere. Carbon dioxide concentrations in the atmosphere have grown from 280 parts per million since fossil fuel burning began with the Industrial Revolution in the middle of the last century to 361 parts per million in 1995—a 30-percent increase.[5] (See Figure 2.)

Although the rate of increase in emissions slowed in the early nineties, this was mainly due to the collapse of the centrally planned industries in the former Eastern bloc, while emissions continued to grow in many industrial countries. At 1.4 billion tons, the United States remained the world's largest source of carbon emissions in 1995; other leading emitters were China, Russia, Japan, and Germany.[6] The United States also had the highest per capita emissions: at 5.25 tons of carbon annually, its per capita emissions were more than seven times those of China, and 25 times those of India.[7]

Yet developing countries' contribution to global carbon emissions is growing fast due to the rapid economic expansion and increasing energy consumption that nations such as China, India, and Brazil are experiencing.[8] In 1994, developing countries accounted for an estimated 40 percent of global carbon emissions—up from 30 percent in 1990.[9] (See Figure 3.)

Emissions in some developing countries are of particular concern. China, for example—with its heavy reliance on coal (three fourths of its commercial energy), inefficient energy use, and continually increasing energy demand—could soon surpass the United States as the world's largest carbon emitter.[10] Currently, it is in second place, producing more than 870 million tons of carbon, nearly 15 percent of global emissions.[11] Ironically, China itself would be hit hard by the consequences of global warming, as the predicted one-meter rise in sea level by 2100 would displace 70 million people in its coastal provinces.[12]

Developing countries such as China are not yet covered by emission reduction targets under the climate convention.[13] Industrial countries, on the other hand, aimed to cut their carbon emissions back to 1990 levels by the end of this decade.[14] However, many are falling short—particularly Australia, Canada, and the United States—and are expected to miss this target.[15]

If policies are not changed and dependence on fossil fuels not reduced, global carbon emissions from fossil fuel burning could reach 7 billion tons by 2000, and 8 billion by 2010, according to International Energy Agency predictions.[16] The 1995 report of the Intergovernmental Panel on Climate Change states that emission reductions are already technically and economically feasible, and can be achieved by replacing carbon-intensive fossil fuels with natural gas and renewable energy sources and by improving energy efficiency.[17]

So far, however, policies to achieve that goal have been slow in coming. At the first Conference of the Parties in March 1995, delegates deferred concrete action on cutting emissions until 1997: they decided to set up a two-year negotiation process to approve a protocol to the convention, which is expected to set legally binding reduction targets for the early twenty-first century.[18]

WORLD CARBON EMISSIONS FROM FOSSIL FUEL BURNING, 1950–95, AND ATMOSPHERIC CONCENTRATIONS OF CARBON DIOXIDE, 1960–95

YEAR	EMISSIONS (mill. tons of carbon)	CARBON DIOXIDE (parts per mill.)
1950	1,620	n.a.
1955	2,020	n.a.
1960	2,543	316.8
1965	3,095	319.9
1966	3,251	321.2
1967	3,355	322.0
1968	3,526	322.8
1969	3,735	323.9
1970	4,006	325.3
1971	4,151	326.2
1972	4,314	327.3
1973	4,546	329.5
1974	4,553	330.1
1975	4,527	331.0
1976	4,786	332.0
1977	4,920	333.7
1978	4,960	335.3
1979	5,239	336.7
1980	5,172	338.5
1981	5,000	339.8
1982	4,960	341.0
1983	4,947	342.6
1984	5,109	344.3
1985	5,282	345.7
1986	5,464	347.0
1987	5,584	348.8
1988	5,801	351.3
1989	5,912	352.7
1990	5,943	354.0
1991	6,010	355.5
1992	5,926	356.2
1993 (est)	5,940	357.0
1994 (est)	5,990	358.8
1995 (prel)	6,056	360.7

SOURCES: Marland, Andres, and Boden, electronic database, Oak Ridge National Laboratory, 1995; 1993–95, Worlwatch estimates based on Marland et al., on OECD, and on BP.

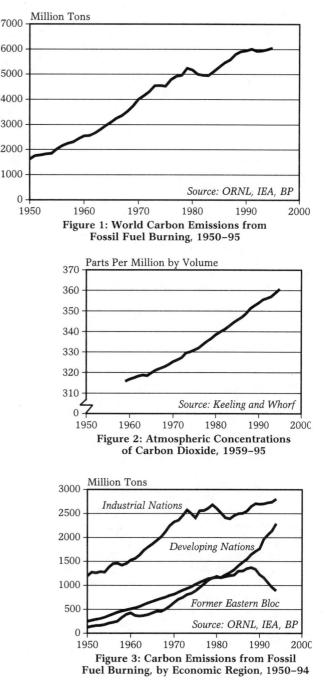

Figure 1: World Carbon Emissions from Fossil Fuel Burning, 1950–95

Figure 2: Atmospheric Concentrations of Carbon Dioxide, 1959–95

Figure 3: Carbon Emissions from Fossil Fuel Burning, by Economic Region, 1950–94

Global Temperature Sets New Record   Odil Tunali

The average temperature of the atmosphere at the earth's surface rose to a record high in 1995, according to preliminary figures. At 15.39 degrees Celsius, 1995 was on average 0.01 degrees warmer than 1990—previously the warmest year since records were first kept in 1866.[1] (See Figure 1.)

These figures are maintained by the Goddard Institute for Space Studies at NASA, and are one of two sets of long-term surface temperature data.[2] Despite slight variations in individual measurements, the two sets concur that 1995 was the hottest year on record, despite an unusually cold December in North America and Europe.[3]

The 1995 average temperature represents a 0.3-degree Celsius increase since mid-1992—a year after the Mount Pinatubo eruption spewed millions of tons of dust into the atmosphere, which blocked radiation from the sun, lowering global temperatures for about two years.[4] Since 1994 the warming has resumed and, even with the Pinatubo cooling, the early nineties have been as warm as the late eighties, which was the warmest half-decade on record.[5] James Hansen, a climate scientist at the Goddard Institute, predicts that at least one more new record will be set before the millennium closes.[6]

The global average surface temperature has risen by 0.3–0.6 degrees Celsius in the past century—the fastest warming since the end of the last ice age more than 10,000 years ago—and the 10 hottest years in recorded human history have all occurred in the eighties and nineties.[7]

What makes the high average temperature of 1995 all the more significant is that it occurred without the influence of natural phenomena that at times contribute to warm temperatures: El Niño, the warm-water pool that appears in the Pacific every four years or so, was absent, and the solar energy cycle was at its lowest point.[8] This supports the theory that what is altering the earth's climate is the accumulation in the atmosphere of greenhouse gases caused by human activity.

In a report released in December 1995, the Intergovernmental Panel on Climate Change (IPCC), a U.N. advisory group of 2,500 scientists, concluded for the first time that the observed warming is "unlikely to be entirely natural in origin."[9] The dominant human influence on climate is the heat-trapping effect of increasing carbon dioxide (CO_2) concentrations in the atmosphere, released largely by the burning of fossil fuels.[10]

The IPCC projects that if emissions of carbon keep increasing at recent rates so as to lead to a doubling of atmospheric CO_2 concentrations by the end of the next century, average temperatures could increase by 1–3.5 degrees Celsius.[11] The key concern of scientists is not just warmer temperatures but how these would affect other natural phenomena. Among the expected effects of a warmer world are rising sea levels, more frequent floods and droughts, and an increase in the number and severity of hurricanes, all of which would create major disruptions.[12]

Despite the clear evidence of warming at the earth's surface, however, some press reports in 1995 pointed to an apparent inconsistency with temperature readings taken by satellites.[13] These are more precise and comprehensive than surface measurements, but because they take the average temperature of the lowest seven kilometers of the atmosphere rather than measuring at the surface where human activity occurs, they show a similar but slightly different trend than the surface data do.[14] (See Figure 2.)

Since the greenhouse effect is strongest at the surface, where the atmosphere is densest, surface data show warmer temperatures than the broader band of the atmosphere covered by the satellite data.[15] In addition, the depletion of the ozone layer appears to be cooling portions of the upper atmosphere, which is also thought to contribute to the discrepancy.[16] And compared with 130 years of surface measurements, the satellite data cover only the last 17 years—too short a time span to conclude whether the atmosphere is warming or not.[17]

Still, Dr. John Christy of the University of Alabama notes that the satellite data, which he assembles, track the surface data closely, and, in time, are expected to show a clear warming trend.[18]

Global Temperature Sets New Record

GLOBAL AVERAGE TEMPERATURE, 1950–95

YEAR	TEMPERATURE (degrees Celsius)
1950	14.86
1955	14.92
1960	14.98
1965	14.88
1966	14.95
1967	14.99
1968	14.93
1969	15.05
1970	15.02
1971	14.93
1972	15.00
1973	15.11
1974	14.92
1975	14.92
1976	14.84
1977	15.11
1978	15.06
1979	15.09
1980	15.18
1981	15.29
1982	15.08
1983	15.24
1984	15.11
1985	15.09
1986	15.16
1987	15.27
1988	15.28
1989	15.22
1990	15.38
1991	15.36
1992	15.11
1993	15.14
1994	15.23
1995 (prel)	15.39

SOURCES: Goddard Institute for Space Studies, New York, January 19, 1996.

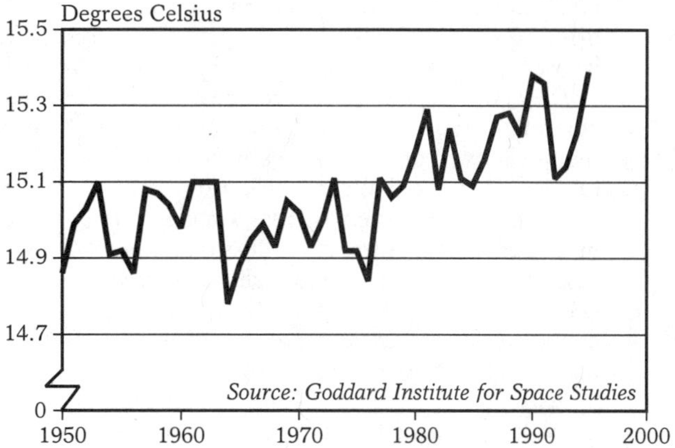

Figure 1: Average Temperature at the Earth's Surface, 1950–95

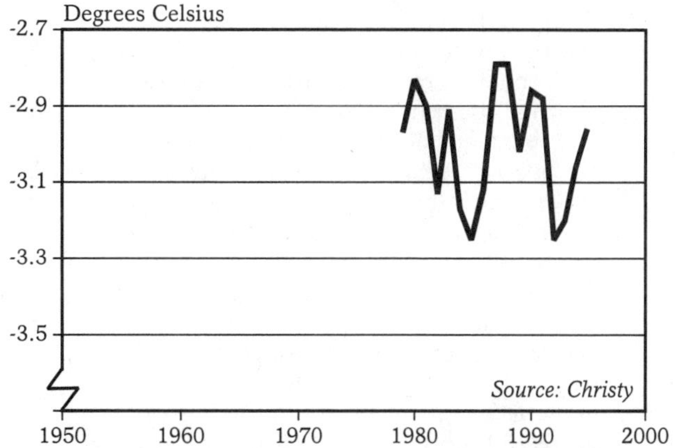

Figure 2: Average Temperature of the Lower Atmosphere Based on Satellite Measurements, 1979–95

CFC Production Drop Continues
Anjali Acharya

Global chlorofluorocarbon (CFC) production declined by more than 20 percent in 1995—falling for the seventh consecutive year and bringing production levels down to 77 percent below their peak in 1988.[1] (See Figure 1.)

Observed increases in concentrations of chlorine in the stratosphere—primarily from the breakdown of CFCs—have been widely implicated in the depletion of lower-stratospheric ozone over the past two decades.[2] This in turn lets more ultraviolet (UV) radiation reach the earth's surface, which can increase skin cancer and cataracts in humans, damage crops and other plants, and destroy the phytoplankton that underly the marine food chain.[3]

Scientific evidence has firmly established the link between CFCs and other ozone-depleting substances and the destruction of the ozone layer.[4] The problem is most pronounced over Antarctica, where up to 60 percent of total ozone is depleted each September, causing the "ozone hole."[5] (See Figure 2.) Ozone depletion has also been observed over mid-latitude regions. Globally, stratospheric ozone is declining at a rate of close to 3 percent per decade.[6]

The ozone hole at its maximum has exceeded 20 million square kilometers during each of the last seven years.[7] The hole over Antarctica in 1995 was the longest lasting one on record.[8] Ozone losses of more than 10 percent were observed over northern middle latitudes in the spring, reaching an unprecedented 35 percent over Siberia.[9] Due to their long lifetimes, CFCs and other ozone-depleting substances already present in the atmosphere will continue to wreak havoc until perhaps the middle of the next century.[10]

Global efforts to reverse this damage began with the signing of the Vienna Convention in 1985 and the Montreal Protocol in 1987, which established a phase-out schedule for ozone-depleting substances.[11] The protocol was amended in 1990 and 1992 to expand the list of regulated substances and accelerate their phaseout.[12]

The 1992 amendments committed industrial countries to eliminating CFC production by the end of 1995.[13] Halons were banned in 1994.[14] (Developing countries have an extra 10 years to meet all deadlines.)[15] In December 1995, the 150 parties to the protocol revised it once again. Industrial countries agreed to phase out methyl bromide by 2010; developing countries will only freeze production of this potent ozone-depleter in 2002.[16] New controls were also introduced on hydrochlorofluorocarbons, which are currently used as a replacement for CFCs.[17]

Although most countries have complied with these targets, there are loopholes in the process: industrial countries can still manufacture these chemicals for export to developing countries, which may import and make CFCs through 2005.[18] Also, the first cases of noncompliance are being reported. Russia and four other "transition" economies announced in late 1995 they might not meet the CFC phaseout date of January 1, 1996—and they got an extension of four years.[19]

Furthermore, there is growing concern about the expanding emissions of the developing world—where CFC production surged by 87 percent between 1986 and 1993, while exports of CFCs rose seventeenfold.[20] (By 1993, developing countries accounted for about 20 percent of global CFC production).[21] While consumption of CFCs decreased by 74 percent in industrial countries from 1986 to 1993, it increased by more than 40 percent in developing ones.[22]

Evasion of controls on CFCs is evidenced by the rapid growth of a black market—with CFCs being smuggled into the United States and Europe from Russia, India, and China. At least 10,000 tons of CFCs came into the United States illegally in 1995.[23] A further 10,000 tons of smuggled CFCs are believed to be entering the European Union.[24]

A multilateral fund was established in 1991 to facilitate the transfer and finance of technology to developing countries.[25] Payments are falling short of commitments, however; the fund has received only $422 million of the $537 million promised by industrial nations for 1991–95.[26] This lack of funds, developing countries say, has delayed their transition to ozone-safe technologies.

WORLD CFC PRODUCTION,
1950–95

YEAR	TOTAL[1] (thousand tons)
1950	42
1955	86
1960	150
1965	330
1966	390
1967	440
1968	510
1969	580
1970	640
1971	690
1972	790
1973	900
1974	970
1975	860
1976	920
1977	880
1978	880
1979	850
1980	880
1981	890
1982	870
1983	950
1984	1,050
1985	1,090
1986	1,130
1987	1,250
1988	1,260
1989	1,150
1990	820
1991	720
1992	630
1993	520
1994	388
1995 (prel)	300

[1]Includes all CFCs (CFC-11, CFC-12, CFC-113, CFC-114, and CFC-115). The totals are increasingly uncertain because a growing percentage of use occurs in regions where data are not readily available.
SOURCES: 1950 and 1955, Worldwatch estimates based on Chemical Manufacturers Association; 1960–95 from DuPont, Wilmington, Del., private communications.

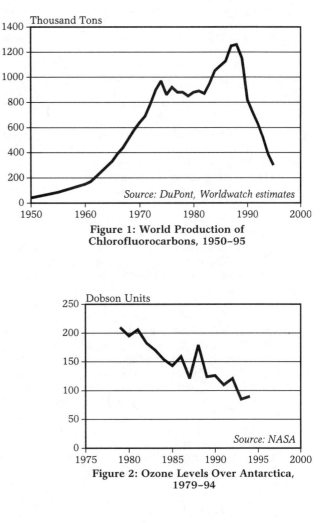

Figure 1: World Production of
Chlorofluorocarbons, 1950–95

Figure 2: Ozone Levels Over Antarctica,
1979–94

Sulfur and Nitrogen Emissions Steady   Hal Kane

World emissions of sulfur from the burning of fossil fuels fell by a half-million tons in 1993, to 69.5 million tons, while those of nitrogen rose by 200,000 tons, to 26.7 million tons.[1] (See Figures 1 and 2.) These figures are the most recent data available because no official organization tracks global emissions of these pollutants.

Additional human-caused emissions of sulfur, possibly as much as 20 percent more, came from other industrial processes such as metal smelting; additional emissions of nitrogen of approximately one third came from the burning of vegetation, such as forests.[2]

Both sulfur and nitrogen emissions increased steadily from mid-century except for just after the oil shocks of 1973 and 1979.[3] This growth stopped in 1989, however, largely because industrial production in the Soviet Union and Eastern Europe began to plummet, and also because of the adoption of emission controls in many countries.[4]

With emissions of each gas more or less flat since 1989, the world may have seen the end of growth in sulfur and nitrogen pollution. The former Soviet Union and Eastern Europe are unlikely to readopt heavily polluting industrial systems, and Western Europe, North America, and other regions are switching from coal to natural gas, which contains little sulfur.[5] Indeed, although the data on sulfur emissions go only until 1993, world use of coal remained flat during 1994 and grew little during 1995, so at least two more years of little or no growth of sulfur emissions seems likely.[6]

Scrubbers and other cleaning technologies have the ability to take most of the sulfur out of waste gases from power plants before they reach the atmosphere.[7] And technologies that burn fuel more efficiently and at more precise temperatures release considerably less nitrogen into the atmosphere than less well tuned equipment, while catalytic converters can also remove nitrogen oxides from emissions.[8]

Future emissions trends depend on whether developing countries such as China and India adopt cleaner technologies. If they do not, their heavy reliance on high-sulfur coal and nineteenth-century technologies will overwhelm successes of cutting sulfur and nitrogen pollution elsewhere. If cleaner machinery reaches these countries, then the reduction of sulfur and nitrogen pollution could become a worldwide success story.

Cleaner technologies brought European emissions of sulfur down by 40 percent between 1980 and 1993, and although nitrogen oxide emissions there rose between 1980 and 1989, they have since dropped back to their 1980 levels.[9] Nevertheless, the latest survey of acid rain damage to European forests found more than 25 percent defoliation in a quarter of Germany's trees, 55 percent of Poland's trees, and 28 percent of Norway's trees.[10]

In the United States, efforts to control emissions have been tied to a system of tradable pollution credits under the Clean Air Act.[11] Corporations are allotted a certain number of credits by the government; if they produce less pollution than expected, they can sell any leftover credits to other companies. If they pollute more, they can buy the surplus credits of others.

Much to the surprise of industry analysts who had predicted that compliance with the Clean Air Act would cost utilities $4–5 billion a year, a November 1995 headline in the *Wall Street Journal* read "Electric Utilities Are Overcomplying With Clean Air Act."[12] Utilities—the country's largest sulfure dioxide emitters—were discharging only about 60 percent of the sulfur allowed by law because the price of low-sulfur coal fell below that of high-sulfur coal, making it cheaper to burn cleaner fuel.[13] Industry analysts had predicted that each pollution allowance, which carries the right to emit one ton of sulfur dioxide, would trade at more than $1,000; today the figure is less than $130 each.[14] This unexpected result pointed to two miscalculations in the Clean Air Act: industry exaggerated the costs of reducing its emissions, and the U.S. government made its requirements far softer than necessary, given the ease of reducing emissions.

WORLD SULFUR AND NITROGEN
EMISSIONS FROM FOSSIL FUEL
BURNING, 1950–93

YEAR	SULFUR (mill. tons)	NITROGEN (mill. tons)
1950	30.1	6.8
1960	46.2	11.8
1970	57.0	18.1
1971	56.9	18.6
1972	58.2	19.5
1973	60.9	20.6
1974	60.9	20.8
1975	56.4	19.9
1976	58.6	21.0
1977	60.1	20.8
1978	61.0	22.3
1979	62.6	22.4
1980	62.9	22.3
1981	61.9	22.1
1982	62.1	22.2
1983	63.0	22.5
1984	64.5	23.3
1985	64.2	23.4
1986	65.2	23.6
1987	66.5	24.3
1988	68.4	25.3
1989	70.8	26.5
1990	68.7	26.3
1991	69.9	26.7
1992	70.0	26.5
1993	69.5	26.7

SOURCES: J. Dignon, unpublished data series, private communication, February 12, 1996; Hameed and Dignon, *Journal of the Air & Waste Management Association*, February 1991; Dignon and Hameed, *JPCA*, February 1989.

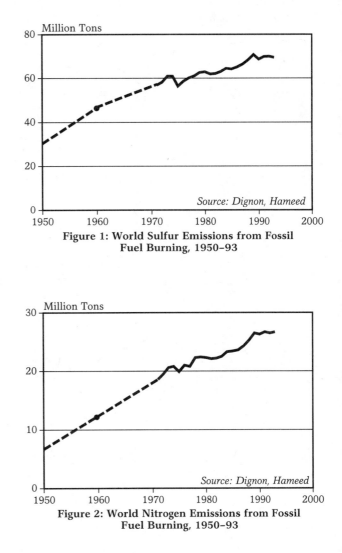

Figure 1: World Sulfur Emissions from Fossil Fuel Burning, 1950–93

Figure 2: World Nitrogen Emissions from Fossil Fuel Burning, 1950–93

Economic
Trends

World Economy Expanding Steadily   Lester R. Brown

In 1995, the global economy grew by an estimated 3.7 percent, up slightly from the 3.6-percent increase in 1994 and the largest expansion since the 4.6-percent growth of 1988.[1] (See Figure 1.) For the second year in a row, income per person increased by more than 2 percent.[2] (See Figure 2.)

This robust year of growth was led by developing countries, whose output of goods and services expanded by 6 percent, more than double the 2.5 percent of industrial countries.[3] Within the developing regions, Asia—by far the largest—expanded by 8.7 percent, with China leading the way at 10.2 percent.[4] With a fourth consecutive year of double-digit growth, the Chinese economy expanded by 57 percent between 1991 and 1995, raising income per person by more than half in just four years.[5] Even more remarkable, early forecasts indicate the economy will grow at more than 10 percent again in 1996.[6]

Other standouts among the fast-paced Asian economies were Korea at 9.7 percent, Vietnam at 9.0 percent, and Thailand at 8.4 percent.[7] Indonesia—with 200 million people, the world's fourth most populous country—expanded at 7.5 percent.[8]

The Indian subcontinent is also picking up the economic pace. India, now successfully attracting record amounts of foreign investment, expanded by 5.5 percent, up from 4.9 percent in 1994.[9] Pakistan and Bangladesh were close behind, at 5.1 percent and 4.9 percent, respectively.[10] Overall, the Indian subcontinent—with 1.2 billion people, as many as in China—expanded by more than 5 percent.[11]

For Latin America, the growth rate in 1995 dropped to 1.8 percent, barely a third the 4.6 percent recorded in 1994.[12] The principal reason was Mexico, where the economy shrank by 5 percent.[13] The Brazilian economy expanded at 5.1 percent in 1995, down slightly from the 5.7 percent registered in 1996.[14] The growth leaders in the region were Chile and Peru, at 7.0 and 6.5 percent, respectively.[15]

Africa, expanding by 3.0 percent in 1995, chalked up its best year since 1989.[16] It was led by Sudan at 7.2 percent, Uganda at 6.5

percent, and Côte d'Ivoire at 6.4 percent.[17] Other African countries growing by 4 percent or more were Ghana, Tanzania, and Tunisia.[18]

Within the industrial world, the U.S. economy—the world's largest—grew at 2.9 percent.[19] Germany, France, Italy, and the United Kingdom all expanded between 2.6 and 3.0 percent.[20] This preliminary estimate for France may be adjusted downward as a result of the strike of government workers during the year's closing quarter.

Japan completed its third year of little or no growth, with its economy rising by an average of 0.3 percent a year from 1992 to 1995.[21] It is, however, recovering from the bursting of the real estate speculation bubble of several years ago, and is projected by the International Monetary Fund (IMF) to expand by 2.2 percent in 1996.[22]

Within the transition economies of Eastern Europe and the former Soviet Union, things are also looking up. There are, however, wide variations within this region. Nearly all the East European economies expanded in 1995.[23] Poland and Romania each completed their third year of growth, registering expansions of 5.5 and 4.5, respectively.[24] The transition from centrally planned economies to market ones is largely completed in these countries.

In contrast, the Russian economy contracted by 4.3 percent in 1995, although at least this was much smaller than the 15-percent decline recorded in 1994.[25] For the Ukraine, the decline in 1995 continued at double-digit levels, suggesting that a turnaround there is still not near.[26] Among the former Soviet republics, the standouts in 1995 were Estonia, Lithuania, and Armenia, whose economies all expanded between 5 and 6 percent.[27]

Overall, the IMF projects the world economy will grow by at least 4 percent in 1996, the highest rate in this decade.[28] Among other things, this assumes the resumption of growth in Japan, recovery in Mexico, and a better performance in the former Soviet republics as the transition to market economies progresses.

GROSS WORLD PRODUCT, 1950-95

YEAR	TOTAL (trill. 1987 dollars)	PER CAPITA (1987 dollars)
1950	3.8	1,487
1955	4.9	1,763
1960	6.1	2,008
1965	7.9	2,362
1966	8.3	2,430
1967	8.6	2,468
1968	9.1	2,560
1969	9.7	2,673
1970	10.1	2,727
1971	10.5	2,776
1972	11.0	2,850
1973	11.7	2,973
1974	11.8	2,941
1975	11.9	2,912
1976	12.5	3,006
1977	13.0	3,073
1978	13.5	3,137
1979	14.0	3,197
1980	14.1	3,165
1981	14.3	3,156
1982	14.4	3,124
1983	14.8	3,156
1984	15.4	3,228
1985	16.0	3,297
1986	16.4	3,321
1987	17.0	3,382
1988	17.8	3,480
1989	18.4	3,534
1990	18.8	3,549
1991	18.7	3,471
1992	19.0	3,448
1993	19.5	3,464
1994	20.1	3,577
1995 (prel)	20.8	3,629

SOURCES: World Bank and International Monetary Fund tables.

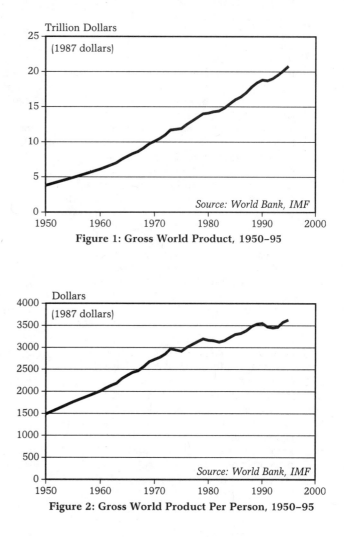

Trillion Dollars

(1987 dollars)

Source: World Bank, IMF

Figure 1: Gross World Product, 1950–95

Dollars

(1987 dollars)

Source: World Bank, IMF

Figure 2: Gross World Product Per Person, 1950–95

Global Trade Continues Upward Gary Gardner

Global trade rose an estimated 2 percent in value to some $4.3 trillion in 1995, continuing the rapid growth of the nineties.[1] (See Figures 1 and 2.) The increase was spurred by falling tariffs, the growing strength of regional trading groups, expanded investment in developing nations, and the recovery of trade activity in Eastern Europe and the former Soviet Union.[2] Growth in trade is expected to remain strong throughout the decade.[3]

The economies of Europe and Japan are strengthening and stimulating trade, but the largest increases continue to come from developing countries.[4] Since the mid-eighties, imports into developing nations have grown faster than those in industrial ones.[5] In 1996, they are projected to rise almost twice as much as those of industrial nations.[6]

Trade increased more than twice as fast as world economic output in 1995, a reflection of the growing integration of the global economy.[7] Many firms now make product components in one or more countries and assemble the product elsewhere.[8] In addition, many companies have set up regional or global headquarters for particular products that they then export around the world.[9] Integration, in turn, is stimulated through increased investment in factories and other real assets in foreign countries. Such direct investment in developing countries has tripled in the past four years; it now accounts for more than 40 percent of net flows of capital into Asia.[10] (The remainder is investments in stocks and bonds, and loans.)

To a large extent, the increase in global trade is regionally driven; trade within regions is growing faster than trade across them. This is prompted in part by the formation of regional trading blocs, which have proved stronger in the nineties than similar organizations of decades past were. The new over-arching global body that was set up in 1995, the World Trade Organization (WTO), reports that nearly a third of all regional trade agreements concluded since 1948 came into being between 1990 and 1994.[11]

Latin America was especially active in regional trade in 1995. Mercosur (a trade zone consisting of Brazil, Argentina, Paraguay, and Uruguay) became the second largest customs union after the European Union (EU).[12] (A customs union not only governs trade within the region, it sets duties for trade with nations outside the region.) The EU negotiated a protocol for a free trade pact with Mercosur, an arrangement that could compete with the proposed hemispheric free trade zone stretching from Tierra del Fuego to Alaska.[13] Meanwhile, the Andean Pact (Bolivia, Colombia, Ecuador, Peru, and Venezuela), an active free trade zone, developed plans to form a customs union.[14] The Central America Common Market and the Caribbean Common Market also became more active.[15]

Many developing countries are experiencing greater trade stability as the share of manufactured exports in their trade mix rises; manufactured goods prices tend to be less volatile than the prices of raw materials. In Asia, manufactured goods accounted for 70 percent of total exports in 1990; for developing countries in the western hemisphere, the figure was 34 percent.[16] In Africa, by contrast, manufactures dropped to 22 percent of total exports in 1990.[17]

At the same time, foreign debt, which eats up foreign exchange that could otherwise be used to purchase imports, is down in much of the developing world; next year, it is expected to reach its lowest level (as a share of export earnings) since 1982.[18] Again, Africa is an exception: indebtedness to foreign creditors continues to rise there.[19]

In its first major judgment of a trade dispute, the WTO ruled that the U.S. Clean Air Act, which sets different cleanliness standards for U.S. and imported gasoline, is discriminatory, and ordered the United States to change its rules or face sanctions.[20] The WTO also received complaints in 1995 of trade discrimination stemming from various national health and labor standards.[21] The organization's approach to such complaints is still developing. Trade/environment disputes are on the agenda of the WTO's first ministerial meeting, set for Singapore in December 1996.[22]

Global Trade Continues Upward

World Exports, 1950–95

YEAR	EXPORTS (bill. 1990 dollars)
1950	330
1955	451
1960	586
1965	804
1966	860
1967	905
1968	1,031
1969	1,150
1970	1,270
1971	1,336
1972	1,460
1973	1,643
1974	1,732
1975	1,640
1976	1,828
1977	1,897
1978	1,994
1979	2,132
1980	2,207
1981	2,222
1982	2,147
1983	2,200
1984	2,393
1985	2,483
1986	2,502
1987	2,659
1988	2,933
1989	3,142
1990	3,334
1991	3,482
1992	3,658
1993	3,857
1994	4,235
1995 (prel)	4,317

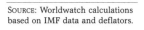

Source: Worldwatch calculations based on IMF data and deflators.

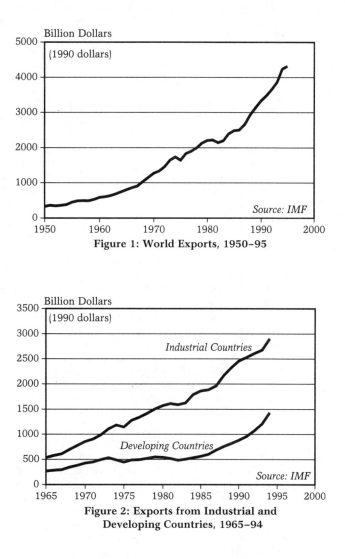

Figure 1: World Exports, 1950–95

Figure 2: Exports from Industrial and Developing Countries, 1965–94

Steel Production Rebounds Slightly   Hal Kane

World production of steel rose by almost 19 million tons in 1995, to more than 748 million tons, rebounding from a decline in the early nineties and from essentially flat production during the mid-nineties.[1] (See Figure 1.) Despite the rise, steel output is now only slightly higher than it was in 1979. Per person output rose by 2 kilograms in 1995, to 131 kilograms, but has mostly fallen since its 1973 peak of 177 kilograms.[2] (See Figure 2.)

The most dramatic changes in steel production have come in the former Soviet Union and Eastern Europe. (See Figure 3.) In 1989, the Soviet Union made 160 million tons of steel, more than 20 percent of the world total.[3] By 1994, output had dropped by more than half—to 78 million tons.[4] In 1995, though, the fall in production stopped for the first time in the nineties, and output stayed about constant.[5] East European production fell as fast, from 61 million tons in 1988 to less than 30 million in 1993, before a slight recovery to 34 million in 1995.[6]

East Asia, meanwhile, has partially offset those declines at the global level. China's production has risen continually: from only 24 million tons in 1977, the nation now produces 93 million tons.[7] Still, that is a far smaller proportion of world output than its population and growing economic strength would dictate. South Korea's economic growth has similarly raised its steel output, from little more than 4 million tons in 1977 to almost 37 million in 1995.[8] And Taiwan's production jumped from under 2 million in 1977 to nearly 12 million in 1995.[9]

Indonesia, Thailand, and Vietnam produce little steel, but if they follow in Japan's footsteps, production in this part of the world will be high in the future. Japan made 102 million tons of steel in 1995, but even that large total was down from 110 million tons in 1990 and 1991.[10]

India's steel production is rising as well. Output did not pick up there until 1984, but from under 11 million tons that year, production topped 20 million in 1995 as the national economy expanded.[11] Nevertheless, production there is also small considering the size of the population: with more than seven times as many people as Japan, India still makes only about one fifth as much steel.[12]

Other parts of the world produce little steel. Africa makes only slightly more than 13 million tons—but more than 8 million tons of that are produced in South Africa.[13] South America produces only 35 million tons in the whole continent, with Brazil dominating with some 25 million tons.[14] The Middle East produces about 8 million tons, although that amount is double its production just five years earlier.[15]

Steel production is growing in countries like China and India because these nations are building their physical infrastructure. In some areas, they are putting up buildings with steel girders for the first time. They are expanding their fleets of cars, and building highways and bridges. They are putting refrigerators in homes. And they are housing their quickly growing populations. Many regions of industrial countries, on the other hand, are past this stage.

This means a changing geographical distribution of steel production, from industrial countries to developing. And it means that the pollution associated with steel production has moved. Chinese cities are bearing a growing burden of air and water pollution and of respiratory diseases, as are many other regions of the developing world. Meanwhile, some areas of North America, Europe, and the former Soviet Union once famous for skies thick with smog and pollution have now become cleaner. Pittsburgh, Pennsylvania, is often cited for its dramatic reversal from a symbol of pollution to one of the more "livable" cities in the United States.[16]

Some of the declines in pollution are due to major improvements in manufacturing processes, however. Many of the new plants being built are electric arc "minimills" that recycle scrap steel from girders, cars, and appliances while using a fraction of the energy that plants relying on virgin ore use.[17] The United States, for example, raised the average recycled content of the new steel it produces from 39 percent in 1984 to more than 58 percent in 1994.[18]

WORLD STEEL PRODUCTION, 1950–95

YEAR	TOTAL (mill. tons)	PER PERSON (kilograms)
1950	190	74
1955	271	97
1960	347	114
1965	451	135
1966	469	137
1967	493	142
1968	524	147
1969	571	157
1970	595	161
1971	582	154
1972	631	163
1973	696	177
1974	703	175
1975	644	157
1976	675	162
1977	675	160
1978	717	166
1979	747	171
1980	716	161
1981	707	156
1982	645	140
1983	664	141
1984	710	149
1985	719	148
1986	714	144
1987	736	146
1988	780	152
1989	786	151
1990	770	145
1991	736	137
1992	724	132
1993	731	132
1994	730	129
1995 (prel)	748	131

SOURCE: International Iron and Steel Institute, *Steel Statistical Yearbook* (Brussels: various years).

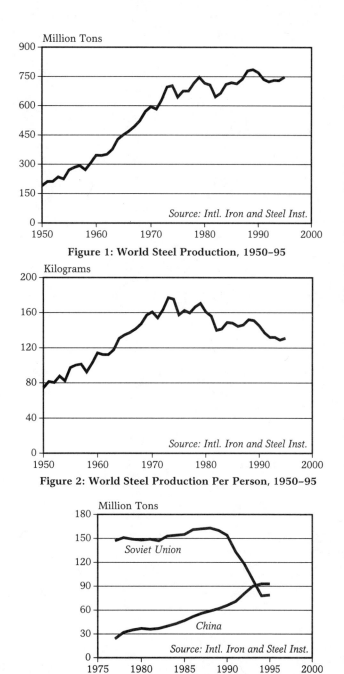

Figure 1: World Steel Production, 1950–95

Figure 2: World Steel Production Per Person, 1950–95

Figure 3: Steel Production, China and Soviet Union, 1977–95

Transportation Trends

In 1995, the world produced an estimated 114 million bicycles, up from 111 million in 1994.[1] (See Figure 1.) The upward trend, broken only twice in the past 45 years, reflects the bicycle's continuing popularity as an inexpensive and reliable form of transportation.

Asia leads world production, with more than two thirds of the global share in 1994.[2] Four nations—China, India, Taiwan, and Japan—accounted for more than 60 percent of the global total.[3] China remains by far the world's largest manufacturer of bicycles, producing more than 41 million in 1994, a quarter of which are for export.[4] India has emerged in recent years as a competitive exporter of bicycles, with shipments growing more than 12 percent in 1994.[5] (See Figure 2.)

Brazil, the world's seventh largest producer, is a rising bicycle power.[6] With close to 5 million bikes produced in 1994, Brazil makes more than either Germany, the United Kingdom, France, or Canada.[7] Industry sources assert that the Brazilian market is potentially as large as that in the United States, and project domestic sales there to rise from 3.9 million units in 1994 to 10 million units by 1997.[8]

Trends in bicycle use differ widely from region to region. Probably the greatest surge in bicycle use in modern times is under way in Cuba, where in just three years the number of bikes rose tenfold in Havana alone, from 70,000 to 700,000.[9] Bicycles there are used for a multitude of purposes, from commuting to hauling to recreation. The product of an acute shortage of oil, the high cycling level is probably temporary, but it nevertheless offers a vision of a city transport system dominated by the bicycle.

By contrast, several Asian cities are increasingly hostile to bicycles. In Ho Chi Minh City, cyclos (load-hauling tricycles) were banned from the city center in 1995, as they have been in Jakarta, Dhaka, and Shanghai in the past three years, allegedly for fostering an image of backwardness and for clogging city streets.[10] Economic prosperity in Vietnam has also cut into the bicycle's popularity: bike use has declined since the mid-eighties as use of motorcycles has picked up.[11] Bikes now account for only 43 percent of total trips, down from 65 percent in 1975.[12]

Government policies can be instrumental in promoting bicycle use. In the Netherlands, where bicycles account for up to half the trips in some cities, governments actively encourage cycling through provision of safe and convenient cycling routes and through disincentives to drive: civil servants are now required to make all official trips by bus, rail, or bicycle.[13] In Palo Alto, California, city employees are reimbursed for business trips made on bikes, and are given $20 per month in vouchers for use at area bike stores.[14] In Lima, Peru, where transportation expenses eat up 12–25 percent of the incomes of low and very low income persons, the city is facilitating cycling by building bikeways and by providing financing so that buyers can pay for their bikes in manageable monthly installments.[15]

Nonmotorized vehicles continue to find wide use as worktools in many parts of the world. They are increasingly popular among law enforcement agencies in the United States, with bike patrol divisions now found in more than 400 U.S. police departments.[16] Even the U.S. Secret Service uses bicycles to patrol the White House grounds.[17] In Uganda, bicycles now dominate the transport of agricultural commodities produced within 35 kilometers of various markets around Kampala, the capital.[18] They help make commercial production possible for many farmers previously isolated from the markets. In Bogotá, Colombia, the largest industrial bakery replaced 200 delivery trucks with 800 tricycles to service its 22,000 daily customers.[19]

Bicycles are now included in transportation planning even at the national and international level. For the first time, the World Bank is considering authorizing lending for projects on nonmotorized transport.[20] The United States has since 1991 required states to incorporate bicycle use into their transportation planning.[21] As the bicycle becomes accepted and promoted at various levels of society, its full potential moves closer to realization.

WORLD BICYCLE PRODUCTION, 1950–95

YEAR	PRODUCTION (million)
1950	11
1955	15
1960	20
1965	21
1966	22
1967	23
1968	24
1969	25
1970	36
1971	39
1972	46
1973	52
1974	52
1975	43
1976	47
1977	49
1978	51
1979	54
1980	62
1981	65
1982	69
1983	74
1984	76
1985	79
1986	84
1987	98
1988	105
1989	95
1990	90
1991	96
1992	103
1993	108
1994	111
1995 (prel)	114

SOURCES: 1950, 1955, and 1990–95, Worldwatch estimates based on *Interbike Directory*, various years; United Nations, *The Growth of World Industry 1969 Edition*, Vol. II, and *Yearbooks of Industrial Statistics 1979 and 1989 Editions*, Vol. II.

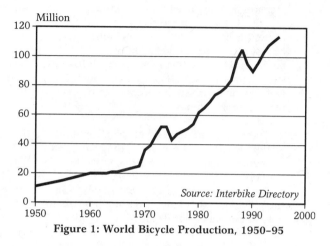

Source: Interbike Directory

Figure 1: World Bicycle Production, 1950–95

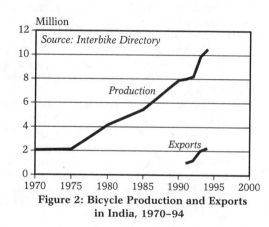

Source: Interbike Directory

Production

Exports

Figure 2: Bicycle Production and Exports in India, 1970–94

Auto Production Rises Again

Odil Tunali

Global automobile production continued to increase in 1995, reaching 35.6 million.[1] (See Figure 1.) Although the rise was a mere 1 percent from 1994, total output came the closest so far to the 1990 peak of 36.1 million.[2] The resulting increase in global fleet size was once again offset by the growth in world population, so the number of people per automobile did not change.[3] (See Figures 2 and 3.)

The sales of new cars, however, remained at 1994 levels: at 34.6 million, they were only 4.5 percent higher than in 1993, when they hit a six-year low of 33.1 million.[4]

Production in the United States fell from the previous year's high of 6.6 million cars to 6.3 million, and sales declined to 8.6 million—down by 3.5 percent.[5] European sales grew by only 0.6 percent, to 12 million cars, down from 1991's peak of 13.5 million.[6] They slowed considerably in September 1995 when government-sponsored incentives to replace highly polluting old cars expired in several countries.[7] Japanese sales did go up, although by a modest 3.5 percent; production, however, in both Japan and Europe declined slightly.[8]

By contrast, production and sales in much of Asia, Latin America, and Eastern Europe were booming. Asia (excluding Japan) recorded a 17.5-percent increase in production, nearing 3 million cars in 1995; meanwhile, sales grew by 8 percent.[9] South Korea, which rivals Japan as the leading Asian car manufacturer, produced 2 million automobiles, about half of which were exported.[10] In Latin America, Brazil—with 1.3 million cars—has emerged among the world's 10 largest carmakers.[11] Poland was the fastest-growing car market of the former Eastern bloc: production and sales both grew by more than 10 percent in 1995.[12]

The global auto industry is moving rapidly to capitalize on the surging demand from developing-country markets. Asia is the most enticing of these since it is the world's most populous region and has the fastest-growing economies.[13] And vehicle sales in China, India, Indonesia, Malaysia, Thailand, and Vietnam are growing faster than the economies.[14] American, European, Japanese, and even South Korean manufacturers have major investments planned in these countries.[15]

China—with its recent economic boom, large consumer market, and rising car demand—is the preferred site of investment for foreign carmakers. Between 1979 and 1995, the number of cars in China grew from 150,000 to 1.9 million, most of which are bought by state enterprises, government offices, and taxi firms.[16] But a new auto policy of the Chinese government announced in 1994 gives foreign firms a major role in the production of cars for individuals or families. Many foreign automakers, among them Mercedes-Benz, Chrysler, Honda, and Ford, are competing to win a contract to produce cars for families. Meanwhile, some are also establishing joint ventures with Chinese firms to manufacture cars and light vehicles.[17]

India is another popular market for foreign carmakers. With recent economic reforms and easier consumer credit, car demand there has been surging.[18] Sales grew by nearly 40 percent in a year—from 180,000 in 1994 to 250,000.[19]

This dramatic increase in production and sales of automobiles in some of the most populous countries of the world raises serious health and environmental concerns. Many urban centers there already have critical levels of air pollution, congestion, and noise, yet few or no regulations are in place to control these problems. For example, nearly 500 new vehicles enter Bangkok's notoriously congested and polluted streets each day, where traffic crawls at average speeds of 1 mile per hour at peak periods.[20] The automotive expansion will not only make these problems worse, it will also increase carbon emissions, contributing to global climate change.

Meanwhile, in the United States the popularity of sport utility vehicles, vans, minivans, and pickups continues to hold. Widespread use of such gasoline-guzzling vehicles is reversing advances in fuel efficiency, while their high level of carbon emissions is cancelling out gains attained in curbing emissions in other sectors.[21]

WORLD AUTOMOBILE PRODUCTION
AND FLEET, 1950–95

YEAR	TOTAL (million)	FLEET (million)
1950	8	53
1955	11	73
1960	13	98
1965	19	140
1966	19	148
1967	19	158
1968	22	170
1969	23	181
1970	22	194
1971	26	207
1972	28	220
1973	30	236
1974	26	249
1975	25	260
1976	29	269
1977	30	285
1978	31	297
1979	31	308
1980	29	320
1981	28	331
1982	27	340
1983	30	352
1984	30	365
1985	32	374
1986	33	386
1987	33	394
1988	34	413
1989	36	424
1990	36	445
1991	35	456
1992	35	470
1993	34	470
1994	35	480
1995 (prel)	36	486

SOURCES: American Automobile Manufactureers
Association; DRI/McGraw-Hill.

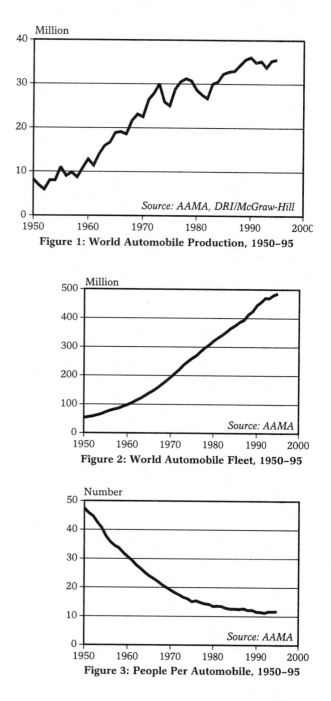

Figure 1: World Automobile Production, 1950–95

Source: AAMA, DRI/McGraw-Hill

Figure 2: World Automobile Fleet, 1950–95

Source: AAMA

Figure 3: People Per Automobile, 1950–95

Source: AAMA

Social
Trends

Population Increase Slightly Down   Aaron Sachs

The world's population now stands at just over 5.7 billion.[1] In 1995, we added close to 87 million people, equivalent to about three times the current population of Canada.[2] (See Figures 1 and 2.)

The new addition represented a decrease of about 1 million from the previous year's population growth.[3] This very slight slowdown in the annual increment reflects a few important trends around the world. But its statistical significance is limited.

The significant trend is that annual growth seems to have reached a plateau, having remained at approximately 88 million for the last decade.[4] The average annual growth rate—the net annual population gain expressed as a percentage of the total population—should continue its gradual decline. (See Figure 3.) But most demographers predict that the net gain itself will probably not begin a steady drop from its perch between 85 and 90 million for another 30 years or so.[5]

The existence of the plateau, however, does suggest that population growth may have peaked. Forecasters are no longer predicting a new doubling of the world's people by sometime in the first half of the next century.[6] The world's population may still be below 10 billion in the year 2050.[7] Of course, even low levels of population growth can be destabilizing: women's health is already being compromised by multiple pregnancies, many cities are overcrowded, and some natural resources are in short supply.

Unfortunately, the slight decrease in last year's net addition to the world's population is in part linked to higher mortality rates in a few areas. In Russia and many neighboring countries, for example, economic instability and a legacy of severe environmental contamination have caused death rates to exceed birth rates by a large margin.[8]

Russia itself, because of an influx of immigrants from even less stable countries, experienced only a slight drop in population last year—about 100,000 people.[9] But annual births are down by close to 1 million since 1987, while annual deaths have climbed by about the same amount.[10] Demographers are guessing that by 2005 Russia's population

may have shrunk by some 9 million.[11]

In sub-Saharan Africa, the devastating impact of AIDS is now starting to show up in census data. Some countries whose populations were growing at a rate of about 3 percent a year in the eighties now have annual growth rates of barely 1 percent.[12] As recently as 1992, Zimbabwe added 250,000 people to its population, but the net gain in 1995 was just 100,000—a decrease attributable almost entirely to AIDS deaths.[13]

Other developments contributing to the slowdown in world population growth are more promising. India, for instance, has seen its net annual addition fall from nearly 17 million in 1993 to 15.6 million in 1995, with no increase in mortality.[14] And demographers have lowered their estimate of the country's total fertility rate—the average number of children born to a woman in her lifetime—from 3.9 in 1993 to about 3.4 currently.[15]

Maintaining such positive trends depends on the international community's willingness to continue making population issues a priority. The long process of implementing the Program of Action agreed on at the International Conference on Population and Development (ICPD) held in Cairo in September 1994 at least got off to a promising start in 1995.

At a May 1995 workshop in Jakarta, delegates from 29 countries emphasized cooperation among governments, nongovernmental groups, and the private sector, and pointed to effective programs addressing women's reproductive health, gender equality, and sex education for adolescents as the keys to population-centered development.[16] And in September 1995, the delegates to the Fourth World Conference on Women, in Beijing, confirmed that upholding women's rights—expanding their access to health care, education, and income-generating employment—is perhaps the world's most crucial development goal, both for its own sake and also because it is probably the only sure way to slow population growth.[17]

WORLD POPULATION, 1950–95

YEAR	TOTAL (billion)	ANNUAL ADDITION (million)
1950	2.555	37
1955	2.779	53
1960	3.038	41
1965	3.345	70
1966	3.414	69
1967	3.484	71
1968	3.555	74
1969	3.629	75
1970	3.704	78
1971	3.782	77
1972	3.859	77
1973	3.936	76
1974	4.012	74
1975	4.086	73
1976	4.159	73
1977	4.231	73
1978	4.304	76
1979	4.380	77
1980	4.457	77
1981	4.533	81
1982	4.614	81
1983	4.695	80
1984	4.775	81
1985	4.856	83
1986	4.941	87
1987	5.029	88
1988	5.117	88
1989	5.205	90
1990	5.295	86
1991	5.381	88
1992	5.469	88
1993	5.556	88
1994	5.644	88
1995 (prel)	5.732	87

SOURCE: U.S. Bureau of the Census, Center for international Research, private communication, January 23, 1996.

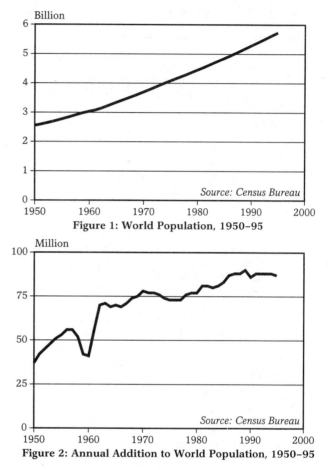

Figure 1: World Population, 1950–95

Figure 2: Annual Addition to World Population, 1950–95

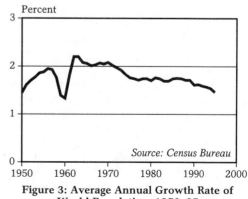

Figure 3: Average Annual Growth Rate of World Population, 1950–95

Cigarette Production Hits New High   Hal Kane

World cigarette production reached an all-time high of more than 5.5 trillion in 1995—50 billion cigarettes above the output in 1994—reversing some years of decline in the early nineties.[1] (See Figure 1.) Nevertheless, worldwide population growth meant that six fewer cigarettes were produced per person in 1995.[2] (See Figure 2.) Production per person has now fallen to 966 pieces per year, 63 below its peak in 1988.[3]

East Asia leads the world in the increase of cigarette production. Fueled by economic growth that has made smoking affordable, China's output rose by 20 billion pieces in 1995 (see Figure 3), and Indonesia's rose by 10 billion.[4] But production fell by almost 4 billion in Japan and by 6 billion in South Korea.[5]

Another large increase was registered in the former Soviet Union and Eastern Europe. Russia made 12 billion more cigarettes, Poland made 4 billion more, and Bulgaria made an additional 2 billion.[6] All these countries are trying to recover from the massive drops in output following the breakup of the Soviet Union and the economic changes in Eastern Europe. Pent-up hunger for tobacco fueled the growth, and foreign investment—much of it from the United States—made higher production possible.[7]

South America's production rose by more than 15 billion pieces—led by Brazil, which produced some 11 billion more than in 1994, and Venezuela, which produced 5 billion more.[8]

In the wealthy countries in North America and Europe, production mostly fell. Higher cigarette taxes and other efforts to cut down on smoking-related disease have been effective there. The United States produced 9 billion fewer cigarettes in 1995 than in 1994.[9] The European Union also reduced output by more than 9 billion, with cuts in Belgium, Germany, Portugal, and Spain.[10] The Netherlands, on the other hand, raised production by 2 billion.[11]

Among wealthy countries, though, the surprise came from Canada, which produced 2.5 billion more cigarettes in 1995, on top of a rise in 1994 of some 9 billion.[12] This is massive growth in the tobacco industry of a country whose government has long discouraged tobacco use. Much if not most of the growth can be traced to the sudden reduction of tobacco taxes in 1994, which had effectively dampened smoking. After being a world leader in cigarette taxation, Canada dropped the price of cigarettes by half in 1994 through the tax cut, and so boosted smoking.[13]

In the course of a year, tobacco kills about 3 million people—2 million in industrial countries and 1 million in developing ones, where large-scale smoking started later.[14] When the waiting period between the start of smoking and the appearance of disease is over in developing countries, the annual toll from tobacco use everywhere is expected to reach 10 million deaths.[15]

As it does every year, new research appeared in 1995 about the ill effects of smoking. It was found, for example, that among people in their thirties, the heart attack rate in smokers was 6.3 times that of nonsmokers, and for those in their forties, the rate was 4.7 times higher.[16] By the World Health Organization's count, smokers who die before the age of 70 on average lose 22 years of life expectancy.[17] Another study found that the risk for facial wrinkling was two to three times greater among smokers than nonsmokers—though the effect of smoking on the face does not become evident until middle age.[18]

In countries where smoking started later, the health effects of tobacco are taking a steadily growing toll. During World War II, although cigarettes were found everywhere in North America and Europe, tobacco consumption declined in Japan.[19] But since 1960 consumption there has risen steadily to be near the top of the world.[20] The mortality rate due to lung cancer has grown in a straight line since the mid-fifties in Japan, even as it began to decline in countries that cut back on smoking. From about 5 deaths per 100,000 people, it is now about 35 and rising steadily.[21] Japan has almost caught up to the United Kingdom in lung cancer deaths.[22]

WORLD CIGARETTE PRODUCTION, 1950–95

YEAR	TOTAL (billion)	PER PERSON (number)
1950	1,686	660
1955	1,921	691
1960	2,150	708
1965	2,564	767
1966	2,678	784
1967	2,689	772
1968	2,790	785
1969	2,924	806
1970	3,112	840
1971	3,165	837
1972	3,295	854
1973	3,481	884
1974	3,590	895
1975	3,742	916
1976	3,852	926
1977	4,019	950
1978	4,072	946
1979	4,214	962
1980	4,388	985
1981	4,541	1,002
1982	4,550	986
1983	4,547	968
1984	4,689	982
1985	4,855	1,000
1986	4,987	1,009
1987	5,128	1,020
1988	5,266	1,029
1989	5,257	1,010
1990	5,418	1,023
1991	5,351	994
1992	5,362	980
1993	5,299	954
1994	5,485	972
1995 (prel)	5,535	966

SOURCES: USDA, FAS, unpublished printouts; data for 1950–58 estimates based on U.S. data.

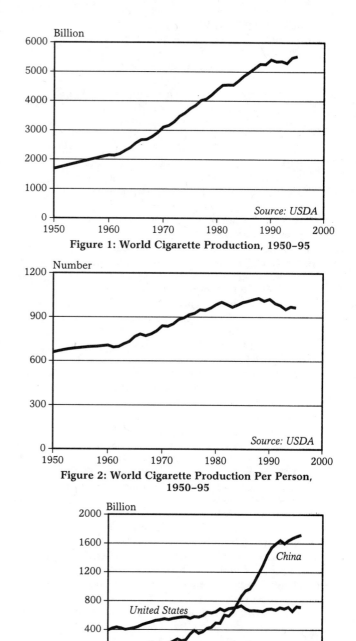

Figure 1: World Cigarette Production, 1950–95

Figure 2: World Cigarette Production Per Person, 1950–95

Figure 3: Cigarette Production, United States and China, 1950–95

HIV/AIDS Pandemic Spreading Faster   Aaron Sachs

More than 4.7 million people contracted HIV in 1995, up from 1994's previous record-high of some 4 million.[1] Each day, then, an average of about 13,000 people became infected, most of them in Southeast Asia and sub-Saharan Africa.[2] The 1.9 million new AIDS cases last year were also a record high.[3] And 1.7 million people died from AIDS in 1995—also more than in any previous year.[4]

AIDS has been with us for about 15 years now, and the human immunodeficiency virus (HIV) has infected some 30.6 million people in that time.[5] (See Figure 1.) Of these carriers, an estimated 10.4 million have developed full-blown AIDS (see Figure 2), and 89 percent of these AIDS patients—or 9.2 million people—have died.[6]

In just the past six years, the total number of adult HIV infections tripled.[7] Judging by current epidemiological trends, it appears that some 60–70 million people will have contracted the virus by the end of this decade, resulting in a global infection rate of about 1 percent.[8] In the hardest-hit areas, more than 30 percent of the local adult population will likely be stricken—as has already occurred in certain cities and towns in Africa.[9]

Though the disease has been centered in Africa since its inception, the number of new infections there seems to have reached a plateau. In the densely populated, rapidly industrializing countries of Southeast Asia, meanwhile, HIV is spreading faster than it ever has anywhere in the world. In 1995, for the first time, there were more new infections in Southeast Asia than in sub-Saharan Africa: while the African number held steady at 1.9 million, the Asian figure climbed from 1.7 million to 2.5 million.[10]

The economic impact of the HIV/AIDS pandemic in the developing world—where more than 90 percent of all HIV infections have occurred—has already begun to destabilize many communities.[11] In Tanzania, a few months of care and a funeral for an AIDS victim cost the equivalent of an average adult's yearly income.[12] And just during this decade, the epidemic will cost Thailand about $9 billion in health care services and productivity losses among adults aged 15–45.[13] Yet about 90 percent of the global HIV/AIDS budget is spent in the industrial world, mostly at advanced research institutes where scientists are testing drugs that most people in the developing world will never be able to afford.[14]

The United Nations' new HIV/AIDS program, launched in January 1996 and called UNAIDS, will attempt to direct more attention and funding to the developing world, where program officers will emphasize affordable care and low-tech prevention techniques.[15] One World Bank–funded project in Kenya that emphasized condom use averted an estimated 10,000 new infections annually at a cost of only about 50¢ each.[16]

Perhaps the most important preventive strategy, though, is the protection of the people who are most vulnerable to catching the virus—who, several studies have shown, turn out to be members of communities already suffering from some sort of discrimination or marginalization.[17] HIV is spreading most quickly among impoverished people who have no access to health services or even basic information about the virus and among people who cannot afford to avoid or refuse sexual encounters with potential carriers.

Married women in parts of East Africa, for instance, are in one of the highest-risk communities in the world because of their low social status and lack of civil rights. They have no legal protection against domestic violence, and divorce is usually crippling both socially and economically. So an African woman will often hesitate to ask even an admittedly promiscuous husband to use a condom simply out of fear that the request will anger him.[18]

The civil rights of people who are already infected often get overlooked as well—which represents an injustice in and of itself, and also raises more obstacles to prevention campaigns. Infected people facing stigmatization and severe social consequences—such as losing their job or being barred from entering a certain country—often avoid the public health care system altogether and end up endangering others, sometimes without realizing it.[19]

ESTIMATES OF CUMULATIVE
HIV/AIDS CASES WORLDWIDE,
1980–95

YEAR	HIV INFECTIONS (million)
1980	0.2
1981	0.6
1982	1.1
1983	1.8
1984	2.7
1985	3.9
1986	5.3
1987	6.9
1988	8.7
1989	10.7
1990	13.0
1991	15.5
1992	18.5
1993	21.9
1994	25.9
1995 (prel)	30.6

YEAR	AIDS CASES (million)
1980	0.0
1981	0.1
1982	0.1
1983	0.1
1984	0.2
1985	0.4
1986	0.7
1987	1.1
1988	1.6
1989	2.3
1990	3.2
1991	4.2
1992	5.5
1993	6.9
1994	8.5
1995 (prel)	10.4

SOURCE: Global AIDS Policy Coalition,
Harvard School of Public Health,
Cambridge, Mass., private communication,
January 18, 1996.

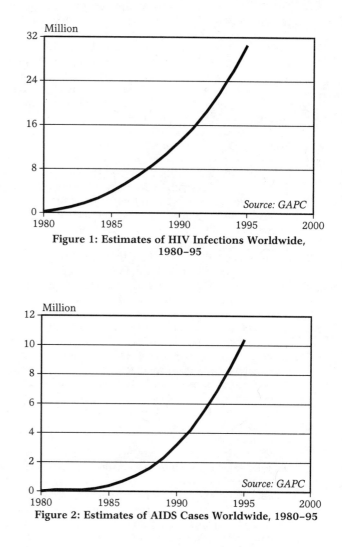

Source: GAPC

Figure 1: Estimates of HIV Infections Worldwide, 1980–95

Source: GAPC

Figure 2: Estimates of AIDS Cases Worldwide, 1980–95

Rapid Urbanization Continues David Malin Roodman

The ranks of city dwellers swelled 250 percent between 1950 and 1995.[1] In rural areas, the population climbed only 75 percent.[2] As a result, 45 percent of people—2.58 billion according to the most recent U.N. estimate—now call a city home, up from 29 percent in 1950.[3] (See Figures 1 and 2.) The figure is projected to pass 50 percent in 2005, when humanity will be predominantly urban.[4]

In 1800, only one city had a million inhabitants: London, capital of the country where the Industrial Revolution began.[5] Well into the twentieth century, most large cities were found in the industrialized democracies and Eastern bloc nations.[6] But around mid-century this began to change. (See Figure 3.) In response to industrialization and population growth, cities in developing countries began to mushroom, so that by 1970, half the world's city dwellers were found in developing countries.[7] By 1995, two thirds were.[8]

Industrialization drives urbanization in two ways. On the one hand, new technologies let farmers, fishers, loggers, and miners produce more with fewer hands, letting more people move off the land. On the other hand, most other enterprises—from weavers' guilds to software companies—have historically tended to function best in areas with higher population densities. Cities and towns have more potential customers, better infrastructure and transportation links, and the rich fabric of suppliers and skilled workers that are essential for getting a new business off the ground.[9]

In the United States, for example, the number of farms sank from 6.3 million to 2.1 million between 1930 and 1990—though the amount of cropland tilled remained stable and production skyrocketed.[10] Partly as a result, the urban fraction of population grew from 56 to 75 percent.[11] In Japan, the government has long protected its farmers—who are inefficient by global standards—from international competition. But recently the country has reduced some import barriers to foreign fruit, beef, and rice that are often many times cheaper than domestic produce.[12] Lower food prices have made it harder for many farmers to get by, and for many young adults, this is one more reason to seek better-paying work in the cities.[13]

In many poorer countries, rural population growth also pushes people into the cities. In nations such as Vietnam and China, where rural populations densities are high but still increasing, it is becoming impractical to subdivide farms or rice paddies any further to accommodate more people.[14] More than 100 million rural Chinese have left their farms to search for work in the country's booming cities, and another 100 million could probably follow without hurting agricultural output.[15]

Cities may be a natural artifact of economic development, but they are exceedingly unnatural from a biological point of view. They require enormous concentrations of food, water, energy, and materials, and generate equally dense concentrations of sewage, pollution, and garbage.[16] In poor countries, where municipal budgets are limited and cities are exploding in size, the side effects of population density have often overwhelmed government attempts to solve them. Millions of people now crowd into improvised shantytowns; struggle to get to work each day; breathe poisonous air; and live without clean water, sanitation, or affordable energy supplies. Fortunately, richer countries have shown that technological fixes such as water works and catalytic converters can reduce or solve many of these problems.

Yet even in rich countries, city living is often impractical, unhealthy, and environmentally unsustainable. One of the biggest culprits is low-density land development patterns that have placed homes far away from shopping and working areas, enforcing a car-based life-style. The apparent freedom that automobiles offer comes with many hidden costs, including long commutes, air pollution, and heavy dependence on oil.[17] The more environmentally sustainable alternative—development at densities that were common before World War II, combined with mass transit, bike paths, and sidewalks—can only be realized when governments take a much larger role in shaping the physical growth of cities.[18] Thus city planning is another key to making modern cities livable.

WORLD URBAN POPULATION, 1950–95

YEAR	POPULATION (billion)
1950	0.738
1955	0.864
1960	1.033
1965	1.186
1970	1.353
1975	1.538
1980	1.752
1985	1.994
1990	2.277
1995 (prel)	2.584

SHARE OF WORLD POPULATION THAT IS URBAN, 1950–95

YEAR	SHARE (percent)
1950	29.3
1955	31.4
1960	34.2
1965	35.5
1970	36.6
1975	37.7
1980	39.4
1985	41.2
1990	43.1
1995 (prel)	45.2

SOURCE: United Nations, *World Population Prospects: The 1994 Revision* (New York: 1995).

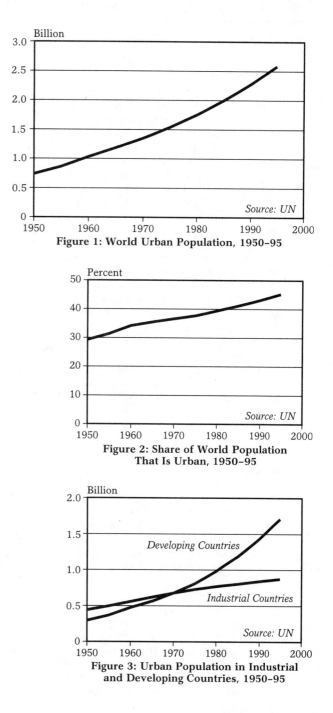

Figure 1: World Urban Population, 1950–95

Figure 2: Share of World Population That Is Urban, 1950–95

Figure 3: Urban Population in Industrial and Developing Countries, 1950–95

Refugees on the Rise Again   Hal Kane

At the beginning of 1995, the world had 27.4 million people who were refugees or were in refugee-like situations and who were deemed eligible for assistance by the office of the U.N. High Commissioner for Refugees (UNHCR).[1] (See Figure 1.) This number does not include everyone who had fled from a home or who needed shelter and other assistance, but it does cover those who qualified for refugee assistance under international law and whose governments or host nations allowed to receive help.

This total was 4.4 million higher than one year earlier, and 17 million more than 10 years ago, marking a continuation of rapid growth despite the end of the cold war and attempts at economic and social development throughout the world.[2]

Until the early nineties, all U.N. refugee assistance went to people who had left their countries; in 1993 and 1994, in contrast, the growth came from people displaced within their own countries.[3] The United Nations and the international community have become more willing and better able to help internally displaced people.[4]

In 1993 and 1994, for example, the number of refugees who had crossed international borders actually fell, according to the UNHCR.[5] From a figure of 19 million at the beginning of 1993, the total dropped to 16.4 million in early 1994 and 14.5 million in early 1995.[6] This is the first reduction in their numbers since 1950.

This welcome trend has been offset by the rising numbers of internally displaced and other people needing assistance.[7] The internally displaced helped by UNHCR grew from 3.7 million in 1994 to 5.4 million in January 1995, and the agency helped an additional 7.5 million people who were in the process of returning to their countries or who otherwise needed assistance.[8]

Perhaps the largest cause for the shift from international to internal refugees is today's wars. Almost all these are internal battles, caused by the breakup of countries or other internal conflicts.[9] Civil wars have created not only millions of international refugees but also as many or more internal refugees.

Several counts of the internally displaced—people who left for many reasons, of which war is only one—have estimated the number at about 26-27 million worldwide; this figure includes all those who fled their homes, not just those receiving U.N. help.[10] Yet people who move internationally are more likely to be counted than those who move within countries because of the national security and diplomatic significance of their movements. Internal refugees sometimes appear to just be ordinary people who moved from the countryside to a city or from one region to another; a fuller count might put their numbers far higher than those of international refugees.[11] Also, most of these people who remain within their countries cannot be reached by international aid because they are an internal concern of sovereign nations that refuse access to them.

The largest source of international refugees in the world is Afghanistan, which has dominated that position since the end of the seventies.[12] As of October 1995, 2.6 million Afghans were living in Iran, Pakistan, India, and the former Soviet Union.[13] The second largest source of refugees is Rwanda, with 1.8 million citizens currently in Burundi, Tanzania, Uganda, and Zaire.[14] No other country comes close to those two. The next is Liberia, with 785,000 people outside their native country, followed by Somalia with 526,000 and Sudan with 525,000.[15]

For internally displaced people, Bosnia and Herzegovina tops the list, with 2.7 million—more even than Afghanistan's international refugees.[16] Liberia has 1.5 million, above and beyond the Liberians who fled the country.[17] Sierra Leone has 782,000; Azerbaijan, 663,000; and Croatia, 425,000.[18]

The locations with the most international refugees around the world have changed dramatically in the last few years. Africa has surged past Asia to have the most, with 11.8 million.[19] (See Figure 2.) Europe's refugee population, both international and internally displaced, has also surged, and at 6.5 million is nearly as large as Asia's 7.9 million.[20]

REFUGEES RECEIVING U.N.
ASSISTANCE, 1961–95

YEAR	TOTAL (million)
1961	1.4
1962	1.3
1963	1.3
1964	1.3
1965	1.5
1966	1.6
1967	1.8
1968	2.0
1969	2.2
1970	2.3
1971	2.5
1972	2.5
1973	2.4
1974	2.4
1975	2.4
1976	2.6
1977	2.8
1978	3.3
1979	4.6
1980	5.7
1981	8.2
1982	9.8
1983	10.4
1984	10.9
1985	10.5
1986	11.6
1987	12.4
1988	13.3
1989	14.8
1990	14.9
1991	17.2
1992	17.0
1993	19.0
1994	23.0
1995 (prel)	27.4

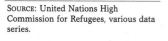

SOURCE: United Nations High
Commission for Refugees, various data
series.

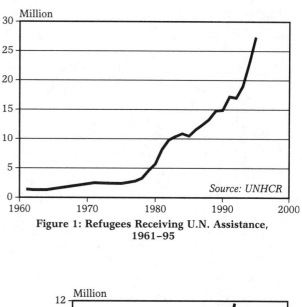

**Figure 1: Refugees Receiving U.N. Assistance,
1961–95**

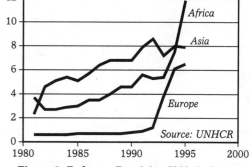

**Figure 2: Refugees Receiving U.N. Assistance
in Asia, Africa, and Europe, 1981–95**

Military
Trends

Nuclear Arsenals Continue to Decline   Michael Renner

The number of nuclear warheads worldwide declined from an estimated 44,500 in 1994 to 40,640 in 1995, a drop of 9 percent. Since its 1986 peak, the size of the global nuclear arsenal has dropped by 42 percent and is now slightly below the 1968 level.[1] (See Figure 1.)

The Nuclear Non-Proliferation Treaty (NPT) was signed in 1968.[2] It was intended to forestall the emergence of additional nuclear weapons states, but part of the bargain was for the existing nuclear powers to move toward disarmament. Yet the opposite happened in terms of the second goal. In May 1995, the NPT was extended indefinitely, but not without considerable debate over the nuclear powers' past record and future action with regard to fulfilling their pledge.[3]

The United States and Russia together account for 97 percent of all nuclear warheads.[4] (The United Kingdom, France, and China together control about 1,200 warheads.)[5] Both are continuing to dismantle warheads and launchers. During the past 10 years, the number of warheads in the former Soviet Union declined by about 20,000, and U.S. warheads fell by almost 10,000.[6] (See Figure 2.)

Three years after the second U.S.-Russian strategic arms treaty, START II, was signed, the U.S. Senate ratified it, but strong opposition in Russia casts doubt on whether it will actually enter into force.[7] Even as both countries dismantle older weapons, modernization continues, though to a lesser degree in Russia.[8] Further, the United States is planning to create a "hedge" stockpile—warheads removed from deployment but kept in reserve instead of being dismantled. Russia might do the same with a portion of the 12,000 warheads currently in storage.[9]

Non-nuclear countries agreed to the indefinite extension of the NPT with the expectation that a comprehensive test ban treaty (CTBT) would be speedily concluded. CTBT negotiations have been held in Geneva since January 1994. Lack of political will prevented their conclusion in time for the April 1995 NPT extension conference.[10] The hope now is that a treaty will finally be finished by mid-1996, in time for signature by the U.N.

General Assembly in September 1996.

Although the nuclear weapons states pledged at the NPT conference to "exercise utmost restraint," China (the only nuclear state not to observe a testing moratorium) conducted a test only three days after the meeting.[11] Then France broke its three-year testing moratorium, provoking worldwide protests, and went on to set off five nuclear bombs during 1995.[12] So a total of seven nuclear tests took place in 1995, up from two in 1994.[13] (See Figure 3.) (In January 1996, France triggered another bomb blast and then announced that it had ended its test program.)[14]

Russia and the United States are maintaining their own testing moratoria, but political change—both countries are to hold presidential elections in 1996—could bring test ban opponents to power. All nuclear states except China have endorsed a comprehensive test ban treaty, but opposition among their respective military complexes remains strong and could gain the upper hand if the current CTBT talks stall.[15]

Further, the political dynamics in South Asia could throw sand into the test ban machinery. In December 1995, reports circulated that India may be preparing for its first test since 1974.[16] An Indian test would have immediate ripple effects in Pakistan and China, and likely beyond.[17]

Efforts to delegitimize and abolish nuclear weapons received several boosts in 1995. Joseph Rotblat, a long-time disarmament advocate, was awarded the Nobel Peace Prize.[18] The U.N. General Assembly and the World Health Organization asked the International Court of Justice to rule whether use of nuclear weapons is illegal; a ruling is expected in the spring of 1996.[19] African nations are preparing to join Latin America and the South Pacific in formally establishing a nuclear-weapons free zone.[20] And in December 1995, the Australian government announced the formation of the Canberra Commission on the Elimination of Nuclear Weapons, which is to formulate practical steps toward a world free of nuclear weapons.[21]

WORLD NUCLEAR ARSENAL, 1945–95

YEAR	NUCLEAR WARHEADS (number)
1945	2
1950	301
1955	2,632
1960	20,368
1965	39,047
1966	40,348
1967	41,697
1968	41,209
1969	39,891
1970	39,871
1971	41,371
1972	44,020
1973	47,591
1974	50,690
1975	52,173
1976	53,104
1977	54,953
1978	56,882
1979	59,120
1980	61,652
1981	63,537
1982	65,454
1983	67,093
1984	68,327
1985	69,294
1986	70,298
1987	69,322
1988	67,974
1989	65,165
1990	61,946
1991	57,886
1992	53,450
1993	48,359
1994	44,500
1995 (prel)	40,640

SOURCE: Robert Norris, NRDC, private communication, January 17, 1996.

Figure 1: World Nuclear Arsenal, 1945–95

Figure 2: U.S. and Soviet Strategic and Tactical Nuclear Warheads, 1945–95

Figure 3: Nuclear Warhead Tests, 1945–95

Peacekeeping Expenditures Level Off   Michael Renner

Expenditures for United Nations peacekeeping operations reached an estimated $3.36 billion in 1995, abruptly capping a rapid growth of outlays in recent years.[1] (See Figure 1.) The 1995 amount is less than New York City spends on its Police, Fire, and Corrections Departments combined.[2] It is equivalent to less than half of 1 percent of global military spending.[3] Slightly more than half of the 1995 expenditures were accounted for by the twin operations in Bosnia-Herzegovina and Croatia. And the next four largest missions were together responsible for another quarter of the outlays.[4]

Before the late eighties, the number of peacekeepers deployed in any given year was typically below 15,000.[5] But by 1993, the peacekeeping ranks (military troops, observers, and police) had expanded to close to 80,000 from some 80 countries.[6] (See Figure 2.) The number of civilian members, insignificant until the late eighties, rose from 1,500 in 1990 to some 12,000 in 1994 and about 10,000 in 1995.[7]

As operations in Somalia, Mozambique, and El Salvador ended during the first half of 1995, the number of troops and observers declined again to about 53,000 by November 1995.[8] At the end of 1995, the U.N. handed over operations in Bosnia to IFOR, a NATO-led force deployed to enforce the U.S.-brokered Dayton Peace Agreement.[9] And the Croatia mission ended in January 1996, replaced by a much smaller, 5,000-strong force in the Eastern Slavonia region.[10] Together, these changes reduced the number of peacekeepers by another 30,000 troops. Hence, the enormous buildup in personnel since the late eighties has largely been reversed.

Since 1945, a total of 1,280 U.N. peacekeepers from 65 countries have lost their lives, due either to hostile acts or accidents.[11] During 1995, 90 peacekeepers were killed, compared with 135 in 1994 and 203 in 1993.[12]

The rise of peacekeeping in the post–cold war era found expression in a newly energized U.N. Security Council. Between 1946 and 1990, a total of 646 Council resolutions were passed, but 201 others were vetoed.[13]

With the fading of the East-West standoff, use of the veto disappeared almost entirely. The number of resolutions adopted rose from 15 in 1987 to 78 in 1993 and 70 in 1995.[14]

U.N. peacekeeping has repeatedly suffered from halfhearted support by member states. Their collective arrears on peacekeeping assessments reached a record in August 1995: $2.95 billion, or close to a full year's expenditures.[15] Though declining to $1.7 billion by year-end, unpaid assessments were still one third higher than a year earlier.[16] (See Figure 3.)

The United States remains by far the biggest debtor, paying only 45 percent of its assessed share.[17] In 1995, U.S. peacekeeping debts briefly surpassed the $1 billion mark, prompting severe criticism even by Washington's closest allies.[18] U.N. officials have been forced to delay reimbursing governments that contribute personnel and equipment to peacekeeping operations. The reimbursement backlog is now about $1 billion.[19]

Much of peacekeeping's future depends on U.S. attitudes. Though more supportive of peacekeeping than the Republican-dominated Congress, the Clinton administration adopted a set of policy guidelines in 1994 that restricted U.N. action in Rwanda, Burundi, Georgia, and Angola.[20] Republican efforts to curtail U.S. contributions sharply did not fully succeed, but nevertheless they pushed the U.N. to the edge of financial collapse.[21]

In 1996, peacekeeping involves far more limited finances and personnel than it did during the past four years. The U.N. is also expected to withdraw from Rwanda and Haiti during 1996.[22] Without these missions, annual expenditures are likely to fall to about $950 million.[23]

The peacekeeping boom is over. Although the U.S.-dominated Security Council is disinclined to support large or ambitious new operations (such as in Burundi, where a slow-motion civil war could erupt into massive violence at any moment), the world's conflicts will not simply go away, however.[24] Peacekeeping is here to stay as a challenge.

U.N. PEACEKEEPING OPERATION
EXPENDITURES, 1986–95

YEAR	EXPENDITURE (mill. dollars)
1986	242
1987	240
1988	266
1989	635
1990	464
1991	490
1992	1,767
1993	3,059
1994	3,342
1995	3,364

SOURCE: Field Operations Division, Department of Peace-Keeping Operations, United Nations, New York, private communications, October 23 and December 20, 1995.

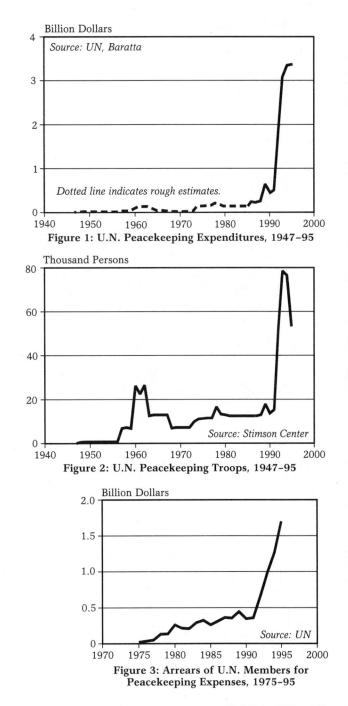

Figure 1: U.N. Peacekeeping Expenditures, 1947–95

Figure 2: U.N. Peacekeeping Troops, 1947–95

Figure 3: Arrears of U.N. Members for Peacekeeping Expenses, 1975–95

Part

Special Features

Agricultural Features

Efforts to Control Pesticides Expand   Toni Nelson

As the human and environmental costs of pesticides become better understood, a growing number of countries are banning the most toxic of these chemicals. National bans on 18 of the most hazardous and widely used pesticides increased from 53 in 1983 to 689 in 1995, according to the San Francisco–based Pesticide Action Network.[1] (See Table 1.) Many of the new bans were enacted in developing countries, where pesticide use has been increasing in recent years.[2]

Modern synthetic pesticides, especially the organophosphate insecticides, were developed from chemicals tested for their potential as nerve gas weapons during World War II.[3] During the forties, industrial countries began to use these chemicals for agricultural pest control. Usage increased rapidly in subsequent years, and annual global consumption is now estimated at 2.5 million tons (5.5 billion pounds).[4] The 1994 world pesticide market was valued at $27.8 billion, and the pesticide industry projects sales over $34 billion by 1998.[5] In the United States alone, 860 active-ingredient pesticide chemicals are formulated into 21,000 commercial products registered with the Environmental Protection Agency.[6] Of those, 278 are directly used on raw agricultural crops.[7]

Awareness of the costs associated with pesticide use is also growing, however. Rachel Carson's *Silent Spring*, published in 1962, constituted the first attempt to document the increase in wildlife deaths associated with pesticide use.[8] More recently, the effects of pesticides on human health have been observed. The World Health Organization estimates that as many as 20,000 deaths occur annually from pesticide poisoning, while a 1990 study calculated that some 25 million agricultural workers in developing countries are acutely poisoned each year.[9]

One group of chemicals, including many of the organochlorine pesticides such as DDT, chlordane, and heptaclor, is suspected of causing reproductive abnormalities in wildlife and humans by disrupting the endocrine systems of living organisms.[10] Scientists have

TABLE 1: NATIONAL PESTICIDE BANS, SELECTED YEARS			
YEAR	DEVELOPING COUNTRIES	INDUSTRIAL COUNTRIES	TOTAL
	(number of bans)		
1983	n.a.	n.a.	53
1989	176	114	290
1991	254	162	416
1993	305	220	525
1995	455	234	689

SOURCE: Pesticide Action Network, "Demise of the Dirty Dozen Chart," San Francisco, Calif., various editions.

linked both the increase in breast and testicular cancers and the decline in male sperm production in industrial countries reported in several recent studies to the presence of endocrine-disrupting chemicals in the environment.[11]

In addition, pesticides can be deleterious to the agricultural and other systems they are intended to benefit. One of the most problematic consequences of pesticide use is the destruction of natural pest predators, which typically account for about half of the pest control in agricultural systems.[12] This can lead to explosions in both target pest populations and secondary pests. In Indonesia, pesticide use in the early eighties dramatically decreased the number of natural predators for the brown planthopper, resulting in an estimated $1.5 billion in rice losses over a two-year period in the mid-eighties.[13]

Problems associated with the destruction of natural predators are frequently exacerbated by the development of pesticide resistance in target populations. More than 900 species of insects, plant diseases, and weeds have developed resistance to the pesticides commonly used to control them.[14] As a result, increasing amounts of pesticides are required to maintain low pest populations. In the United States, at least 10 percent of pesticide use is devoted to combatting resistance in pest species.[15] Pesticides can also endanger bees and other pollinating insects; agricultural losses resulting from reduced pollination may reach $4 billion annually in the United States alone.[16]

As concern about pesticides has grown, countries have tried to regulate the use of these chemicals. Global efforts to control the use and trade of pesticides led the United Nations in 1989 to develop the Prior Informed Consent (PIC) procedure, which enables countries to prohibit pesticide imports without having to take legislative action domestically.[17] Since PIC was implemented in 1991, 136 countries have registered more than 700 bans on the import of the first 12 pesticides included in the system.[18]

PIC consititued the first international effort to shift control over hazardous chemicals from industry to national governments. Its effectiveness is limited, however. Currently, the procedure includes only 12 pesticides and 6 industrial chemicals, although by March 1994 some 127 chemicals had been identified as possible candidates.[19] The process is cumbersome and lengthy, and one expert has calculated that at the current rate it will take roughly until 2050 to incorporate all the pesticides that already have at least one ban against them (the basic requirement for inclusion in PIC).[20]

An additional criticism of PIC is its failure to incorporate many of the world's most widely used pesticides. Most of the initial 12 pesticides included in PIC are insecticides that have already been banned in industrial countries.[21] Although these insecticides pose a serious threat to the people and ecosystems of the developing countries where they are still used, they represent a small percentage of global pesticide use.[22] Industrial countries, which account for some 80 percent of total pesticide consumption, primarily apply herbicides and fungicides to crops.[23] Yet most of these chemicals are not yet in PIC.

PIC's status as a voluntary procedure also limits its effectiveness, since no enforcement mechanism exists to preclude exports from occurring. However, work is currently under way to prepare a legally binding instrument for the application of the PIC procedure.[24] The precedent has been set by the European Union, where participation in the PIC system is mandatory for all members. In 1992, a European Community regulation made PIC binding on all member-states, who must now comply with the import decisions registered by PIC participants.[25]

Meanwhile, a new effort to obtain an international ban on persistent organic pollutants (POPs) is aimed at completely eliminating the production and use of nine pesticides and three industrial chemicals suspected of having endocrine-disrupting effects.[26] At the 1995 U.N. Conference for the Protection of the Marine Environment, 110 countries agreed to begin working on a legally binding international ban on 12 POPs.[27] As with PIC, regional organizations have taken the lead: the signatories of the North American Free Trade Agreement as well as countries at the International Ministerial North Sea Conference are working toward phasing out all production and use of the 12 POPs targeted at the U.N. meeting.[28]

Due to the embryonic nature of these international efforts, trade in banned pesticides persists, even where national laws prohibit their use. A recent U.N. study on international trade in widely prohibited chemicals found that banned or severely restricted chemicals are produced in all geographic regions by both developing and industrial countries.[29] More than 110,000 tons of the 44 chemicals studied were made between 1990 and 1994, including 32,000 tons of DDT produced by three developing countries and one industrial nation.[30]

Although only 9 of the 21 chemicals produced in 1990 were still being manufactured four years later, more than 30 of these widely prohibited chemicals were still being traded.[31] Similarly, a study by the Foundation for Advancements in Science and Education examining U.S. pesticide exports between 1992 and 1994 found that at least 7,000 tons (15 million pounds) of banned pesticides were exported, with some heading to nations where their use is also forbidden.[32] Countries that received shipments of domestically banned pesticides from the United States included Argentina, Brazil, Mozambique, the Netherlands, Singapore, and South Korea.[33]

Organic Farming Up Sharply
Gary Gardner

Output from organic farming is up sharply this decade, with organic agriculture now regarded as a high-growth industry in some countries.[1] Although global data are unavailable, several national and regional indicators reveal clear trends: organically cultivated area in the European Union expanded fourfold between 1987 and 1993, while the number of farmers in organic production doubled.[2] In the United States, sales of organic farm products more than doubled between 1990 and 1994.[3] (See Figure 1.)

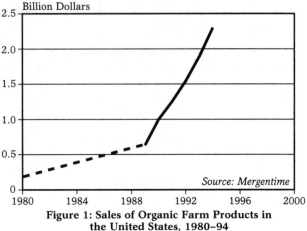

Figure 1: Sales of Organic Farm Products in the United States, 1980–94

Source: Mergentime

Although organic food captures only a small share of the total food market in most industrial countries—typically 2 percent or less—the half-decade of solid growth indicates that interest is more than fleeting.[4] This stands in contrast to previous spurts in these sales, which were prompted by passing concerns about food safety.[5]

The definition of "organic" varies from country to country, and even within nations, but most definitions focus on highly restricted use of chemical fertilizers and pesticides.[6] Because agriculture is a prime source of water and soil pollution in many countries, this shift away from chemical inputs is welcome environmental news.

The label "organic" is now applied to a variety of products beyond fresh produce, including personal care items and materials such as cotton.[7] In the United States, land planted to organically grown cotton skyrocketed from just over 60 hectares in 1990 to more than 13,000 hectares certified or pending certification in 1994.[8] The achievement is especially impressive given that cotton typically receives heavy pesticide treatments, accounting for some 25 percent of world insecticide use.[9]

The blossoming of organic agriculture has several roots. Consumer demand for healthy food and increased awareness overall of agriculture's toll on the environment have driven much of the increase. A study by the Food

Marketing Institute in the United States reports that 24 percent of U.S. shoppers purchase some natural or organic produce at least once a week.[10] Such high demand has brought organics into mainstream supermarkets: 42 percent of U.S. supermarkets now carry some organic produce; these outlets posted a 23-percent rise in such sales in 1994.[11] In Japan, where an estimated 3-5 million consumers buy organic produce regularly, demand for organics was the primary source of an 80-percent increase in U.S. exports of organic produce in 1994.[12]

Latin American producers increasingly view organic production as an entree to lucrative niche markets. Mexico, for example, is now the world's largest producer of organic coffee, with thousands of certified growers.[13] Aztec Harvests, an organic Mexican coffee, is marketed by peasant organizations directly to big-name clients such as United Airlines and Ben and Jerry's ice cream in the United States.[14] Organic sesame, beans, bananas, vanilla, and vegetables are also being exported by peasant organizations in Mexico.[15]

Some producers see organic production as a way to reduce farming costs. In India, the Karnataka Farmers Association, representing a third of the state's 30 million farmers, has formed an International Institute for Sustainable Agriculture to help increase farmer incomes by weaning them from dependence on expensive chemicals.[16] In the United States, economic pressures, coupled with rising demand for organics, have prompted several corporations to switch to organic production: Fetzer and Gallo vineyards in California now use primarily organically produced grapes, and the Patagonia clothing company has pledged to switch to all-organic cotton in its 1996 product line.[17]

In Germany, government subsidies for conversion to organic farming have boosted production. In an effort to reduce the environmental impact of farming and to meet consumer demand for healthier food, the government paid farmers 300-500 deutsche marks ($190-316) per hectare between 1989 and 1992 if they converted to organic farming.[18] The subsidies help farmers through the risky transition period, when yields are suppressed as soils "withdraw" from dependence on chemical fertilizers and when organic produce cannot command a premium because certification is pending. Organic farms increased sixfold, and their area tenfold, throughout the newly reunited Germany as a result of the subsidies.[19]

Without support, many farmers are hesitant to risk the shift to organic production: a survey of Danish farmers revealed that one in five would like to switch, but find the prospect difficult and financially risky.[20] The survey results prompted the government to devise an action plan to help farmers make the transition.[21]

Organic produce is often more expensive than conventionally grown food. In Germany, organics are typically priced 20-100 percent higher than conventional produce, in part because of a lack of competition at all levels of the processing chain.[22] Higher labor costs and lower yields also contribute to the price difference, but these are not insurmountable obstacles. Scientists at the Rodale Institute in the United States note that most agricultural research has focused for decades on conventional agriculture; little attention was given to organic production.[23] More research and greater competition could make organic produce competitive with conventionally grown

foods.

The cost of organic produce and risks to organic farmers are both lessened in Japan through an innovative system known as *teikei*. Under this system, consumers—whether individually or as members of a cooperative—negotiate directly with farmers for delivery of organic produce during the growing season.[24] The arrangement gives the organic farmer a guaranteed market for his or her goods, and provides consumers with organic produce at prices below those found in retail outlets.[25] More than 1 million Japanese households participated in the *teikei* system in 1990 (before the current surge in organic production, which began in Japan in 1993).[26] A similar system of production and distribution, known as community sustainable agriculture, is used in the United States.

Expansion of organic agriculture is limited, however, by the availability of organic nutrients at the farm level. Most urban organic waste is not returned to the farm; even if it were, one study noted that urban organic waste in the United States could meet only 10 percent of agricultural demand for nutrients.[27] As a consequence, chemical fertilizers, which are shunned by organic farmers, are necessary for viable farming on a national scale.

Nevertheless, strong growth in organic agriculture is expected to continue. One analyst in Germany expects organic food's share of the market there to increase from 1.3 percent in 1993 to 8 percent by 2000.[28] In the United States, federal standards for organic agriculture—along with a government seal for its products—are set to be issued in 1996, which is expected to boost both confidence and sales.[29] Such trends are hopeful signs of a decreased dependence on polluting and unhealthy agricultural inputs.

Economic Features

Environmental Taxes Spread

David Malin Roodman

Governments have increasingly taxed environmental destruction over the last two decades. In the sixties and seventies—the early years of modern environmental law—public authorities relied mostly on regulations and standards in their efforts to control pollution and conserve resources. More recently, they have begun turning to environmental taxes as flexible tools that can supplement or replace many regulations. Since the new taxes raise revenue, unlike other environmental policies, they are also reducing the need for standard levies on wages, income, capital gains, and sales—taxes that tend to discourage generally desirable activities such as employment, investment, and commerce. Thousands of environmental levies have now appeared worldwide. (See Table 1.)[1]

Surprisingly, some of the countries with the least experience with market economics—former and current centrally planned economies—levy what are, on paper at least, the world's most sophisticated environmental taxes. Pollution tax codes in China, Russia, and most other former Eastern bloc countries now cover hundreds of air and water pollutants, toxic and radioactive wastes, and even noise.[2] These systems have developed over the last 20 years out of a communist tradition of using fines to enforce environmental standards (at least in the breach), and in response to the particularly ruinous environmental toll of central planning.[3]

In practice, these pollution tax systems suffer several major deficiencies. Emissions below officially permitted levels are usually exempt from taxation. Corruption and inflation have often reduced the charges to token payments.[4] In addition, many companies are still state-run and pass their costs on to customers or the central government, making them less responsive to market signals.[5] Nevertheless, these tax systems are a foundation for what could eventually become a robust set of environmental taxes.

Many developing countries use environmental taxes, but rarely with the same sophistication. Malaysia, for instance, has adjusted its gas taxes to make leaded fuel 2.8 percent more expensive than unleaded.[6] Partly as a result, the market share of unleaded gas has shot from zero to 60 percent since 1991.[7] Thailand and Turkey also favor unleaded fuel with lower taxes.[8] To phase out the use of ozone-depleting chlorofluorocarbons (CFCs), Singapore has been auctioning off limited numbers of permits every three months for producing or importing the chemicals—in effect, taxing CFC use.[9]

In western countries, hundreds of environmental taxes are now in place, on everything from car batteries in Canada to fertilizers in Finland.[10] The city of Victoria, British Columbia, instituted a trash tax of $1.20-2.10 per bag in 1992, along with a strong recycling program.[11] A year later, residents were throwing away 18 percent less trash.[12]

The United States, Denmark, and Australia have each combined regulations and taxes to phase out production of ozone-depleting chemicals.[13] After the U.S. tax started in 1990, it raised $3.8 billion by late 1995.[14] In the Netherlands, a system of water pollution taxes between 1976 and 1991 played a dominant role in reducing industrial emissions of heavy metals into rivers and lakes by 83-97 percent.[15] It also stimulated the development of a world-class water pollution control equipment industry.[16]

One group of environmental taxes easily brings in the most money in industrial countries. Taxes on motor fuels raise more than $170 billion a year, or 2.6 percent of total tax revenues, mostly from gasoline sales.[17] The United States has by far the lowest gasoline taxes, averaging 9¢ per liter (34¢ per gallon) in 1993. Taxes in Australia, Canada, Japan, and New Zealand range between 20¢ and 30¢ per liter (75¢–$1.14 per gallon).[18] In the European Union, though, taxes of 40-85¢ per liter ($1.51-3.22 per gallon) make gasoline prices two to four times higher than in the United States.[19]

Gasoline is dearest in Portugal, at $1.21 a liter ($4.58 a gallon) in 1993, and partly as a result it is used most sparingly there—only 235 liters per person in 1993.[20] At the opposite extreme, U.S. gasoline use was the highest among industrial countries, at 1,600 liters per person, contributing to problems ranging from smog and traffic congestion to global warming.[21]

The nations of northern Europe are at the cutting edge of the environmental tax movement. In 1991, Sweden enacted the world's first "tax shift": a large, revenue-neutral shift in the tax base from constructive activities such as work and investment to destructive ones such as pollution. Specifically, it shifted 1.3 percent of the total tax burden from national income taxes to several environmental taxes, including ones on emissions of sulfur dioxide, which cause acid rain, and of carbon dioxide, which add to the greenhouse effect.[22]

In 1993 and 1995, Denmark followed suit, introducing a 3-percent shift in the government funding burden from income to an array of new environmental levies.[23] Over 1996 and 1997, the Netherlands is shifting 0.8 percent of total tax revenue from income and profits to energy.[24] Momentum for tax shifting is growing in other European countries, including Austria, Norway, and Germany.[25]

Environmental taxes, in contrast with most regulations, give companies and consumers the freedom to decide how and how much to reduce their pollution or resource use. Yet policymakers can still be confident that the higher a tax, the less environmental harm will occur. Generally, those for whom cleaning up is cheapest do it most. Many companies also pass part of their tax bills on to their customers through higher prices, thus encouraging consumers to switch to less pollution-intensive products. Taxes also stimulate the development of cleaner technologies, which can reduce the price of pollution reduction and resource conservation in the long run. In effect, taxes seek the path of least economic resistance to protecting the environment.

TABLE 1: PARTIAL LIST OF ENVIRONMENTAL TAXES

TAX BASE	WHERE TAXED[1]
Solid or Hazardous Waste Generation	Australia, Austria, China, Finland, France, Netherlands, Poland, United States, many municipalities in industrial countries
Fresh Water Use	Australia, Belgium, Denmark, Finland, France, Germany, Ireland, Netherlands, Poland, Turkey, most former Soviet republics
Sales of Fertilizers or Pesticides	Austria, Finland, Norway, Sweden
Water Pollution	Australia, Belgium, Canada, China, France, Germany, Netherlands, Portugal, Spain, most former Eastern bloc nations
Air Pollution[2]	China, Denmark, France, Japan, Norway, Portugal, Sweden, most former Eastern bloc nations
Production of Ozone-Depleting Chemicals	Australia, Denmark, Singapore,[3] United States
Carbon Dioxide Emissions	Netherlands, Scandinavian countries
Motor Fuel Sales and Car Ownership	almost all countries

[1]Place lists are not necessarily exhaustive. [2]Includes taxes on sulfur content of fuels. [3]Takes the form of quarterly government auctions of rights to import or produce limited amounts of ozone-depleting chemicals.
SOURCE: Worldwatch Institute, based on sources listed in endnote 1.

Private Finance Flows to Third World
Hilary F. French

Private capital flows to developing countries are continuing to grow in response to a range of changes in international economic conditions. In 1995, they reached $167 billion—nearly four times higher than in 1990.[1] Meanwhile, flows of official development finance are stabilizing as donor countries around the world are increasingly preoccupied with cutting budget deficits. Official flows amounted to $64 billion in 1995, a substantial increase over 1994 because of the Mexican rescue package, but still below the 1991 figure of $65 billion.[2] (See Figure 1.) As a result of these twin trends, the share of private finance in total net resource flows has increased from 48 percent in 1990 to 72 percent in 1995.[3]

Not only the scale but also the nature of private capital flows has changed markedly. Investments in emerging stock markets ("portfolio equity") increased sharply as a share of total private transfers in the early nineties, rising from 8 percent of total private flows in 1990 to 30 percent in 1993.[4] However, this form of investment declined substantially in 1994 and again in 1995, partially in reaction to the Mexican peso crisis.[5] Meanwhile, "foreign direct investment" in projects to build factories, power plants, roads, and other undertakings through legal mechanisms such as joint ventures increased steadily, as did the issuance of bonds.[6]

On an aggregate level, the increase in private finance has reversed the negative net transfers that developing countries experienced in the eighties. In 1988, developing countries sent $1.5 billion more to the North in interest payments on their debt and in the repatriation of profits on foreign investment than they received in new private and public finance; by 1995, net transfers from North to South amounted to $126 billion.[7]

The surge in private flows remains concentrated in a small number of countries, however. More than half of all stock market investments over 1989–93 were in just three countries: Brazil, Mexico, and South Korea.[8] As for foreign direct investment, five countries—Argentina, China, Malaysia, Mexico, and Thailand—received more than half of the total in this same period.[9] And Argentina, Brazil, and Mexico accounted for some 40 percent of all long-term bond issues.[10]

Meanwhile, debt burdens remain high in many countries around the world. As Robin Broad and John Cavanagh note in a recent article in *Foreign Policy*, "The inescapable conclusion is that the North-South economic gap is narrowing for about a dozen countries but continues to widen for well over 100 others."[11] This reality points to the continued need for public finance and debt relief in countries that the private sector is passing by.

Much of the private investment taking place today is underwriting environmentally unsustainable economic activity. For instance, private investors are vying for position in China's booming electric power market.[12] Emissions from new coal-fired power plants could help make China the world's largest emitter of carbon by 2025.[13] Elsewhere, large timber conglomerates from China, Indonesia, and Malaysia are attempting to secure logging rights to 3.4 million hectares of rain forest in Suriname—an area equal to nearly a quarter of the country.[14]

Yet private investment can also facilitate the development of environmentally sound businesses in the Third World. For instance, joint ventures with Danish firms to produce wind turbines are contributing to a boom in wind power development in India.[15] And in Suriname, international uproar over the proposed logging deals has prompted a search for alternatives—including more environmentally benign forms of investment such as ecotourism and prospecting for "rainforest pharmaceuticals."[16]

The challenge is to determine how to shape private capital flows to the developing world so that they support environmentally sustainable development. Environmentalists have lobbied for years for the "greening" of official development assistance. As a result, bilateral aid agencies and multilateral lending sources such as the World Bank have taken steps to integrate environmental considerations into their programs.[17] With private-sec-

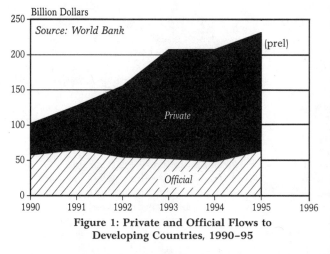

Figure 1: Private and Official Flows to Developing Countries, 1990–95

tor investment, it is far more difficult to know how to influence its course.

One tactic is to encourage public and private sources of finance and other support for private investment to adhere to more stringent environmental criteria in their operations. Toward this end, environmental groups are pressing the World Bank's International Finance Corporation and its Multilateral Investment Guarantee Agency (MIGA) to implement tougher environmental policies.[18] Significantly, 30 private banks from around the world came together before the June 1992 Earth Summit to sign a statement expressing their commitment to promoting environmental protection and sustainable development through their lending practices. The number of signatories to the statement had expanded to 74 by mid-1995.[19] National agencies such as the U.S. Overseas Private Investment Corporation (OPIC) and the U.S. Export-Import Bank are also working to strengthen their environmental stance.[20]

Because all these sources of support are critical to the viability of many private endeavors, they potentially possess considerable leverage. In one promising indication that this leverage may increasingly be used, OPIC recently announced it would withhold $100 million in political risk insurance it had designated for an environmentally destructive gold mining project in Indonesia.[21] MIGA is

now under pressure to follow suit.[22]

Another useful step would be the further development of internationally agreed environmental criteria or standards for international investment. The U.N. Centre on Transnational Corporations drafted "Criteria for Sustainable Development in Management" in 1991.[23] A number of industry groups have drawn on these in crafting their own voluntary codes, as did the Earth Summit's *Agenda 21.*[24] But more work is needed, as a number of companies appear to recognize: two thirds of some 200 companies polled in the 1993 *Benchmark Corporate Environmental Survey* thought the United Nations should work toward standardizing national environmental rules and regulations. A majority felt the U.N. should also be active in setting international policy guidelines.[25]

One possible route would be to incorporate environmental considerations into international investment agreements. An important precedent is provided by the investment provisions of the North American Free Trade Agreement (NAFTA), which stipulate that it is a violation of the treaty to lower environmental standards or to weaken enforcement of them in order to attract investment.[26] Under the environmental side agreement to the accord, countries can be penalized with trade sanctions if they fail to uphold these parts of NAFTA.[27]

With the Uruguay Round on world trade now concluded, negotiators are next likely to take up the need for international investment rules.[28] Just as trade and environment deliberations have become linked, international investment discussions are also likely to become enmeshed with environmental deliberations in the years ahead.

Insurance Industry Reels

Christopher Flavin

As global temperatures rise due to the greenhouse effect, "the incidence of floods, droughts, fires and heat outbreaks is expected to increase in some regions," according to the 1995 report of the Intergovernmental Panel on Climate Change (IPCC), an expert group of scientists that reports to the United Nations.[1]

Such changes could be devastating for the insurance industry, which saw claims for weather-related disasters rise from $16 billion for the entire decade of the eighties to $48 billion for just the first half of the nineties.[2] (See Figure 1.) This dramatic rise cannot be definitively linked to global warming, but it has convinced many insurance executives that it is time for them to get serious about climate change. Franklin Nutter, President of the Reinsurance Association of America, sums up the dilemma: "The insurance business is first in line to be affected by climate change...it could bankrupt the industry."[3]

A scientific assessment done for Munich Re, a German insurance company, notes, "A warmer atmosphere and warmer seas result in greater exchange of energy and add momentum to the vertical exchange processes so crucial to the development of tropical cyclones, tornadoes, thunderstorms, and hailstorms."[4] Already, a study by the National Oceanic and Atmospheric Administration indicates a steady increase in precipitation from extreme one-day storms in the United States in recent decades.[5]

The 3–4 degree Celsius rise in sea temperatures projected by atmospheric models could increase the destructive potential of hurricanes by 50 percent and cause sustained storm winds as high as 350 kilometers (220 miles) per hour.[6] Donald Friedman, former director of the Natural Hazards Research Program for the Travelers Insurance Company, calculates that such a warming would lengthen the current hurricane season in North America by two months or more, and allow the storms to move further north before petering out—possibly striking major urban areas such as New York.[7]

The past five years have witnessed unprecedented damage from weather-related disasters. In May 1991, for example, a cyclone (hurricane) with winds of 270 kilometers per hour hit Bangladesh, flooding vast areas of the country's flat coastal plain.[8] An estimated 139,000 people were killed, more than a million homes were damaged or destroyed, and financial losses were put at $3 billion—more than 10 percent of Bangladesh's annual economic output.[9] Within the next year, at least five devastating tropical storms caused billion-dollar-plus losses from China to Pakistan and Hawaii.[10]

After two decades of relative calm, the southeastern United States has been struck by several serious hurricanes in recent years, including 1995, which had the most active Atlantic hurricane season since the thirties.[11] Although sophisticated warning systems have limited the loss of life, economic damage has been unprecedented because of burgeoning coastal development.

South Florida's vulnerability was demonstrated on August 24, 1992, when Hurricane Andrew came ashore with sustained winds of 235 kilometers per hour—the third most powerful hurricane to

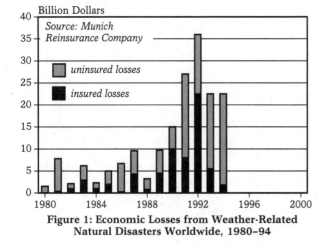

Figure 1: Economic Losses from Weather-Related Natural Disasters Worldwide, 1980–94

make landfall in the United States in the twentieth century.[12] Andrew virtually flattened 430 square kilometers of Dade County in Florida, destroying 85,000 homes and leaving almost 300,000 people homeless.[13] Total losses were estimated at $25 billion—equivalent to the combined losses of the previous three most costly U.S. storms.[14] Robert Sheets, then director of the National Hurricane Center, estimated that if Andrew had moved just 30 kilometers further north, it would have caused damages of $100 billion, and covered New Orleans in 6 meters of water.[15]

Whether or not hurricane severity is increased by climate warming, such losses could be multiplied by another feature of a warming world: rising seas. Water expands as it warms, and higher temperatures also tend to melt the glacial ice found near the world's poles. During the past century, sea levels have already risen by 20-40 centimeters, and scientists believe that by 2100 the sea level in local areas will rise between 10 and 120 centimeters above current levels.[16]

Such increases would threaten coastal communities, as well as the estuaries and aquifers on which societies depend. According to the IPCC, these increases could flood many deltas, and make portions of some cities uninhabitable.[17] The IPCC's mid-range projections indicate that most of the beaches on the East Coast of the United States will disappear during the next 25 years.[18]

Such projections, together with mounting disaster claims in the early nineties, made many insurance companies painfully aware of their vulnerability. In 1990, H.R. Kaufmann, the General Manager of Swiss Re, one of Europe's largest insurance companies, noted: "There is a significant body of scientific evidence indicating that last year's record insured loss from natural catastrophes was not a random occurrence....Failure to act would leave the [insurance] industry and its policyholders vulnerable to truly disastrous consequences."[19]

The dilemma is that companies' rates and coverage policies have always been based on

the law of averages. They look to past weather trends and assume that, over time, the frequency of catastrophes will stay the same. But as the Allstate company notes: "We purchased our catastrophe protection based on the company's historical loss record before Andrew happened....We're reassessing that protection now."[20]

Some analysts believe that another series of "bad years," or even one particularly catastrophic storm, could force major companies out of business. With this risk in mind, industry leaders such as Munich Re and Lloyd's of London participated in the First Conference of the Parties to the Framework Convention on Climate Change in Berlin in March and April 1995.[21]

The entry of the insurance industry into the debate on climate change is a potential watershed. As a business on the front lines of society's most risky activities, the industry has a long tradition of spurring policy changes to help reduce risks—fire codes for buildings and air-bag requirements for automobiles being two important examples. The insurance industry's total size is similar to the huge fossil fuel industry, which has worked so hard in recent years to discourage governments from taking strong action to slow global warming. These two titans may soon go head-to-head on the global climate issue.

Environmental Features

Forest Loss Continues

Anjali Acharya

Between 1980 and 1990, the world lost an average of 9.95 million hectares of net forest area annually—roughly the size of South Korea.[1] Forests once covered more than 40 percent of the earth's land surface.[2] Today, their expanse has been reduced by one third, to 3.4 billion hectares, or 27 percent of the land area.[3] (See Table 1.) (Total wooded area, which includes open woodland and brushland, amounts to some 5.1 billion hectares.)[4] Most of the decline in forest area has occurred since 1950.[5]

Over the past decade or so, most of the world's deforestation has been concentrated in the tropics, with 9.65 million hectares of forest area lost annually between 1980 and 1990.[6] Tropical forests, most of which lie in developing countries, cover almost 1.8 billion hectares and include rain forests as well as moist deciduous and dry zone ecosystems.[7]

Vast forest areas in Latin America, Southeast Asia, and Africa are being destroyed to expand cropland, build cattle ranches, and extract timber. In many developing countries, farmers are clearing virgin forest to grow food—a step they are forced into by growing populations, inequitable land tenure, and the use of much of the best cropland for export crops.

A comparison of per capita forest cover gives an idea of how severe these pressures are. While the average proportion of forested land is almost the same for industrial and developing regions, the per capita figures differ significantly: 1.1 hectares per person in industrial regions compared with 0.5 hectares in developing regions.[8] Agricultural pressures are expected to increase significantly in the years ahead.

Forests are also being logged to feed a growing world demand for wood. Logging has increased in all three tropical regions—Africa, Asia, and Latin America—with a consistent rise over the past decade in both total area logged and total volume of wood removed.[9] As many as 5.9 million hectares are logged annually in the tropics, 4.9 million of which is primary forest.[10] Depending on the terrain and the intensity of the logging,

the ecological effects range from local changes in forest composition to widespread devastation.[11]

The problems faced by temperate forests are different from those of tropical forests, but they can be equally severe. Temperate forests covering about 1.6 billion hectares are found mostly in industrial countries.[12] They are dominated by broad-leaved species in the mid-latitudes and by conifers farther north.

Although the area of temperate forests has remained constant or even increased in the last half-century, this statistic disguises a major degradation in temperate forest quality.[13] A great deal of primary forest has been replaced by plantations—often just even-aged monoculture tree farms that do not support nearly as high a level of biodiversity as an ecologically complex, natural forest does. In Western Europe, the process is perhaps at its most advanced. Only about 1 percent of the region's forests can be classified as old growth—and much of that now consists of small isolated remnants.[14]

Public attention has been focused primarily on tropical forest destruction, but timber companies have recently been clear-cutting vast tracts of boreal forest in Canada and Russia. As many as 1 million hectares of Canada's forests are logged annually; Siberia may be losing 4 million hectares of forest a year—twice the deforestation rate of Brazil.[15] A recent report by the World Wide Fund for Nature states that timber trade is now undoubtedly the primary cause of natural forest loss in temperate northern countries that still have substantial old-growth forests.[16]

In addition, air pollution is increasingly playing a role in forest decline, especially in Europe. A 1994 survey of 32 countries by the European Commission and the U.N. Economic Commission for Europe estimated that 26.4 percent of the continent's trees had moderate to severe defoliation caused mainly by air pollutants, drought, and nutrient loss.[17] That figure represents a 3.8-percent increase over 1993.[18]

With the destruction of forests worldwide, thousands of plant and animal species are threatened with extinction. Rain forests, which are disappearing at the rate of 4.6 million hectares a year, support an incredible diversity of species.[19] Temperate forests are also losing many plant and animal species.[20]

And in both temperate and tropical environments, forest loss is causing damage well beyond the forests themselves. Large-scale clear-cutting often leads to severe soil erosion, which can choke rivers and streams. Forest loss can also radically reduce an area's water-retaining capacity, thereby causing extensive floods.

In addition, forests play a crucial role in regulating the amount of carbon dioxide (CO_2) in the atmosphere. The cutting of tropical forests is releasing to the atmosphere each year more than 1.5 billion tons of carbon stored in biomass and surrounding soils, according to the U.N Food and Agriculture Organization.[21] However, scientists who have carefully assessed the atmosphere's shifting CO_2 balance believe that the world's forests as a whole are actually absorbing a net total of roughly 1.5 billion tons of carbon each year, equivalent to one quarter of the carbon released by fossil fuel combustion.[22]

Most of the carbon is being absorbed by temperate and boreal forests, apparently in response to the fertilizing effects of the additional CO_2 now in the atmosphere.[23] The dynamics of this process are poorly understood and potentially unstable, however, and if climate change accelerates in the future, it could kill large areas of forest, causing billions of tons of additional carbon to be released, which would further accelerate the process of change.[24]

Over the past decade, several international initiatives have been launched and national forestry policies formulated in an attempt to reduce deforestation, especially in tropical regions. Yet forest loss continues unabated. What is needed more than ever is increased local participation in the management and protection of forests. In the tropics, appropriate incentive policies, adequate tenure rights and security, and research and technical assistance would encourage forest protection and conservation.[25] In temperate regions, programs to manage, protect, and rehabilitate forests should receive a high priority, particularly in eastern and southern Europe, North Africa and the Middle East.[26]

TABLE 1: GLOBAL FOREST STATUS, BY REGION

REGION	FOREST AND OTHER WOODED LAND (million hectares)	ANNUAL CHANGE (thousand hectares)	FORESTS PER CAPITA (hectares)	FORESTS AS SHARE OF LAND (percent)
Industrial regions	2,064	−79	1.1	27
Europe	195	+191	0.3	27
Former Soviet Union	942	+51	2.2	35
North America	749	−317	1.7	25
Developed Asia and Oceania	178	−4	0.5	9
Developing regions	3,057	−9,874	0.5	26
Africa	1,137	−2,828	0.9	8
Asia/Pacific	660	−999	0.2	19
Latin America and Caribbean	1,260	−6,047	2.2	48
All regions	5,120	−9,953	0.6	27

SOURCE: U.N. Food and Agriculture Organization, *Forest Resources Assessment 1990: Global Synthesis*, Forestry Paper 124 (Rome: 1995).

Aquatic Species Disappearing   Janet N. Abramovitz

Humankind is placing increasing demands and stresses on the natural resources that support us. Nowhere is this more evident than in freshwater systems—an extremely sensitive barometer of planetary health. As biological assets, freshwater systems are both disproportionately rich and disproportionately imperilled.

First, 12 percent of all animal species—including 41 percent of all recognized fish species—live in the 1 percent of the earth's surface that is fresh water.[1] At the same time, at least one fifth of all freshwater fish have become extinct, threatened, or endangered in recent years, and entire freshwater faunas have disappeared.[2] Dramatic declines in freshwater species are occurring in every part of the world.[3] (See Table 1.)

The Nature Conservancy reports that in North America, the most thoroughly studied continent, 67 percent of mussels, 65 percent of crayfish, 37 percent of fish, and 38 percent of amphibians are either in jeopardy or—in some cases—already gone.[4] Forty-two percent of Europe's 193 freshwater fish species are threatened, endangered, or of special concern.[5] In biologically unique South Africa, two thirds of its 94 fish species need special protection to avoid extinction.[6]

These high levels of extinction and endangerment are not artifacts of earlier perturbations; they are recent and increasing.[7] Ten fish species became extinct in North America during the last decade alone.[8]

Many species require several different habitat types during different stages of life. Outright habitat destruction and structures such as dams that interfere with the movement of nutrients or species between the habitats have serious implications for species survival. Indeed, extinctions of riverine species over large areas have already occurred. Many other species, whose populations have become too fragmented to remain viable, are also likely doomed to extinction in the near future.[9]

The decline of freshwater mussel species helps demonstrate the interdependence of species with each other and their environment. The Mississippi River basin and the eastern part of North America are home to the world's most diverse freshwater mussel fauna; one third of the world's freshwater mussel species are found there.[10] They serve as food for many species, and they filter and cleanse vast quantities of water each day. Each mussel species has a particular fish species it depends on during a brief but critical part of its life cycle. If the fish disappear, the mussels cannot reproduce. If the mussels disappear, the water is not cleansed.

Freshwater mussels are excellent indicators of habitat and water quality. During their 30–130 year life span, these sedentary creatures remain in the same spot, filtering water and eating microscopic plankton.[11]

The mussels have declined in both abundance and diversity in North America. Ten percent of these species have become extinct since 1900.[12] Sixty-seven percent of the remaining 297 native freshwater mussel taxa (281 species and 16 subspecies) are endangered, threatened, or of special concern.[13] Many may already be extinct. Only 24 percent (70 species) are considered stable.[14] Habitat destruction has been the single biggest threat. After the Little Tennessee River was impounded in 1979 by a dam, 44 of its 50 native mussel species disappeared.[15]

Many species are being lost before they are even named or understood. Today, some of the most rapid changes are occurring in the species-rich tropics, little studied by science. A study of the Cross River Basin in Cameroon and Nigeria, for example, found that earlier tallys had undercounted the diversity of fish species by 73 percent.[16] The Amazon River, the world's largest, contains perhaps one third of the planet's 9,000 known fish species—many still being discovered.[17]

Even more ominous than the absolute number of extinctions is the increase in extinction rates. Recent extinction rates are 100–1,000 times higher than before humans existed.[18] Further, if now-threatened species become extinct in the next century, rates will continue accelerating to 1,000–10,000 times prehuman levels.[19] Thus we are running a "biodiversity deficit": we are destroying species (and ecosystems) faster than nature can create new ones.[20]

The stresses on freshwater biodiversity come not just from the number of people but also where they are located and the nature and scale of their activities. Today, more than 60 percent of the world's 5.6 billion people live within one kilometer of surface water.[21] Freshwater systems around the globe are threatened by habitat degradation and fragmentation, the introduction of nonnative species, excessive water withdrawals, pollution, commercial exploitation, and global climate change.

By far the biggest threat comes from physical habitat alteration, cited in 93 percent of the declines in North American freshwater fish species, according to the American Fisheries Society.[22] In the northern third of the world, 77 percent of the water in the 139 largest river systems has been significantly affected by fragmentation of the rivers and their tributaries by dams, water flow regulation from reservoir operation, irrigation, and interbasin transfers.[23] More than 85 percent of U.S. inland waters are artificially controlled and at least half of the country's original wetlands (excluding those in Alaska) have been drained.[24] Between the 1780s and the 1980s, more than 24 hectares (60 acres) of wetlands were lost every hour of the 200 years.[25]

Aquatic habitats are also degraded as their watersheds are logged, mined, or converted to agriculture or grazing; wetlands and coastal areas are converted to fish farms; and rain-fed or flood-dependent agriculture is replaced by irrigation schemes. Human settlement and industrialization also brings roads, ports and factories, and land covered by impermeable surfaces. The impacts of human activities can last far longer than the apparent disturbance. Overfishing of selected species can change the food web relationships of aquatic communities long after the fishing pressure has ceased.

Freshwater ecosystems are not just a part of the environment; they are a part of our economies as well. The prospects for human well-being today are bound up in their fate, as are future options for evolution and human use.

TABLE 1: FRESHWATER FISH SPECIES: STATUS AND THREATS IN SELECTED AREAS

AREA	KNOWN FRESHWATER FISH SPECIES (number)	EXTINCT (percent)	IMPERILLED (percent)	PRINCIPAL THREATS
Global	9000+	{ 20 combined }		
Amazon River	3000+	—	—	Habitat degradation; overharvesting
Asia	1500+	—	—	Habitat degradation; competition for water; overharvesting
North America	950	2	37	Habitat degradation; introduced species
Mexico (arid lands)	200	8	60	Competition for water; pollution
Europe	193	—	42	Habitat degradation; pollution
South Africa	94	—	63	Habitat degradation; pollution; competition for water
Lake Victoria	350	57	43	Introduced species
Costa Rica	127	—	9	Habitat degradation
Sri Lanka	65	—	28	Habitat degradation
Iran	159	—	22	Habitat degradation; competition for water
Australia	188	—	35	Habitat degradation; competition for water

SOURCE: See endnote 3.

Environmental Treaties Strengthened   Hilary F. French

L ast year was a busy one for environmental diplomats. Though no entirely new treaties were signed in 1995, many existing agreements were strengthened. In addition, the groundwork was laid for future actions. This represents important progress in environmental treaty implementation, which is increasingly characterized by flexible processes through which agreements can be updated as scientific understanding advances and political will coalesces.

The most noteworthy event of the year was an agreement struck in August on managing international fisheries.[1] (See Table 1.) It elaborates on provisions of the original Law of the Sea accord that relate to fish stocks that straddle the boundaries of economic zones and fish species that migrate long distances.[2] The new agreement was opened for signature on December 4, 1995, in New York, and will enter into force after it has been ratified by 30 countries.[3]

Negotiations toward this treaty were set in motion at the June 1992 Earth Summit in Rio de Janeiro. They got off to a slow start, with most observers expecting no more than a nonbinding agreement. But the political will to reach a tougher accord began to grow as the magnitude of the global overfishing crisis became clear. For instance, the U.N. Food and Agriculture Organization reports that 69 percent of fish stocks worldwide are now either fully exploited, overfished, depleted, or rebuilding from previous overfishing.[4] Passions reached a high peak in mid-March 1995, when shots were fired in a dramatic high-seas conflict between Canada and Spain over access to turbot stocks in the waters off Newfoundland.[5]

The final accord represents a compromise between coastal states, such as Canada, that worried about the actions of foreign fishers in international waters adjacent to their own and countries with long-distance fishing

---

TABLE 1: SELECTED INTERNATIONAL ENVIRONMENTAL AGREEMENTS: TIMELINE AND NUMBER OF PARTICIPANTS

YEAR	AGREEMENT, PLACE SIGNED, AND NUMBER OF PARTICIPANTS
1946	International Convention for the Regulation of Whaling. Washington. 57 parties
1959	Antarctica Treaty. Washington. 43 parties.
1972	Convention on the Prevention of Marine Pollution by Dumping of Wastes and Other Matter (London Dumping Convention). London. 74 parties.
1973	Convention on International Trade in Endangered Species of Wild Fauna and Flora (CITES). Washington. 130 parties.
1973	International Convention for the Prevention of Pollution from Ships (MARPOL). London. 92 parties.
1982	United Nations Convention on the Law of the Sea. Montego Bay. 158 signatories, 84 parties.
1987	Montreal Protocol on Substances that Deplete the Ozone Layer. Montreal. 154 parties.
1989	Basel Convention on the Control of Transboundary Movements of Hazardous Wastes and Their Disposal. Basel. 98 parties.
1992	United Nations Framework Convention on Climate Change. New York. 166 signatories, 153 parties.
1992	Convention on Biological Diversity. Rio de Janeiro. 168 signatories, 140 parties.
1994	Convention to Combat Desertification in those Countries Experiencing Serious Drought and/or Desertification. Paris. 115 signatories, 25 parties.
1995	Agreement for the Implementation of the Provisions of the United Nations Convention on the Law of the Sea of 10 December 1982 Relating to the Conservation and Management of Straddling Fish Stocks and Highly Migratory Fish Stocks. New York. 32 signatories.

SOURCE: See endnote 1.

fleets, such as Spain, that focused more on the failure of coastal states to manage fisheries adequately within their waters. In a nod to the concerns of the latter group, the final accord contains some provisions that are aimed at promoting the sustainable management of fish stocks in all waters.

The main target of the treaty, however, is fishing on the high seas.[6] The agreement defers to the quotas and conservation measures set by regional fishing organizations for these areas, but expressly allows the boarding and inspection of vessels to monitor compliance. Where there are conflicts between nations over fishing rights, the agreement requires compulsory and binding third-party dispute settlement under the terms set out in the Law of the Sea.[7]

One other initiative launched in 1995 may bring added hope for the health of the oceans. In late October 1995, environmental diplomats convened in Washington to finalize a Global Program of Action for protection of the marine environment from land-based sources of pollution.[8] This action plan includes a call for nations to initiate negotiations toward a binding treaty on reducing persistent organic pollutants such as DDT and dioxins that can accumulate in marine species.[9]

Efforts to protect another global commons—the atmosphere—also moved forward slowly in 1995. Negotiatiors met in Berlin in March for the first Conference of the Parties to the U.N. Framework Convention on Climate Change.[10] There they agreed to what has become known as the Berlin Mandate—a commitment to begin negotiations aimed at agreeing within two years on targets for greenhouse gas emissions after 2000 for industrial countries, which the current treaty is notably silent on.[11]

Later in the year, the members of the Montreal Protocol on ozone depletion agreed in the meeting of their Conference of the Parties—held from November 28 to December 7 in Vienna—to phase out methyl bromide use in industrial countries by 2010.[12] Methyl bromide is a widely used pesticide that is also a potent ozone depleter. They also decided to accelerate the schedule for phasing out the use of hydrochlorofluorocarbons.[13] Though a step forward, many had urged more aggressive action, particularly for developing countries, which have been given extra time to carry out the provisions of both the original accord and its subsequent amendments.[14]

Steps were also taken in 1995 to strengthen the Convention on Biological Diversity. In November, the second Conference of the Parties to the accord convened in Jakarta.[15] The meeting reached agreement to begin work on a protocol governing the transboundary movement of living organisms modified through biotechnology, and decided to undertake further work on biodiversity in coastal and marine ecosystems and in forests.[16] Notably, the United States is not a party to the treaty, as it has not yet been ratified by the U.S. Senate.[17]

Finally, the Basel Convention on the hazardous waste trade was amended in Geneva in September to formalize an earlier, unofficial decision to go beyond regulation to an outright ban on trade in hazardous wastes between industrial and developing countries.[18] The amendment proved controversial, however, with some countries concerned that the ban would prevent trade bound for legitimate recycling operations.[19] Again, the United States has yet to ratify even the original Basel accord.[20]

As all this activity indicates, the environment is becoming a steadily more prominent issue in international relations. Yet while the number of meetings and treaties grows, the health of the global environment continues to deteriorate. Unfortunately, in all too many cases the political will does not yet exist for the decisive actions needed to reverse the decline.

Social
Features

Infectious Diseases Return
Anne E. Platt

In 1993, the last full year for which estimates are available, infectious diseases accounted for an estimated one third of all deaths in the world—16.4 million out of 51 million. By comparison, 9.7 million people were killed by heart disease that year and 6 million people died from cancer.[1] More than 99 percent of deaths from infectious diseases occur in developing countries, where these illnesses cause 42 percent of deaths (16.3 million).[2] In industrial countries, in contrast, infectious diseases are responsible for only 1.2 percent of deaths (135,000).[3]

Infectious diseases also cause chronic and debilitating illness for millions of people worldwide. For example, there were an estimated 1.8 billion episodes of diarrheal diseases in 1993, primarily in sub-Saharan Africa.[4] Between 300 million and 500 million people contend with malaria each year, while more than 240 million people suffer from acute respiratory infections, particularly pneumonia.[5] (See Table 1.)

An estimated 8.3 million people contracted tuberculosis in 1993, with nearly 3 million dying from this severe pulmonary infection.[6] During the nineties, 30 million people are expected to die from tuberculosis as the number of cases complicated by coinfection with HIV and drug-resistant strains of tuberculosis rises.[7]

Several other diseases thought to have been well under control, such as diphtheria, cholera, and malaria, have made recent comebacks due to waning health programs and increased poverty and urbanization. For example, an epidemic of diphtheria—a flu-like disease that kills 5-10 percent of its victims—originally began in 1990 in Russia and has since spread throughout the former Soviet Union.[8] The incidence of diphtheria shot up from 839 cases in the newly independent states in 1989 to 47,802 in 1994, with three fourths of this traditional childhood illness striking people over the age of 15.[9]

Cholera is on the upswing too. An epidemic that began in Peru in 1991 spread through water supplies and shellfish and caused more than 500,000 cases throughout Latin America, with 200,000 in Peru alone.[10] Cholera has also plagued refugees in Rwanda and Zaire, and a new, more virulent strain has spread rapidly through Bangladesh, China, India, and other parts of Asia, killing thousands of people.[11]

In many cases, outbreaks of infectious diseases are linked to and sometimes caused by changes in the environment. Human-induced changes in the environment, such as deforestation, agriculture, and even changes in weather patterns, have exposed more people to diseases that would otherwise be dormant or of limited seriousness. People moving into new environments also play a role, as does the simple increase in population. And these

TABLE 1: POPULATIONS AFFECTED BY VARIOUS TRADITIONAL INFECTIOUS DISEASES, 1993

DISEASE	DEATHS	INCIDENCE[1]
Acute Respiratory Infections	4.1 mill.	248 mill.
Diarrheal Diseases	3 mill.	1.8 billion
Tuberculosis	2.7 mill.	8.3 mill.
Malaria	2 mill.	300-500 mill. (prevalence[2])
Measles	1.2 mill.	45 mill.
Hepatitis B	1 mill.	2.2 mill.
Whooping Cough (pertussis)	360,000	43 mill.
Bacterial Meningitis	210,000	1.2 mill. (prevalence[2])
Schistosomiasis	200,000	200 mill. (prevalence[2])
Leishmaniasis	197,000	7.2 mill.
Yellow Fever	30,000	200,000
Dengue/DHF	23,000	560,000
Japanese Encephalitis	11,000	40,000
Cholera	6,800	380,000
Polio	5,500	110,000

[1]Number of new cases of a particular disease reported during a certain period of time. [2]Number of all cases of a particular disease estimated to occur worldwide.
SOURCE: Report of the Director-General, *The World Health Report 1995: Bridging the Gaps* (Geneva: World Health Organization, 1995); malaria data from "World Malaria Situation in 1992, Part I: Middle South Asia, Eastern Asia and Oceania," *Weekly Epidemiological Record*, October 21, 1994.

and other factors interact in complex ways to aggravate problems.

For example, cases of dengue—also known as breakbone fever because of the hemorrhaging, vomiting, diarrhea, and painful bones it causes—have been on the rise in Latin America since the eighties as urbanization and poverty increased. Mosquito spraying programs were cut back, which led to an increase in mosquitoes and a subsequent rise in cases of dengue fever.[12] Between 1956 and 1980, an average of 29,000 cases of dengue hemorrhagic fever, the most severe form, were reported annually.[13] Between 1986 and 1990, the number increased nearly tenfold, to more than 260,000 per year.[14]

In developing countries, 80 percent of all diseases are caused by consuming water contaminated with pathogens and pollution.[15] Diarrhea, which causes severe dehydration and malnutrition, kills nearly 3 million children under age five every year and accounts for one fourth of the deaths in this age group.[16] In some regions, underlying conditions of malnutrition and poor hygiene have worsened and increased vulnerability to minor infections. One in five people in the world does not have clean drinking water.[17] Providing safe drinking water and improving sanitation could reduce the suffering from water-related diseases.

Specialists refer to "manmade malaria" to describe the routine phenomenon of the disease flaring up near irrigation projects, dams, construction sites, standing water, and poorly drained areas where malaria is already present but usually only during a certain time of the year, when conditions are right for mosquitoes.[18] This is common throughout the tropical areas of Asia, Africa, and the Americas.

Microorganisms themselves are also changing. Some are becoming more virulent and others are resisting antibiotic treatment.[19] In Europe, penicillin-resistant pneumococci is causing a range of infections including pneumonia and the often fatal blood infection septicemia.[20] In 1979, only 6 percent of pneumococcus strains were penicillin-resistant; by 1989, this number had grown to 44 percent.[21]

As early as 1956, *Plasmodium*, the parasite that causes malaria, began to develop resistance to chloroquine. Since then, drug-resistant strains of malaria have spread throughout the tropics and have developed immunity to other antimalarial drugs, causing more severe cases of malaria. In Vietnam, for example, between 1987 and 1990 severe drug-resistant cases of malaria and mortality tripled due to a combination of multidrug-resistant malaria, migration into forested areas, mining activity, and inadequate medical resources, care, and delivery.[22]

Despite these grim statistics, considerable progress in the fight against infectious diseases has been made during this century. Smallpox was officially eradicated in 1979 thanks to the vaccination of 250 million people.[23] Polio has been eliminated in 145 countries. Worldwide, cases of this crippling viral disease dropped 80 percent between 1988 and 1994.[24] Only 100,000 people suffer from Dracunculiasis, or Guinea Worm disease, a seriously debilitating illness that causes grotesque swelling of the limbs—down from 3.5 million in 1986.[25]

A campaign by UNICEF during the seventies and eighties to immunize children saved millions of lives. In 1993, nevertheless, 2.4 million children died from vaccine-preventable diseases—measles, neonatal tetanus, tuberculosis, and pertussis.[26] Despite the effectiveness and low cost of vaccines and other treatments—such as oral rehydration therapy, which helps to rebuild fluid loss from diarrhea—many treatments are not distributed widely. Basic infrastructure and administrative problems as well as a lack of money, supplies, personnel, and knowledge hamper further improvements.[27]

As old diseases come back and new ones emerge, human-induced environmental changes continue to accelerate. Until environmental causes of infectious diseases are recognized and taken into consideration, outbreaks of these and other diseases will continue to plague the world.

Landmines Proliferate

Michael Renner

In a landmine-infested area of Mozambique, villagers were recently asked to list their problems. They mentioned land, water, health, and education, but not landmines. Why? To the villagers, the reasoning was simple: problems have solutions.[1] This disheartening tale seems to encapsulate the global landmine predicament.

More than 250 million landmines have been produced over the past 25 years, including approximately 200 million antipersonnel mines.[2] Production ranges from 10 million to 30 million each year.[3] Some 100 companies in 48 countries are producing more than 340 different types of mines.[4]

It is estimated that 110 million landmines are currently scattered in 64 countries. In some of the worst affected nations, 20–60 mines are found per square kilometer.[5] (See Table 1.) Given that mines could remain deadly for decades if not hundreds of years and that capacities to get rid of them are severely limited, many countries will suffer for generations. At the current pace of demining, it would take 4,000 years to clear just one fifth of the landmines in Afghanistan.[6]

In fact, mines continue to be laid far faster than they are being removed: in an average year, clearing operations worldwide struggle to retrieve roughly 100,000 mines, even as an estimated 2 million—or 5 million, some say—additional mines are being laid.[7] Under current conditions, the number of uncleared mines will reach 120–135 million by the end of this decade.

Scattered randomly, landmines have become a ubiquitous threat to the normal functioning of many societies, even long after a conflict has ended. Without effective demining programs, large areas of land remain inaccessible, refugees are discouraged from returning home, peasants cannot work their fields or get their produce to markets, economic activity grinds to a halt, and reconstruction is hindered. In Afghanistan, more than a third of the families in one survey thought they would be able to grow more crops in the absence of landmines.[8]

Landmines are not so much weapons of war as instruments of terror. Of approximately 1 million persons who have been killed or maimed by landmines since 1975, some 80 percent were civilians, many of them children.[9] Landmines kill some 10,000 people each year and maim another 20,000—every 20 minutes or so, a person steps on a mine.[10] In Cambodia, one out of 234 persons is an amputee.[11]

Mine blasts cause horrific wounds and require multiple surgery. Each surviving victim is estimated to incur lifetime costs of about $3,000 for surgery and prosthetic devices; for the present 250,000 amputee mine victims, this adds up to $750 million.[12] (If adequate treatment were available, the expense would be far higher.)[13] Coping with the needs of mine-blast survivors can easily overwhelm not only their family's resources, but also their country's health and social systems. The World Health Organization notes that no more than 15–20 percent of rehabilitation needs are currently being met.[14]

Experience suggests that it takes 100 times as long to detect, remove, and disarm a mine as to plant it.[15] Mines are extremely cheap to manufacture (typically $3–20), but expensive to remove ($300–1,000).[16] Estimates of the cost to clear all mines worldwide are astronomical, ranging from a minimum of $33 billion to a more plausible $85 billion.[17]

Oil-rich Kuwait signed demining contracts worth about $700–800 million after the Iraqi occupation.[18] It is spending far more than is available in the rest of the world combined, and yet by one estimate the effort could well take 20 years.[19]

But demining efforts elsewhere are severely underfunded. The United Nations is a key actor—its involvement in mine-clearance assistance has grown from operations in just Afghanistan in 1988 to 14 operations in 1994 and 18 in 1995—yet its resources remain highly inadequate.[20] The U.N. is spending some $70 million per year on clearance and awareness programs, most of it funded by voluntary contributions by national governments.[21] A Voluntary Trust Fund for Assistance in Mine Clearance established in

November 1994 attracted pledges of only $21.6 million (with another $7 million going to strengthen the U.N.'s demining standby capacity).[22] The U.N. expects an additional $58 million to be available through bilateral and multilateral programs.[23] Yet this still falls far short of what is needed.

Even if the proliferation of landmines stopped overnight, with the present global demining capacity it would take almost 1,100 years to get rid of all the mines already scattered throughout the world. But because the challenge is a growing one, mine-clearance efforts would have to be increased more than twentyfold just to prevent the problem from getting worse.[24]

During the past few years, an international grassroots campaign—with some 400 organizations in 36 countries—has made considerable progress in delegitimizing antipersonnel mines.[25] In 1993 the U.N. General Assembly called for an export moratorium, and in 1995 the European Parliament called for a complete ban on mines.[26] A growing number of national governments have declared moratoria on exports, and a handful have stopped production, renounced the use, or are destroying existing stocks. By January 1996, 22 countries were on record as calling for a comprehensive international ban on antipersonnel mines.[27]

But there is still significant opposition among several countries, particularly China, India, and Pakistan, and even among the armed forces of some countries that have taken limited measures against mines.[28] Recent efforts to strengthen the weak Inhumane Weapons Convention (Protocol II of which deals with landmines) deadlocked.[29]

Those opposed to a ban argue instead for the production of self-destruct mines or the retrofitting of old ones. The United States supports this option. It might cost about $700 million to fit existing mine stockpiles with self-destruct devices.[30] Yet money spent on refitting and on developing new, "smart" mines would not only fail to address the problem, it would also take funds away from the already meager resources currently available for mine clearance. While mine technology continues to evolve, making mines harder to detect and defuse, mine-clearance techniques essentially date from the forties.[31]

The landmine crisis is of such magnitude and the policy responses so inadequate that the rhetorical question posed by the European Parliament's Committee on Development and Cooperation in 1995 will haunt humanity for a long time to come: "What crop costs a hundred times more to reap than to plant and has no market value when harvested?"[32]

TABLE 1: ESTIMATED NUMBER OF UNCLEARED LANDMINES, MOST AFFECTED COUNTRIES, RELATIVE TO TERRITORY, MID-NINETIES

WORST AFFECTED COUNTRIES	NUMBER OF MINES (million)	MINES PER SQUARE KILOMETER[1] (number)
Afghanistan	10	15
Angola	15	12
Bosnia	3	59
Cambodia	10	55
Croatia	2	35
Egypt	23	23
Eritrea	1	11
Iran	16	10
Iraq	10	23
Kuwait[2]	6	250
Mozambique	2	3
Somalia	1	2

[1]These averages in some cases understate the severity of mine infestation in parts of a country. For instance, as much as 90 percent of the mines in Iraq may be located in the Kurdish region. [2]1991 data. Kuwait now has substantially fewer mines, following an intensive clearing effort.
SOURCES: Country data from United Nations, General Assembly, "Assistance in Mine Clearance. Report of the Secretary-General," September 6, 1994, and from Christopher S. Wren, "Everywhere, Weapons that Keep on Killing," *New York Times*, October 8, 1995; mines per square kilometer ratio calculated from *The New York Times Atlas of the World*, Third Revised Concise Edition (New York: Times Books, 1992).

Violence Stalks Women Worldwide   Toni Nelson

Violence against women around the globe constitutes a violation of their basic human rights as well as a costly impediment to social and economic development. As the *Human Development Report 1995* observed, violence stalks women throughout their lives, from cradle to grave.[1] (See Table 1.) The consequences in both developing and industrial countries include increased health care costs and the loss of women's participation in work and development activities.[2]

Gender-based violence has also led to a reduction in the total number of women. Between 60 and 100 million women are considered "missing"—the victims of the selective abortion of female fetuses, infanticide, neglect and abuse during childhood, and domestic violence.[3]

In many cultures, males are valued more highly than females. Where a strong preference for sons persists, female fetuses are much more likely to be aborted, while female infants are often neglected, malnourished, or killed. The imposition of the one-child-per-family rule has exacerbated this situation in China, where a 1987 census found a half-million fewer female infants than would be predicted given the expected biological ratio of male to female births.[4]

In India, a study of amniocentesis in a large Bombay hospital found that 95.5 percent of fetuses identified as female were aborted, compared with only a small percentage of male fetuses.[5] Female infanticide is still practiced in rural areas of India; in a 1992 study by Cornell University demographer Sabu George, 19 of 33 deaths among female infants (58 percent) within 12 villages in Tamil Nadu were due to infanticide.[6]

Gender-specific forms of violence also occur where male dominance is institutionalized in social, political, and economic systems. To perpetuate discriminatory systems, cultures adopt practices to control women. One of the most notorious is female genital mutilation, which has been performed on 85–114 million women worldwide.[7] Approximately 15 percent of these women have undergone the most severe form, infibulation, in which the clitoris, all of the labia minora, and all or part of the labia majora are removed.[8] The vulva is then stitched together, leaving only a small opening for urine and menstrual blood to pass through.

TABLE 1: SELECTED ESTIMATES OF VIOLENCE AGAINST WOMEN

PRACTICE	ESTIMATED OCCURRENCE
Son Preference	In India, at least 300,000 more girls than boys die every year. In 1987, China was missing 500,000 female infants.
Female Genital Mutilation	Procedure has been performed on 85–114 million girls and women worldwide. More than 2 million girls are at risk each year.
Wife Beating	Large-scale surveys in 10 countries estimate that 17–33 percent of women have been physically assaulted by an intimate partner. In Papua New Guinea, 18 percent of married women receive hospital treatment for injuries inflicted by their husbands.
Murder	In 1987, 62 percent of the women murdered in Canada were killed by an intimate male partner. In India, 1 in 4 deaths among women 16–24 years is due to "accidental burns."
Rape	Between 1 in 5 and 1 in 7 U.S. women will be the victim of a completed rape in her lifetime. More than 20,000 Muslim women were raped in Bosnia in 1992.

SOURCES: Lori L. Heise et al., *Violence Against Women: The Hidden Health Burden*, World Bank Discussion Paper No. 255 (Washington, D.C.: World Bank, 1994); World Bank, *World Development Report 1993* (New York: Oxford University Press, 1993); Lori L. Heise et al., "Violence Against Women: A Neglected Public Health Issue in Less Developed Countries," *Social Science and Medicine*, Vol. 39, No. 9, 1994.

Women who have undergone infibulation have to be repeatedly cut and stitched—on their wedding night and again with each childbirth—and the physical and psychological consequences are severe.[9] The practice is widespread in central Africa and parts of the Middle East and Asia, and also occurs among migrants from these countries in Europe and the United States.[10]

The implicit acceptance across cultures of a man's prerogative to beat his wife provides another example of institutionalized oppression of women. Large-scale surveys in 10 countries estimate that 17–33 percent of women have been physically assaulted by an intimate partner.[11] More limited studies in Latin America, Asia, and Africa report even higher rates of physical abuse among some women, reaching 60 percent or more in select populations.[12]

Women are also the primary victims of sexual crimes, which include sexual abuse and rape. Girls are almost universally the target of child sexual assaults.[13] According to national random surveys, 27–34 percent of women in Norway, the United States, Canada, New Zealand, Barbados, and the Netherlands were sexually abused during childhood.[14] Often, very young children are the victims: studies from Peru, Chile, Mexico, Papua New Guinea, and the United States indicate that 13–32 percent of abused girls are age 10 and under.[15]

Rape haunts women throughout their lifetimes, exposing them to unwanted pregnancy, potentially fatal sexually transmitted diseases, and psychological trauma. In the United States, where some of the best data exist, studies suggest that between 1 in 5 and 1 in 7 women will be the victim of a completed rape during her lifetime.[16] Similarly, a study comparing sexual assault in the cities of 14 developing countries over five years found rates of 10 percent or greater in six cities.[17]

Mass rape in war also presents a grave threat. According to a January 1993 report by a European Community Investigative Mission, more than 20,000 Muslim women in Bosnia were raped during the conflict there, including some held in "rape camps" where they were forced to bear Serbian children.[18]

Because violence against women is a significant cause of disability and death, it undermines social and economic development efforts. Health care costs associated with gender violence represent the use of society's resources for the treatment of a largely preventable social ill. In the United States, a major health maintenance organization found that women who had been raped or beaten had medical costs two and a half times higher than women who had not been victimized.[19]

The World Bank has identified violence as a major risk factor for ill health and disease among women of reproductive age. In their overall analysis, 19 percent of the total disease burden of women aged 15–44 in advanced market economies could be linked to domestic violence or rape.[20] Violence constitutes a comparable threat to women in developing countries, but due to the relatively greater burden of disease in those regions, it represents only 5 percent of their total disease burden.[21]

As recently as the late eighties, violence against women was virtually absent from policy and funding agendas at the international level.[22] Even the 1979 text of the Convention on the Elimination of All Forms of Discrimination Against Women did not specifically mention violence.[23]

But women's groups have successfully lobbied to incorporate gender issues into the international human rights agenda. More than 1,000 women's groups the Campaign for Women's Human Rights in the effort to focus attention on gender issues.[24] These groups collected more than 400,000 signatures in 128 countries demanding that the World Conference on Human Rights in June 1993 declare violence against women to be a violation of human rights.[25] The resulting Vienna Declaration was the first official U.N. document to incorporate this position.[26]

In November 1993, the U.N. General Assembly passed the Declaration on the Elimination of Violence Against Women, which offer the first official U.N. definition of gender-based abuse.[27]

Voters Turn Out in Large Numbers Hal Kane

In many countries that had their first or nearly their first elections in 1995, voters turned out in impressive numbers. Worldwide, though, voting percentages varied considerably among countries and also among elections.[1] (See Table 1.)

The newly independent Central Asian countries had particularly high voter turnouts during 1995. Kyrgyzstan held its first contested presidential election, and 86 percent of registered voters showed up at the polls, many on horseback.[2] In Kazakstan, turnout was even higher, as 91 percent of the entire voting age population—not just of registered voters—reached the polls for a referendum on whether to extend the president's term to the year 2000.[3] And in Uzbekistan, some 92 percent of the registered voters went to the polls for a legislative election.[4]

South Africa's first truly democratic election was held in April 1994, and attracted 85 percent of registered voters—a high turnout by the standards of almost any country.[5] By November 1, 1995, however, voting in local elections in South Africa drew only 42 percent of registered voters.[6] Yet a drop of more than 50 percent in voting participation is common for local elections, since they receive less attention than presidential ones.

Other African countries also boasted high voter turnouts despite continentwide reputations for and problems with corruption and an unwillingness of existing regimes to cede power. In Tanzania, 77 percent of registered voters participated in elections.[7] The polling marked the end of 34 years of one-party rule and was the first time that those who reached voting age since independence from Britain in 1961 had ever had a political voice. Voting was plagued by disputes and fraud, however, and with various recounts and one revote, the election that originally took place on October 29th did not end until November 19th.[8]

Meanwhile, in Namibia some 76 percent of the populace voted.[9] And in Algeria, 76 percent of voters also turned out in an attempt to save that country from violence and disintegration.[10] This was the first contested presidential election since independence from

France in 1962, despite death threats against voters and a call for a boycott by the opposition.[11]

In Niger, in contrast, only 35 percent of voters turned out for a legislative election that threw control of the prime ministry into question when the opposition party won a large portion of the seats in parliament.[12] And in Côte d'Ivoire, few turned out to vote in the first presidential election since the death of the long-governing founding father, Felix Houphouet-Boigny—in part because of opposition calls for a boycott and warnings of fraud, in part because many considered the vote uncompetitive and a mere formality, and in part because of politically related violence that took several lives.[13] In Sierra Leone, a military coup averted a scheduled election.[14]

One of the most important elections came in newly independent Belarus. There, turnout for a legislative election was only 56 percent, but this was a larger showing than was expected and it blocked efforts by President Alexander Lukashenko to dissolve the legislature and strengthen his one-man rule.[15] Lukashenko, who has been ruling Belarus by decree and defying decisions of the Constitutional Court, had urged citizens not to vote and vowed to dissolve the legislature if a turnout of less than 50 percent prevented election of a legislative quorum.[16] During an earlier election, in May 1995, too few voters showed up to produce a quorum for the legislature, as Belarusan law requires a 50-percent turnout for an election to be valid.[17] This issue is not unique to Belarus—Ukraine had several elections in 1995 just trying to fill the parliament.[18]

In Russia, on the other hand, the electoral machinery was pushed to the breaking point as early predictions that cynical voters would stay home proved wrong.[19] Instead, about 61 percent of registered voters went to the polls in wintery weather in Russia's second post-Soviet parliamentary election, voting from a ballot offering a choice of 43 parties.[20] Even as a newly democratized country, this turnout matches or exceeds those in the United States, which prides itself on its democratic traditions. Voter turnout in the 1994 U.S. congressional elections, by comparison, was 59 percent—an unusually high turnout for the United States.[21]

Meanwhile, a real display of emotion was seen in Quebec, Canada, where about 94 percent of all eligible voters cast ballots, and separatists narrowly lost a referendum on independence from Canada for the French-speaking province.[22]

In many other regions of the world, though, citizens showed little interest in voting. Only 28 percent of Haitians turned out at the polls for a presidential election that represented the first opportunity in Haiti's 192 years of independence for a peaceful presidential transition.[23] Some analysts believe that participation was low because President Aristide was not in the running and his handpicked successor, Rene Preval, appeared a heavy favorite to win (and did),

making it unnecessary for people to vote.[24]

And no elections were held in several of the world's largest countries: China and Nigeria are among those whose governments will not hold elections.

Of course, democracy is not a panacea. Voting does not solve all problems, and sometimes can even exacerbate them. Bosnian Muslims, Croats, and Serbs, for example, lived together peacefully and intermarried under dictatorial control, but broke apart into war under democratic governance.[25] And democratic leaders in Armenia and Azerbaijan furthered each country's slide into a brutal war against the other—a war that had previously been held in check, in part, by Soviet totalitarianism.[26] In Rwanda, the establishment of a multiparty system and a coalition government in 1992 and battles over control of the government played a role in hardening the ethnic divisions that erupted in civil war and genocide in 1994.[27]

On the other hand, democracy has been common to most of the world's most prosperous countries. No two established democratic countries have ever gone to war against each other.[28] And no democratic country with a relatively free press has ever suffered a major famine.[29]

TABLE 1: VOTER TURNOUTS IN SELECTED COUNTRIES, 1995

COUNTRY	TYPE	VOTING PERCENTAGE[1]
Uzbekistan	Parliamentary	92
Kazakstan[2]	Presidential	91
Iceland	Parliamentary	87
Kyrgyzstan	Presidential	86
Argentina	Presidential	81
France	Presidential	80
Tanzania	Presidential	77
Namibia	Presidential	76
Algeria	Presidential	76
Peru	Presidential	73
Malaysia	Parliamentary	72
Estonia	Parliamentary	70
Finland	Parliamentary	69
Poland	Presidential	68
Thailand	Parliamentary	62
Belarus	Parliamentary	56
Georgia	Presidential	47
Guatemala	Presidential	47
Niger	Parliamentary	35
Haiti	Presidential	28

[1]Of all registered voters, not all citizens, except where noted. [2]Percent of total voting age population, not of registered voters.
SOURCE: International Foundation for Electoral Systems, Washington, D.C., various computer printouts; various newspaper articles compiled by Worldwatch.

NOTES

WORLD GRAIN PRODUCTION FALLS (pages 24–25)

1. U.S. Department of Agriculture (USDA), Foreign Agricultural Service (FAS), *Grain: World Markets and Trade,* Washington, D.C., December 1995; USDA, Economic Research Service, "Production, Supply, and Demand View" (electronic database), Washington, D.C., January 1996.
2. USDA (electronic database), op. cit. note 1.
3. U.S. Bureau of the Census, Center for International Research, Suitland, Md., private communication, January 23, 1996.
4. USDA (electronic database), op. cit. note 1; Census Bureau, op. cit. note 3.
5. USDA (electronic database), op. cit. note 1; Census Bureau, op. cit. note 3.
6. USDA (electronic database), op. cit. note 1; Census Bureau, op. cit. note 3.
7. USDA (electronic database), op. cit. note 1; USDA, FAS, *Grain: World Markets and Trade,* Washington, D.C., January 1996.
8. K.F. Isherwood and K.G. Soh, "Short Term Prospects for World Agriculture and Fertilizer Use," presented at 21st Enlarged Council Meeting, IFA, Paris, November 15-17, 1995.
9. Ibid.
10. Ibid.
11. Ibid.
12. Census Bureau, op. cit. note 3.
13. Isherwood and Soh, op. cit. note 8.
14. Ibid.

SOYBEAN PRODUCTION DROPS (pages 26–27)

1. U.S. Department of Agriculture (USDA),

"Oilseeds: World Markets and Trade," Washington, D.C., October 1995.
2. Ibid.; U.S. Bureau of the Census, Center for International Research, Suitland, Md., private communication, January 23, 1996.
3. USDA, op. cit. note 1.
4. Ibid.
5. Ibid.
6. Ibid.
7. Ibid.
8. Ibid.
9. Ibid.
10. Ibid.
11. Ibid.
12. Ibid.
13. Ibid.
14. Ibid.
15. USDA, National Agricultural Statistics Service, *Agricultural Statistics 1994* (Washington, D.C.: U.S. Government Printing Office, 1994).
16. Population Reference Bureau, *1995 World Population Data Sheet* (Washington, D.C.: 1995).
17. USDA, op. cit. note 1.
18. Ibid.
19. Ibid.
20. Ibid.

MEAT PRODUCTION CLIMBS SHARPLY (pages 28–29)

1. U.S. Department of Agriculture (USDA), Foreign Agricultural Service (FAS), *Livestock and Poultry: World Markets and Trade*, Washington, D.C., October 1995.
2. Ibid.; U.S. Bureau of the Census, Center for International Research, Suitland, Md., private communication, January 23, 1996.
3. International Monetary Fund, *World Economic*

Outlook, October 1995 (Washington, D.C.: 1995); USDA, op. cit. note 1.
4. USDA, op. cit. note 1.
5. Ibid.
6. Ibid.
7. Ibid.
8. Ibid.; USDA, FAS, *Livestock and Poultry: World Markets and Trade*, Washington, D.C., April 1995.
9. USDA, op. cit. note 1; USDA, op. cit. note 8.
10. USDA, op. cit. note 1; USDA, op. cit. note 8.
11. USDA, op. cit. note 1; USDA, op. cit. note 8.
12. USDA, op. cit. note 1.
13. Ibid.
14. Ibid.
15. Ibid.
16. Ibid.
17. Ibid.
18. Ibid.
19. Ibid.
20. Ibid.
21. Ibid.
22. Ibid.
23. Ibid.
24. Ibid.
25. Ibid.
26. USDA, FAS, *Grain: World Markets and Trade*, Washington, D.C., December 1995.

WORLD FISH HARVEST HITS NEW HIGH (pages 30–31)

1. Data for 1994 from Maurizio Perotti, fishery statistician, Fishery Information, Data and Statistics Service, Fisheries Department, U.N. Food and Agriculture Organization (FAO), Rome, private communications, April 12, 1995, and January 25, 1996; 1984–91 culture and marine data from FAO, *Aquaculture Production Statistics, 1984-1993* (Rome: 1995); 1950–95 world harvest, total catch, and total culture from FAO, *Yearbook of Fishery Statistics: Catches and Landings* (Rome: 1967-1994); before 1984, culture estimates are based on a 1975 aquaculture production estimate from National Research Council, *Aquaculture in the United States: Constraints and Opportunities* (Washington, D.C.: National Academy of Sciences, 1978) and country estimates in Conner Bailey and Mike Skladeny, "Aquacultural Development in Tropical Asia," *Natural Resources Forum*, February 1991; growth rates from FAO, *Marine*

Fisheries and the Law of the Sea: A Decade of Change, FAO Fisheries Circular No. 853 (Rome: 1993).
2. "Fish and Fisheries Products," *Food Outlook*, August/September 1995.
3. FAO, *The State of World Fisheries and Aquaculture* (Rome: 1995).
4. Ibid.
5. FAO, *Yearbook of Fishery Statistics: Catches and Landings* (Rome: various years); 1994 data from Perotti, op. cit. note 1; population data from U.S. Bureau of Census, Center for International Research, Suitland, Md., private communication, January 23, 1996.
6. Alison Maitland, "Poor Endangered By Fall in Fish Stocks," *Financial Times*, October 16, 1995.
7. National Marine Fisheries Service, Southeast Regional Office, *Addressing Finfish Bycatch in Gulf of Mexico and South Atlantic Fisheries: A Report to Congress* (St. Petersburg, Fla.: 1995).
8. FAO, *A Global Assessment of Fisheries Bycatch and Discards*, Technical Paper No. 339 (Rome: 1994), as cited in FAO, op. cit. note 3.
9. William J. Broad, "Creatures of the Deep Find Their Way to the Table," *New York Times*, December 26, 1995.
10. William McCloskey, "Fished Out!" *International Wildlife*, May/June 1993; Dick Russell, "Fishing Down the Food Chain," *Amicus Journal*, Fall 1995.
11. Carl Safina, "Bluefin Tuna in the West Atlantic: Negligent Management and the Making of an Endangered Species," *Conservation Biology*, June 1993; Terry Hall and Nikki Tait, "Asian Fleets Roam in Search of Bluefin Tuna," *Financial Times*, August 30, 1994; "Australia, Japan Sign Agreement to Limit Tuna Fishing," *JPRS Report: Environmental Issues*, January 23, 1995.
12. Carl Safina, "The World's Imperiled Fish," *Scientific American*, November 1995.
13. Anne Swardson, "Canadians Drive Off Spanish Trawler," *Washington Post*, March 27, 1995; Karen Fossli, "Canada/Norway Fisheries Agreement Angers Iceland," *Financial Times*, January 13, 1995; Hugh Carnegy, "Fish May Hinder SDP Plans to Net Iceland's Pro-EU Voters," *Financial Times*, April 5, 1995.
14. John Kurien, "Impact of Joint Ventures on Fish Economy," *Economic and Political Weekly*, February 11, 1995; Nityanand Jayaraman, "Troubled Waters: India's Small Fishermen Say Big Isn't Always Better," *Far Eastern Economic Review*, April 27, 1995.
15. Ted Bardacke, "Fish War Crisis Brings Thai and

Malaysian PMs to the Table," *Financial Times*, December 14, 1995.

16. Fred Pearce, "On the Origin of Revolution," *New Scientist*, September 30, 1995.

17. Barbara Crossette, "Treaty Proposal to Curtail Overfishing Is Approved at U.N.," *New York Times*, August 5, 1995.

18. Alison Maitland, "Delays Feared in Implementing Fish Stocks Treaty," *Financial Times*, December 5, 1995.

19. FAO, "Report of the 21st Session of the Committee on Fisheries (Rome, March 10–13, 1995)," Rome, June 5–16, 1995.

AQUACULTURE PRODUCTION RISES (pages 32–33)

1. U.N. Food and Agriculture Organization (FAO), "Aquaculture Production Statistics 1984–1993," Fisheries Circular No. 815, Revision 7, Rome, 1995.

2. Ibid.

3. Ibid.

4. Ibid.

5. Ibid.

6. Ibid.; FAO, *Yearbook of Fishery Statistics: Catches and Landings 1993* (Rome: 1995).

7. FAO, op. cit. note 1; FAO, op. cit. note 6.

8. FAO, op. cit. note 1; FAO, op cit. note 6.

9. FAO, op. cit. note 1.

10. Ibid.

11. Ibid.; FAO, op. cit. note 6.

12. FAO, op. cit. note 1.

13. Ibid.

14. Hal Kane, "Growing Fish in Fields," *Worldwatch*, September/October 1993.

15. FAO, op. cit. note 1.

16. Ibid.

17. Fish conversion rate from Ross Garnaut and Guonan Ma, East Asia Analytical Unit, Department of Foreign Affairs and Trade, *Grain in China* (Canberra: Australian Government Publishing Service, 1992); grain-to-poultry rate derived from data in Robert V. Bishop et al., *The World Poultry Market—Government Intervention and Multilateral Policy Reform* (Washington, D.C.: U.S. Depatrment of Agriculture (USDA), 1990); poultry data from Linda Bailey, Livestock and Poultry Situation staff, Economic Research Service (ERS), USDA, Washington D.C., private communication, April 27, 1992, and from various issues of *Feedstuffs*; grain-to-pork rate based on Leland Southard, Livestock and Poultry Situation and Outlook staff, ERS, USDA, Washington, D.C., private communication, April 27, 1992; grain-to-beef rate from Allen Baker, Feed Situation and Outlook Staff, ERS, USDA, Washington, D.C., private communication, April 27, 1992.

18. FAO, "Review of the State of the World Fishery Resources: Aquaculture," Fisheries Circular No. 886, Rome, 1995.

19. Malcom C. M. Beveridge, Lindsay G. Ross, and Liam A. Kelly, "Aquaculture and Biodiversity," *Ambio*, December 1994.

20. Ibid.

21. Ibid.

22. Crispino A. Saclauso, "Brackishwater Aquaculture: Threat to the Environment?" *Naga, The ICLARM Quarterly* (International Center for Living Aquatic Resource Management, Philippines), July 1989.

23. FAO, op. cit. note 18.

24. Ibid.

25. Lester R. Brown, "The Acceleration of History," in Lester R. Brown et al., *State of the World 1996* (New York: W.W. Norton & Company, 1996); world fish catch from Maurizio Perotti, fishery statistician, Fishery Information, Data and Statistics Service, Fisheries Department, FAO, Rome, private communications, April 12, 1995, and January 25, 1996.

26. "From Hunting to Farming Fish," Consultative Group on International Agricultural Research, press release, Washington, D.C., May 14, 1995.

27. James Harding, "World Bank Sees Big Future for Fish Farming," *Financial Times*, May 15, 1995.

WORLDWIDE FEEDGRAIN USE DROPS (pages 34–35)

1. U.S. Department of Agriculture (USDA), Foreign Agricultural Service, *Grain: World Markets and Trade*, Washington, D.C., December 1995.

2. Ibid.

3. Ibid.; USDA, Economic Research Service, "Production, Supply, and Demand View" (electronic database), Washington, D.C., January 1996.

4. International Monetary Fund, *World Economic Outlook, October 1995* (Washington, D.C.: 1995).

5. USDA, op. cit. note 3.

6. USDA, op. cit. note 1.

7. Ibid.

8. Ibid.

9. Ibid.

10. Ibid.

11. USDA, op. cit. note 3.

12. Ibid.

13. Ibid.

14. USDA, op. cit. note 1.

15. Ibid.

16. Ibid.

17. Population from Population Reference Bureau, *1995 World Population Data Sheet* (Washington, D.C.: 1995).

18. USDA, op. cit. note 1.

19. Ibid.

GRAIN STOCKS DROP TO ALL-TIME LOW (pages 36–37)

1. U.S. Department of Agriculture (USDA), Foreign Agricultural Service (FAS), *Grain: World Markets and Trade*, Washington, D.C., December 1995.

2. USDA, "Production, Supply, and Demand View" (electronic database), Washington, D.C. January 1996.

3. Ibid.; International Monetary Fund (IMF), *International Financial Statistics Yearbook* (Washington, D.C.: 1994).

4. Grain prices from "Futures Prices," *Wall Street Journal*, various editions.

5. Ibid.

6. USDA, op. cit. note 1.

7. USDA, op. cit. note 2.

8. U.S. Bureau of the Census, Center for International Research, Suitland, Md., private communication, January 23, 1996.

9. USDA, op. cit. note 1.

10. USDA, FAS, *Grain: World Markets and Trade*, Washington, D.C., January 1996.

11. IMF, *World Economic Outlook, October 1995* (Washington, D.C.: 1995).

12. USDA, op. cit. note 1.

13. Ibid.

14. Census Bureau, op. cit. note 8.

15. Christopher Goldthwaite, FAS, USDA, personal communication, April 25, 1995.

16. "Vietnam to Limit Exports of Rice for Four Months," *Journal of Commerce*, May 19, 1995.

17. Deborah Hargreaves, "Wheat Prices Hit 15-Year High as EU Imposes Tax on Exports," *Financial Times*, December 8, 1995.

18. Bruce Barnard, "EU to Conserve Barley By Curbing Exports," *Journal of Commerce*, January 12, 1996.

DECLINE IN FERTILIZER USE HALTS (pages 40–41)

1. K.F. Isherwood and K.G. Soh, "Short Term Prospects for World Agriculture and Fertilizer Use," presented at 21st Enlarged Council Meeting, International Fertilizer Industry Association, Paris, November 15–17, 1995.

2. U.N. Food and Agriculture Organization, *Fertilizer Yearbook* (Rome: various years).

3. Ibid.

4. Isherwood and Soh, op. cit. note 1; U.S. Bureau of the Census, Center for International Research, Suitland, Md., private communication, January 23, 1996.

5. Census Bureau, op. cit. note 4; U.S. Department of Agriculture, Foreign Agricultural Service, *Grain: World Markets and Trade*, Washington, D.C., December 1995.

6. Isherwood and Soh, op. cit. note 1.

7. Ibid.

8. Ibid.

9. Ibid.

10. Population Reference Bureau, *1995 World Population Data Sheet* (Washington, D.C.: 1995).

11. Isherwood and Soh, op. cit. note 1.

12. Ibid.

13. Ibid.

14. Ibid.

15. Ibid.

16. Ibid.

17. Ibid.

18. Ibid.

WORLD GRAINLAND AREA DROPS (pages 42–43)

1. U.S. Department of Agriculture (USDA), Foreign Agricultural Service (FAS), *Grain: World Markets and Trade*, Washington, D.C., December 1995.

2. Ibid.; Lester R. Brown, *Who Will Feed China? Wake-Up Call for a Small Planet* (New York: W.W. Norton & Company, 1995); USDA, Economic Research Service (ERS), *Update on Agricultural Resources and Economic Indicators*, No. 12, Washington, D.C., 1995.

3. USDA, *World Grain Database* (unpublished printouts) (Washington, D.C.: 1992); USDA,

ERS, "Production, Supply, and Demand View" (electronic database), Washington, D.C., January 1996.

4. USDA (unpublished printout), op. cit. note 3; USDA (electronic database), op. cit. note 3; population from U.S. Bureau of the Census, Center for International Research, Suitland, Md., private communication, January 23, 1996.

5. K.F. Isherwood and K.G. Soh, "Short Term Prospects for World Agriculture and Fertilizer Use," presented at 21st Enlarged Council Meeting, International Fertilizer Industry Association, Paris, November 15-17, 1995.

6. USDA, FAS, *October World Agriculture Production*, Washington, D.C., October 1995.

7. USDA, op. cit. note 1.

8. USDA, ERS, *Agricultural Resources Inputs: Situation and Outlook Report*, Washington, D.C., October 1993.

9. Ibid.

10. USDA (electronic database), op. cit. note 3; USDA, FAS, *Grain: World Markets and Trade*, Washington, D.C., January 1996.

11. Wang Rong, "Food Before Golf on Southern Land," *China Daily*, January 25, 1995.

12. Ibid.

13. Scott Thompson, "The Evolving Grain Markets in Southeast Asia," in USDA, FAS, *Grain: World Markets and Trade*, Washington, D.C., June 1995.

14. "Ford Avoids Hanoi Farmland Ban," *The Japan Times*, July 25, 1995.

15. Ibid.

16. Census Bureau, op. cit. note 4.

IRRIGATED AREA DIPS SLIGHTLY
(pages 44–45)

1. U.N. Food and Agriculture Organization (FAO), *FAO Production Yearbook* (Rome: 1994); Bill Quinby, Economic Research Service (ERS), U.S. Department of Agriculture (USDA), Washington, D.C., private communication, January 24, 1996.

2. FAO, op. cit. note 1; FAO, *FAO Production Yearbook*, 1993 (Rome: 1993); interpretation of data from Jean Marc Faures, FAO, private communication, January 6, 1996.

3. FAO, op. cit. note 1.

4. Operations Evaluation Department, "A Review of World Bank Experience in Irrigation," World Bank, Washington, D.C., November 1994.

5. Ibid.

6. FAO, op. cit. note 2.

7. Sandra Postel, "Forging a Sustainable Water Strategy," in Lester R. Brown et al., *State of the World 1996* (New York: W.W. Norton & Company, 1996).

8. USDA, Foreign Agricultural Service, *Grain: World Markets and Trade*, Washington, D.C., December 1995.

9. FAO, *State of Food and Agriculture 1993* (Rome: 1993).

10. Mark Rosegrant and Mark Svendsen, "Asian Food Production in the 1990s: Irrigation Investment and Management Policy," International Food Policy Research Institute, Washington, D.C., 1993.

11. Sandra Postel, *Last Oasis: Facing Water Scarcity* (New York: W.W. Norton & Company, 1992).

12. FAO, "Water Development for Food Security," Rome, March 1995.

13. Operations Evaluation Department, op. cit. note 4.

14. Postel, op. cit. note 7.

15. China from You Wen-Rui, "Environmental Issues in Water Development in China," *Environmental Issues in Land and Water Development* (Bangkok: FAO Regional Office for Asia and the Pacific, 1992); Iran from Anthony Young et al., *Land Degradation in South Asia: Its Severity, Causes, and Effects upon the People* (Rome: FAO, 1994).

16. Maharashtra from Raj Chengappa, "India's Water Crisis," *World Press Review*, August 1986; Gujarat from A. Vaidyanathan, "Second India Series Revisited: Food and Agriculture," Madras Institute of Development Studies, Madras, India, 1994; Haryana from Marcus Moench, "Approaches to Groundwater Management: To Control or Enable," *Economic and Political Weekly*, September 24, 1994.

17. Wendell Holmes and Mindy Petrulis, "Declining Water Levels in the Texas High Plains Translate to Declining Economic Performance," ERS, USDA, Washington, D.C., 1988.

18. Worldwatch calculation based on data in Jamil al Alawi and Mohammed Abdulrazzak, "Water in the Arabian Peninsula: Problems and Perspectives," in Peter Rogers and Peter Lydon, eds., *Water in the Arab World: Perspectives and Prognoses* (Cambridge, Mass.: Division of Applied Sciences, Harvard University, 1994).

19. Ramesh Bhatia, Upali Amerasinghe, and K.A.U.S. Imbulana, "Productivity and Profitability of Paddy Production in the Muda Scheme, Malaysia," *Water Resources Development*, Vol. 11, No. 1, 1995.

20. Ibid.
21. Thomas S. Maddock and Walter G. Hines, "Meeting Future Public Water Supply Needs: A Southwest Perspective," *Water Resources Bulletin*, April 1995.

OIL PRODUCTION RISES (pages 48-49)

1. American Petroleum Institute, *Basic Petroleum Data Book* (Washington, D.C.: 1994); "Worldwide Look at Reserves and Production," *Oil & Gas Journal*, December 25, 1995.
2. David H. Knapp, "Non-OPEC Oil Supply Continues to Grow," *Oil & Gas Journal*, December 25, 1995.
3. "Worldwide Look at Reserves and Production," op. cit. note 1.
4. U.S. Department of Energy (DOE), Energy Information Administration, *Monthly Energy Review December 1995* (Washington, D.C.: 1995).
5. "Saudi Arabian Sands," *Energy Economist*, November 1993.
6. Patrick Crow, "Iraqi Oil Exports Still at Issue," *Oil & Gas Journal*, January 22, 1996.
7. "Worldwide Look at Reserves and Production," op. cit. note 1.
8. Knapp, op. cit. note 2.
9. Arthur Gottschalk, "Phase I of Caspian Oil Project Under Way," *Journal of Commerce*, August 16, 1995.
10. Steve LeVine, "Way Sought to Pass Russia with Oil Line," *New York Times*, September 9, 1995.
11. DOE, op. cit. note 4.
12. "U.S. Still Has Oil, Gas Allure," *Oil & Gas Journal*, March 13, 1995.
13. "Gulf of Mexico Operations Bolster U.S. Oil and Gas Production," *Oil & Gas Journal*, January 22, 1996.
14. David Lascelles, Ronald van de Krol, and Judy Dempsey, "Shell Tense Over Brent Spar," *Financial Times*, June 20, 1995.
15. Cacilie Tohwedder and Peter Gumbel, "Shell Bows to German Greens' Muscle," *Wall Street Journal*, June 21, 1995.
16. Ibid.
17. Steve Kretzmann, "Nigeria's 'Drilling Field,'" *Multinational Monitor*, January/February 1995.
18. David Knott, "Shell the Target After Nigerian Executions," *Oil & Gas Journal*, November 20, 1995.
19. Paul Lewis, "Nigeria's Deadly Oil War: Shell Defends Its Record," *New York Times*, February 12, 1996.

NATURAL GAS PRODUCTION EDGES UP (pages 50-51)

1. Worldwatch Institute estimate based on British Petroleum (BP), *BP Statistical Review of World Energy* (London: Group Media & Publications, 1995), on U.S. Department of Energy, Energy Information Administration, *Monthly Energy Review January 1996* (Washington, D.C.: 1996), on *PlanEcon Energy Report*, and other sources; the Worldwatch figures include natural gas liquids as well as methane.
2. *PlanEcon Energy Report*, January 1996.
3. BP, op. cit. note 1.
4. Ibid.
5. David Hoffman, "Russian's Economic Colossus," *Washington Post*, December 3, 1995.
6. Chang Wimin, "China to Import Gas from Central Asia, Russia," *China Daily*, February 5, 1996.
7. Ben Hirschler, "Going Gets Tougher in Search for Oil and Gas in Nigeria," *Journal of Commerce*, October 17, 1995.
8. "Expanding Natural Gas Markets Top Industry Agenda in Latin America," *Oil & Gas Journal*, November 13, 1995.
9. George Baker, "Mexico's Energy Policies Stand at Crossroads," *Oil & Gas Journal*, November 6, 1995.
10. *Oil & Gas Journal*, various issues.
11. Steven Collins, "Special Report: Gas-Fired Power Plants," *Power Magazine*, February 1993.
12. Bob Bjorge, General Electric, Schenectady, N.Y., private communication and printout, August 26, 1993.
13. Ibid.
14. Collins, op. cit. note 11.
15. Brooke Stoddard, "Fuel Cell Update," *American Gas*, June 1993.
16. "The Amazing Shrinking Fuel Cell," *Energy Economist*, October 1995.

COAL USE UP SLIGHTLY (pages 52-53)

1. Coal use in 1995 is Worldwatch estimate based on data for the former Soviet Union and Eastern Europe from Dr. Matthew J. Sagers, "Energy Overview for the Former Soviet Republics and

Eastern Europe Through the First Nine Months of 1995," *PlanEcon Energy Report*, January 1996, on data for China from Vicki McLaine, U.S. Department of Energy (DOE), Energy Information Administration (EIA), Washington, D.C., private communication, February 12, 1996, on extrapolations of data for coal use trends from British Petroleum (BP), *BP Statistical Review of World Energy* (London: Group Media & Publications, 1995), and on data for the United States from DOE, EIA, *Monthly Energy Review January 1996* (Washington, D.C.: 1996).

2. Historical data from United Nations, *World Energy Supplies* (New York: various years), from United Nations, *Yearbook of World Energy Statistics* (New York: 1983), and from United Nations, *Energy Statistics Yearbook* (New York: various years); 1994 figure is a Worldwatch estimate, based on U.N. data and on BP, op. cit. note 1.

3. McLaine, op. cit. note 1.

4. BP, op. cit. note 1.

5. Ibid.

6. Sagers, op. cit. note 1; historical decline from BP, op. cit. note 1.

7. BP, op. cit. note 1.

8. Ibid.

9. Ibid.

10. Arthur Gottschalk, "US Coal Output Forecast to Grow By 2.4% to Set Record in 1996," *Journal of Commerce*, January 22, 1996.

11. BP, op. cit. note 1.

12. Ibid.

13. Ibid.

14. Ibid.

15. DOE, EIA, *Annual Energy Review 1994* (Washington, D.C.: 1995).

16. Christopher Flavin and Nicholas Lenssen, *Power Surge: Guide to the Coming Energy Revolution* (New York: W.W. Norton & Company, 1994).

17. Gregg Marland, "Carbon Dioxide Emission Rates for Conventional and Synthetic Fuels," *Energy*, Vol. 8, No. 12, 1983; coal's contribution to carbon dioxide totals is a Worldwatch estimate based on various sources provided in notes 1 and 2.

18. Sheila Tefft, "Rush to Burn Coal Turns China Into Asia's Polluter," *Christian Science Monitor*, August 30, 1995.

19. Jonathan E. Sinton, ed., *China Energy Data Book* (Berkeley, Calif.: Lawrence Berkeley Laboratory, 1992).

NUCLEAR POWER VIRTUALLY STEADY (pages 54–55)

1. Installed nuclear capacity is defined as reactors connected to the grid as of December 31, 1995, and is based on Worldwatch Institute database complied from statistics from the International Atomic Energy Agency (IAEA) and press reports primarily from *European Energy Report, Energy Economist, Nuclear News, New York Times, Journal of Commerce, Financial Times,* and other major publications, including Greenpeace International, WISE–Paris, and Worldwatch Institute, *The World Nuclear Industry Status Report: 1992* (London: 1992).

2. Worldwatch database, op. cit. note 1.

3. Steve LeVine, "Despite U.S. Protests, Armenia Will Restart Nuclear Reactor," *New York Times*, October 24, 1995; "Armenia-2 Restarts After Six-Year Shutdown," *Nuclear News,* December 1995.

4. Worldwatch database, op. cit. note 1.

5. Ibid.; IAEA, *Nuclear Power Reactors in the World* (Vienna: 1995).

6. Worldwatch database, op. cit. note 1.

7. Ibid.

8. Ibid.

9. Ibid.

10. Paul C. Parshley, Deborah F. Grosser, and Daria A. Roulett, "Should Investors Be Concerned About Rising Nuclear Plant Decommissioning Costs?" Shearson Lehman Brothers, New York, January 6, 1993.

11. IAEA, op. cit. note 5.

12. U.S. Department of Energy, Energy Information Administration, *World Nuclear Outlook 1995* (Washington, D.C.: U.S. Government Printing Office, 1995).

13. "New Swedish Government Postpones Power Liberalisation," *European Energy Report,* October 28, 1994.

14. "New U.K. Nuclear Company Drops Plans for New Units as Privatization Nears," *McGraw-Hill's Electric Power Daily,* December 12, 1995.

15. "Decommissioning Clearance for East Germany's Greifswald," *European Energy Report,* September 1, 1995.

16. Worldwatch database, op. cit. note 1.

17. Editorial, *Mainichi Daily News* (Tokyo), December 12, 1995; "Japanese Fear Spill Will Chill Nuclear Program," *Journal of Commerce,* December 12, 1995.

18. "Japan Admits It Hid Extent of Nuclear Leak," *San Francisco Chronicle,* December 21, 1995.

19. Masuro Sugai, "The Anti-Nuclear Power

Movement in Japan," in Helmar Krupp, ed., *Energy Politics and Schumpter Dynamics* (New York: Springer-Verlag, 1992), with an update from Agency of Natural Resources and Energy, *A Handbook of Nuclear Power, 1995* (Tokyo: Denryoku Shimpo Sha, 1995).

20. Mika Obayashi, Citizens Nuclear Information Center, Tokyo, private communication, December 1, 1995; John Willis, Greenpeace Japan, Tokyo, private communication, December 2, 1995.
21. Walter W.L. Shen, "An Overview of Taiwan's Nuclear Program," *Nuclear News,* June 1995.
22. Ibid.
23. *Reuter News Wire,* January 24, 1996.
24. Tony Walker, "China Buys French N-power Reactors in $2.8bn Deal," *Financial Times,* January 17, 1995.
25. Craig S. Smith, "China Angered by Nuclear-Plant Delay," *Wall Street Journal,* April 26, 1995.
26. "Korean Nuclear Project Set Back," *Wall Street Journal,* February 2, 1996.

WIND POWER GROWTH ACCELERATES (pages 56–57)

1. Estimates by Birger Madsen, "International Wind Energy Development," BTM Consult, Ringkobing, Denmark, private communication, February 1996, and by Paul Gipe and Associates, Tehachapi, Calif., private communication, March 1, 1996; the historical wind power series has been adjusted from those published in earlier *Vital Signs* to reflect more recent assessments.
2. Figure of 1 percent is based on figures on total world electricity generation in U.S. Department of Energy, Energy Information Administration, *International Energy Outlook 1995* (Washington, D.C.: 1995).
3. Madsen, op. cit. note 1.
4. Ibid.
5. Gipe and Associates, op. cit. note 1.
6. Madsen, op. cit. note 1; Gipe and Associates, op. cit. note 1. The figures here on annual additions are greater than the increase in cumulative capacity shown earlier, since some of the wind turbines installed in earlier years have been abandoned. The series published this year also includes a significant upward adjustment in new capacity installed in 1994.
7. Deutsches Windenergie-Institut, "Windenergienutzung in der Bundesrepublik Deutschland,

Stand 32.12.1995," February 1996.
8. Madsen, op. cit. note 1.
9. Ibid.
10. *Windpower Monthly,* various issues.
11. Antoine Bonduelle, "France Prepares Market Incentives," *Windpower Monthly,* February 1996.
12. Deutsches Windenergie-Insitut, op. cit. note 7; Jens Peter Molly and A. Keuper, "Wind Energy Development in Germany," Deutsches Windenergie-Insitut, Wilhelmshaven, Germany, June 6, 1995.
13. Molly and Keuper, op. cit. note 12.
14. William Grant, "European Policies to Promote Cogeneration and Wind Energy Systems," Izaak Walton League of America for the German Marshall Fund, Washington, D.C., 1994.
15. Sarah Knight, "Politicians Unite to Protect Wind Tariffs from Utility Mutiny," *Windpower Monthly,* June 1995.
16. Neelam Matthews, "Business Booming for Villagers," *Windpower Monthly,* July 1995.
17. "Wind Firm Falls on Hard Times," *New York Times,* December 27, 1995.
18. Gipe and Associates, op. cit. note 1.
19. Ibid.

SOLAR CELL SHIPMENTS JUMP (pages 58–59)

1. Paul D. Maycock, "1995 World PV Module Shipments 81.4 MW; 17.2 Percent Increase," *PV News,* February 1996.
2. Cumulative total based on ibid., and assumes a 1-percent annual failure rate of existing systems.
3. Paul D. Maycock, Photovoltaic Energy Systems Inc., Casanova, Va., private communication, February 8, 1996.
4. "U.S. PV Shipment Growth Even Faster Versus Europe, Japan Than Believed," *The Solar Letter,* February 2, 1996.
5. Maycock, op. cit. note 1.
6. "U.S. PV Shipment Growth," op. cit. note 4.
7. Paul D. Maycock, "Led By Sharp and Kyocera, Japanese Shipments Increase 16.4 Percent," *PV News,* February 1996.
8. Ibid.
9. Paul D. Maycock, "European Module Shipment Flat For the First Time Ever!" *PV News,* February 1996.
10. Ibid.
11. Ibid.
12. Maycock, op. cit. note 3.

13. Ibid.
14. Ibid.
15. Paul D. Maycock, "Rest of the World Module Shipments Increase 13 Percent," *PV News*, February 1996.
16. Paul D. Maycock, "1995 PV Cell and Module Shipments Top 80 MW," *PV News*, February 1996.
17. Martin Green, with introduction by Derek Lovejoy, "Multilayer Thin Film Silicon Solar Cells," *Natural Resources Forum*, Vol. 19, No. 4, 1995.
18. Stephen Steubner, "Brave New World for PV: Energy Officials Plot Strategy to Boost PV Throughout the Globe," *PV News*, October 1995.
19. Ibid.; Taylor Moore, "Developing Countries on a Power Drive," *EPRI Journal*, July/August 1995.
20. Currently, conversion efficiencies of thin-film silicon solar cells are around 15 percent; M.A. Green et al., "Enhanced Light-Trapping in 21.5% Efficient Thin Silicon Solar Cells," presented at the 13th European Photovoltaic Solar Energy Conference, Nice, October 1995; Green, op. cit. note 17.
21. Green, op. cit. note 17.

SALES OF COMPACT FLUORESCENTS SOAR (pages 60–61)

1. Data for 1988 from Evan Mills, Lawrence Berkeley Laboratory, Berkeley, Calif., private communication, February 3, 1993; 1989–92 data from Nils Borg, "Global CFL Sales," *International Association for Energy-Efficient Lighting* (IAEEL) *Newsletter*, Stockholm, Sweden, Vol. 4/94; 1993–95 data from Nils Borg, IAEEL/National Board for Industrial and Technical Development, Stockholm, Sweden, private communication, February 5, 1996.
2. Borg, private communication, op. cit. note 1.
3. Ibid.
4. Ibid.
5. Ibid.
6. Ibid.
7. Mark Levine et al., "Electricity End-Use Efficiency: Experience with Technologies, Markets, and Policies Throughout the World," American Council for an Energy-Efficient Economy (ACEEE), Washington, D.C., March 1992.
8. India and Hungary from Steve Nadel, ACEEE, Washington, D.C., private communication, January 19, 1996; Thailand and Indonesia from Peter du Pont, International Institute for Energy Conservation (IIEC), Washington, D.C., private communication, January 17, 1996; Poland and Russia from Sabrina Burner, IIEC, London, private communication, January 29, 1996; Ukraine and Kyrgyzstan from Dana Younger, International Finance Corporation/Global Environment Facility Coordinator, Washington, D.C., private communication, February 7, 1996.
9. Younger, op. cit. note 8.
10. Data on China from Steve Nadel et al., "Lighting Energy Efficiency in China: Current Status, Future Directions" (draft), ACEEE, Washington, D.C., 1996; U.S. data for 1989–91 from Evan Mills, Lawrence Berkeley Laboratory, Berkeley, Calif., private communication, January 17, 1996; U.S. data for 1992 from U.S. Department of Commerce, Bureau of the Census, "Current Industrial Reports: Electric Lamps—MQ36B (92)-5," Washington, D.C., September 1993; U.S. data for 1993–94 from U.S. Department of Commerce, Bureau of the Census, "Current Industrial Reports: Electric Lamps—MQ36B (94)-1," Washington, D.C., July 1995.
11. Nadel et al., op. cit. note 10; Census Bureau, July 1995, op. cit. note 10.
12. Nadel et al., op. cit. note 10.
13. Du Pont, op. cit. note 8.
14. Ibid.
15. Younger, op. cit. note 8.
16. World Bank, *World Development Report 1994* (New York: Oxford University Press, 1994).
17. World Resources Institute, *World Resources 1994-95* (New York: Oxford University Press, 1994).
18. Bhaskar Natarajan, "Market Characteristics for Implementing Energy Efficient Lighting Programmes," Proceedings of Right Light Three, 3rd European Conference on Energy-Efficient Lighting, Newcastle, England, June 18–21, 1995.
19. World Resources Institute, op. cit. note 17.
20. Worldwatch calculation, assuming a CFL purchase price of $15 and a 10,000-hour lifetime, a price of 75¢ and a lifetime of 1,000 hours for the equivalent 75-watt incandescent, an electricity cost of 8¢ per kilowatt-hour, a 3-percent real discount rate, and an operation period of four hours per day.
21. Amory Lovins, "The 'Negawatt' Revolution: New Techniques for Electric Efficiency," *Site Selection*, November 1990. Calculation includes energy savings from the reduced demand for cooling that results from replacing an inefficient

incandescent bulb with a CFL.

22. Younger, op. cit. note 8.

23. Ibid.

CARBON EMISSIONS HIT ALL-TIME HIGH (pages 64–65)

1. The Kuwaiti oil field fires of the Gulf War, which injected 130 million tons of carbon into the atmosphere, were largely responsible for the previous record set in 1991. Carbon emission figures from G. Marland, R.J. Andres, and T.A. Boden, "Global, Regional, and National CO_2 Emission Estimates From Fossil Fuel Burning, Cement Production, and Gas Flaring: 1950-92" (electronic database) (Oak Ridge, Tenn.: Carbon Dioxide Information Analysis Center, Oak Ridge National Laboratory, 1995); 1993 and 1994 figures are Worldwatch estimates based on ibid., and on British Petroleum (BP), *BP Statistical Review of World Energy* (London: Group Media & Publications, 1995); 1995 figure is a preliminary Worldwatch estimate based on ibid., on Marland, Andres, and Boden, op. cit. in this note, on U.S. Department of Energy (DOE), Energy Information Administration (EIA), *Monthly Energy Review January 1996* (Washington, D.C.: 1995), on "Energy Overview for the Former Soviet Republics and Eastern Europe Through the First Nine Months of 1995," *PlanEcon Energy Report*, January 1996, on "Worldwide Look at Reserves and Production," *Oil & Gas Journal*, December 25, 1995, and on David Ivanovich, "World's Oil Supply Gushes Ahead of Growing Demand," *Journal of Commerce*, February 14, 1996.

2. *United Nations Framework Convention on Climate Change, Text* (Geneva: U.N. Environment Programme/World Meteorological Organization Information Unit on Climate Change, 1992).

3. Intergovernmental Panel on Climate Change (IPCC), Working Group I, "1995 Summary for Policymakers," Madrid, November 29, 1995.

4. Christopher Flavin, "Facing Up to the Risks of Climate Change," in Lester R. Brown et al., *State of the World 1996* (New York: W.W. Norton & Company, 1996).

5. Timothy Whorf, Scripps Institution of Oceanography, La Jolla, Calif., private communication and printout, February 5, 1996; C.D. Keeling and T.P. Whorf, "Atmospheric CO_2 Records From Sites in the SIO Air Sampling Network," in Thomas A. Boden et al., eds., *Trends '93: A Compendium of Data on Global Change* (Oak Ridge, Tenn.: Oak Ridge National Laboratory, 1994); Jonathan Weiner, "Winter Forecast: Frigid. But Don't Be Fooled," *New York Times Magazine*, October 23, 1994.

6. Marland, Andres and Boden, op. cit. note 1; Worldwatch estimates based on ibid., on BP, op. cit. note 1, and on DOE, op cit. note 1.

7. Marland, Andres, and Boden, op. cit. note 1; Worldwatch estimates based on ibid., on BP, op. cit. note 1, and on Population Reference Bureau, *1995 World Population Data Sheet* (Washington, D.C.: 1995).

8. DOE, EIA, *International Energy Outlook 1995* (Washington, D.C.: 1995); Organisation for Economic Co-operation and Development, International Energy Agency, *World Energy Outlook—1995 Edition* (Paris: 1995); "Climate Change Declaration at Summit of Local Governments Hits Asian Emissions," *Interna-tional Environment Reporter*, November 1, 1995.

9. Marland, Andres, and Boden, op. cit. note 1; Worldwatch estimates based on ibid., and on BP, op. cit. note 1.

10. BP, op. cit. note 1; Jessica Hamburger, *China's Energy and Environment in the Roaring Nineties: A Policy Primer* (Washington, D.C.: Pacific Northwest Laboratory, 1995).

11. Marland, Andres, and Boden, op. cit. note 1; Worldwatch estimates based on ibid., and on BP, op. cit. note 1.

12. IPCC, Working Group II, "Second Assessment Report, Summary for Policymakers: Impacts, Adaptations and Mitigation Options," October 1995; World Bank, "Issues and Options in Greenhouse Gas Emissions Control: Summary Report," Washington, D.C., December 1994; Patrick E. Tyler, "China's Inevitable Dilemma: Coal Equals Growth," *New York Times*, November 29, 1995.

13. *United Nations Framework Convention on Climate Change*, op. cit. note 2.

14. Ibid.

15. U.S. Climate Action Network and Climate Network Europe, *Independent NGO Evaluations of National Plans for Climate Change Mitigation: OECD Countries, Third Review, January 1995* (Washington, D.C.: U.S. Climate Action Network, 1995).

16. DOE, op. cit. note 8.

17. IPCC, op. cit. note 12.

18. "Concrete Action on Protocol Deferred; Two-

Year Negotiation Process Established," *International Environment Reporter*, April 19, 1995.

GLOBAL TEMPERATURE SETS
NEW RECORD (pages 66–67)

1. James Hansen et al., Goddard Institute for Space Studies Surface Air Temperature Analyses, "Table of Global-Mean Monthly, Annual and Seasonal Land-Ocean Temperature Index, 1950-Present," as posted at http://www.giss.nasa.gov/Data/GISTEMP, January 19, 1996.
2. The other data come from the Climatic Research Unit at the University of East Anglia in England, and are based on a slightly different combination of land and sea measurements from various parts of the world; William K. Stevens, "'95 The Hottest Year On Record As the Global Trend Keeps Up," *New York Times*, January 4, 1996.
3. Hansen et al., op. cit. note 1; Phil Jones et al., Climatic Research Unit, "University of East Anglia Land Air Temperatures With Sea Surface Temperatures," as posted at http://www.cru.uea.ac.ukc/cru/press/pj9601/data.htm, January 1996; Stevens, op. cit. note 2.
4. James Hansen et al., "Global Surface Air Temperature in 1995: Return to Pre-Pinatubo Level" (abstract), submitted to *Geophysical Research Letter*, 1996.
5. Ibid.
6. Cited in Stevens, op. cit. note 2.
7. Hansen et al., op. cit. note 1; Ross Gelbspan, "The Heat Is On," *Harper's Magazine*, December 1995; Fred Pearce, "Global Warming 'Jury' Delivers Guilty Verdict," *New Scientist*, December 9, 1995.
8. Stevens, op. cit. note 2.
9. Intergovernmental Panel on Climate Change (IPCC), Working Group I, "1995 Summary for Policymakers," Madrid, November 29, 1995.
10. Ibid.; Pearce, op. cit. note 7.
11. IPCC, op. cit. note 9.
12. Christopher Flavin, "Facing Up To the Risks of Climate Change," in Lester R. Brown et al., *State of the World 1996* (New York: W.W. Norton & Company, 1996).
13. Robert Balling, Jr., "Keep Cool About Global Warming," *Wall Street Journal*, October 16, 1995; Boyce Rensberger, "Climatology: What's Hot, What's Not," *Washington Post*, January 8, 1996.
14. James Hansen et al., "Satellite and Surface Temperature At Odds?" *Climatic Change*, Vol. 30,

1995; John R. Christy and Richard T. McNider, "Satellite Greenhouse Signal," *Nature*, January 27, 1994.
15. Hansen et al., op. cit. note 14; Christy and McNider, op. cit. note 14.
16. Hansen et al., op. cit. note 14.
17. Christy and McNider, op. cit. note 14.
18. Cited in Stevens, op. cit. note 2.

CFC PRODUCTION DROP
CONTINUES (pages 68–69)

1. Sharon Getamal, DuPont, Wilmington, Del., private communication, February 15, 1996; estimates of CFC production do not include illegally produced compounds, and therefore the global total is likely to be higher than reported here; 1994 preliminary estimate has been revised upwards from 295,000 to 388,000 tons with incoming production reports from developing countries.
2. James M. Russell III et al., "Satellite Confirmation of the Dominance of Chlorofluorocarbons in the Global Stratospheric Chlorine Budget," *Nature*, February 8, 1996.
3. United Nations Environment Programme (UNEP), "Environmental Effects of Ozone Depletion: 1994 Assessment," Nairobi, November 1994.
4. UNEP, World Meteorological Organization (WMO), National Aeronautics and Space Administration, and National Oceanic and Atmospheric Administration, *Scientific Assessment of Ozone Depletion: 1994* (Geneva: WMO, 1995).
5. Ibid.
6. "WMO Reports Worst Ozone Depletion on Record for 1995 Antarctic Winter," *International Environment Reporter*, December 13, 1995.
7. Ibid.
8. Ibid.
9. Kevin Robert Gurney, "Saving the Ozone Layer Faster," *Technology Review*, January 1996; "WMO Reports Worst Ozone Depletion," op. cit. note 6.
10. "Antarctic Ozone Depletion in 1995 Most Rapid Ever Recorded, WMO Reports," *International Environment Reporter*, September 20, 1995.
11. UNEP, "Action on Ozone," Nairobi, September 1993.
12. Ibid.
13. Ibid.
14. Ibid.
15. Ibid.

16. Debora MacKenzie, "Ozone Deal Could Backfire," *New Scientist*, December 16, 1995; Debora MacKenzie, "Ozone's Future is Up in the Air," *New Scientist*, December 16, 1995; "Parties Agree on Dates for MeBr and HCFC Phase Out," *OzonAction*, January 1996.
17. J. Raloff, "U.N. to Oversee Methyl Bromide Phaseout," *Science News*, December 16, 1995.
18. "U.S. Should Prohibit CFC Manufacture for Exports, Environmental Group Says," *International Environment Reporter*, September 20, 1995.
19. Duncan Brack, "Developed World Takes the Pledge," *The Guardian Weekly*, December 31, 1995.
20. UNEP, "Report of the Secretariat on Information Provided by the Parties in Accordance with Articles 4, 7 and 9 of the Montreal Protocol and the Report of the Implementation Committee," submitted at the Seventh Meeting of the Parties to the Montreal Protocol on Substances that Deplete the Ozone Layer, Vienna, December 5-7, 1995; "Holed Up," *Economist*, December 9, 1995.
21. UNEP, op. cit. note 20.
22. Ibid.
23. Jim Vallette, *Deadly Complacency: US CFC Production, the Black Market, and Ozone Depletion* (Washington, D.C.: Ozone Action, Inc., 1995).
24. Mokoto Rich, "Safeguarding Mother Earth," *Financial Times*, October 27, 1995.
25. UNEP, op. cit. note 11.
26. Theodor Kapiga, Multilateral Fund for the Montreal Protocol, Montreal, Canada, private communication, February 12, 1996.

SULFUR AND NITROGEN EMISSIONS STEADY (pages 70–71)

1. Dr. J. Dignon, Lawrence Livermore National Laboratory, Livermore, Calif., unpublished data series, private communication, February 12, 1996.
2. Ibid.
3. Ibid.; Sultan Hameed and Jane Dignon, "Global Emissions of Nitrogen and Sulfur Oxides in Fossil Fuel Combustion 1970-1986," *Journal of the Air & Waste Management Association*, February 1991; Jane Dignon and Sultan Hameed, "Global Emissions of Nitrogen and Sulfur Oxides from 1860 to 1980," *JAPCA*, February 1989.
4. Historical data series from Dignon and Hameed, op. cit. note 3.
5. Christopher Flavin and Nicholas Lenssen, *Power Surge: Guide to the Coming Energy Revolution* (New York: W.W. Norton & Company, 1994).
6. Coal use in 1995 is Worldwatch estimate based on data for the former Soviet Union and Eastern Europe from Dr. Matthew J. Sagers, "Energy Overview for the Former Soviet Republics and Eastern Europe Through the First Nine Months of 1995," *PlanEcon Energy Report*, January 1996, on data for China from Vicki McLaine, U.S. Department of Energy (DOE), Energy Information Administration (EIA), Washington, D.C., private communication, February 12, 1996, on extrapolations of data for coal use trends from British Petroleum (BP), *BP Statistical Review of World Energy* (London: Group Media & Publications, 1995), and on data for the United States from DOE, EIA, *Monthly Energy Review January 1996* (Washington, D.C.: 1996); 1994 coal use is based on historical data from United Nations, *World Energy Supplies* (New York: various years), from United Nations, *Yearbook of World Energy Statistics* (New York: 1983), and from United Nations, *Energy Statistics Yearbook* (New York: various years) and on a 1994 estimate by Worldwatch based on U.N. data and on BP, op. cit. in this note.
7. David Lascelles, "The High Cost of Cleaning Up," *Financial Times*, May 26, 1993.
8. Ibid.
9. "Latest Monitoring," *Acid News*, December 1995.
10. "More Trees Than Ever Damaged," *Acid News*, December 1995.
11. Laurie Morse, "Utilities' Chance to Clean Up," *Financial Times*, June 30, 1993.
12. Jeff Bailey, "Electric Utilities Are Overcomplying With Clean Air Act," *Wall Street Journal*, November 15, 1995.
13. Ibid.
14. Ibid.

WORLD ECONOMY EXPANDING STEADILY (pages 74–75)

1. International Monetary Fund (IMF), *World Economic Outlook, October 1995* (Washington, D.C.: 1995).
2. Ibid.
3. Ibid.

4. Ibid.; Embassy of the People's Republic of China, "Newsletter," Washington, D.C., January 10, 1996.
5. IMF, op. cit. note 1.
6. Bill Coyle, "Grain Trade Outlook for China," *Agricultural Outlook*, December 1995.
7. IMF, op. cit. note 1.
8. Ibid.; population from Population Reference Bureau (PRB), *1995 World Population Data Sheet* (Washington, D.C.: 1995).
9. IMF, op. cit. note 1.
10. Ibid.
11. Ibid.; PRB, op. cit. note 8.
12. IMF, op. cit. note 1.
13. Ibid.
14. Ibid.
15. Ibid.
16. Ibid.
17. Ibid.
18. Ibid.
19. Ibid.
20. Ibid.
21. Ibid.
22. Ibid.
23. Ibid.
24. Ibid.
25. Ibid.
26. Ibid.
27. Ibid.
28. Ibid.

GLOBAL TRADE CONTINUES UPWARD (pages 76–77)

1. Calculated from data in International Monetary Fund (IMF), *World Economic Outlook October 1995* (Washington, D.C.: 1995).
2. Richard Lawrence, "Another Stellar Year for World Trade Growth," *Journal of Commerce*, November 21, 1995.
3. Robert Chote, "Growth in Trade Will Lift World Economy Outlook, Say Forecasters," *Financial Times*, August 4, 1995.
4. Lawrence, op. cit. note 2.
5. Ibid.
6. Ibid.
7. "Spanish Steps," *The Economist*, November 18, 1995.
8. Bhushan Bahree, "World Exports of Goods Rose 9% in '94, Outpacing the Growth of Production," *Wall Street Journal*, April 4, 1995.
9. "...And Other Ways to Peel the Onion," *The Economist*, January 7, 1995.
10. IMF, op. cit. note 1.
11. "Sunshine and Showers," *The Economist*, April 29, 1995.
12. Samuel Silva, "Trade Volumes Rise as Barriers Fall," *IDB*, March 1995.
13. Enrique Yeves, "Observers Hedge Their Bets as Latin America Jockeys for Future Trade Position," *Ceres*, May/June 1995.
14. Silva, op. cit. note 12.
15. Lawrence, op. cit. note 2.
16. IMF, op. cit. note 1.
17. Ibid.
18. Ibid.
19. Ibid.
20. David E. Sanger, "World Trade Group Orders U.S. to Alter Clean Air Act," *New York Times*, January 18, 1996.
21. "US to Use WTO to Open Foreign Food Markets," *Third World Economics*, May 1-15, 1995; Bhushan Bahree, "U.S. Renews Controversial Bid to Tie Labor Principles to Trade Privileges," *Wall Street Journal*, April 5, 1995.
22. "Sunshine and Showers," op. cit. note 11.

STEEL PRODUCTION REBOUNDS SLIGHTLY (pages 78–79)

1. International Iron and Steel Institute (IISI), *Steel Statistical Yearbook 1995* (Brussels: 1995).
2. Historical data from IISI, *Steel Statistical Yearbook* (Brussels: various years); population figures from U.S. Bureau of the Census, Center for International Research, Suitland, Md., private communication, January 23, 1996.
3. IISI, op. cit. note 2.
4. Ibid.
5. IISI, op. cit. note 1.
6. IISI, op. cit. note 2; IISI, op. cit. note 1.
7. IISI, op. cit. note 2; IISI, op. cit. note 1.
8. IISI, op. cit. note 2; IISI, op. cit. note 1.
9. IISI, op. cit. note 2; IISI, op. cit. note 1.
10. IISI, op. cit. note 1; IISI, op. cit. note 2.
11. IISI, op. cit. note 2; IISI, op. cit. note 1.
12. Population figures from Population Reference Bureau, *World Population Data Sheet 1995* (Washington, D.C.: 1995).
13. IISI, op. cit. note 1.
14. Ibid.
15. Ibid.; IISI, op. cit. note 2.
16. Global Tomorrow Coalition, *Global Ecology*

Handbook (Boston: Beacon Press, 1990).

17. William Hogan, *Steel in the 21st Cen tury: Competition Forges a New World Order* (New York: Lexington Books, 1994).

18. Worldwatch calculation based on data from Institute of Scrap Recycling Industries, Washington, D.C., private communication, January 25, 1995.

BICYCLE PRODUCTION UP (pages 82–83)

1. Calculated from data in "World Market Report," *Interbike Directory* (Newport Beach, Calif.: Primedia, Inc., various years).

2. Ibid.

3. Ibid.

4. "World Market Report," *1996 Interbike Directory* (Newport Beach, Calif.: Primedia, Inc., 1996).

5. Ibid.

6. "A Quick Spin on the Global Market," *1996 Interbike Directory* (Newport Beach, Calif.: Primedia, Inc. 1996).

7. "World Market Report," op. cit. note 4.

8. "A Quick Spin on the Global Market," op. cit. note 6.

9. Joseph Scarpaci and Annie Z. Hall, "Havana Pedals Through Hard Times," *Sustainable Transport*, Fall 1995.

10. "Ho Chi Minh City: Free-Market Bicycle Taxis Banned," *Sustainable Transport*, Fall 1995.

11. John Griffin, "Bicyclists Facing Competition from Motorcyclists," *Sustainable Transport*, Winter 1995.

12. Ibid.

13. "Civilized Servants," *IBF News* (International Bicycle Fund, Seattle), No. 2, 1995.

14. Jan Larson, "Rush Hour in Biker Heaven," *American Demographics*, March 1995.

15. "Vamos en Bici," *Medio Ambiente*, April-May 1995.

16. Dennis Martin, National Association of Chiefs of Police, Miami, Fla., private communication, July 12, 1994.

17. Marty Ratchford, U.S. Secret Service, Washington, D.C., private communication, January 29, 1996.

18. William Grisley, "I Have Seen the Future and the Future is...Bicycles," *Ceres*, July/August 1995.

19. Urs Heierli, *Environmental Limits to Motorisation* (St. Gallen, Switzerland: Swiss Centre for Development Cooperation in Technology and Management, 1993).

20. Walter Hook, "ITDP Thinks Globally, Acts Globally," *Sustainable Transport*, Fall 1995.

21. Federal Highway Administration, *The National Bicycling and Walking Study: Transportation Choices for a Changing America* (Washington, D.C.: U.S. Department of Transportation, 1994).

AUTO PRODUCTION RISES AGAIN (pages 84–85)

1. Production in 1950–93 from American Automobile Manufacturers Association (AAMA), *World Motor Vehicle Data*, 1995 ed. (Detroit, Mich.: 1995); 1994 production from AAMA, *AAMA Motor Vehicle Facts & Figures '95* (Detroit, Mich.: 1995); 1995 production from DRI/McGraw-Hill, "DRI World Car Industry Forecast Report," London, November 1995.

2. AAMA, *World Motor Vehicle Data*, op. cit. note 1; AAMA, *Facts & Figures '95*, op. cit. note 1; DRI/McGraw-Hill, op. cit. note 1.

3. AAMA, *World Motor Vehicle Data*, op. cit. note 1; AAMA, *Facts & Figures '95*, op. cit. note 1; DRI/McGraw-Hill, op. cit. note 1; Worldwatch estimates based on ibid. and on AAMA, *World Motor Vehicle Data*, op. cit. note 1; population data from U.S. Bureau of the Census, Center for International Research, Suitland, Md., private communication, January 23, 1996.

4. DRI/McGraw-Hill, op. cit. note 1; earlier industry forecasts and 1993 sales from "World Car Sales Record in Sight," *Financial Times*, December 5, 1994.

5. DRI/McGraw-Hill, op. cit. note 1.

6. John Griffiths, "Vehicle Makers See 3% Growth," *Financial Times*, January 12, 1996; "The Mergers That Never Came," *The Economist*, September 2, 1995.

7. Haig Simonian, "European Car Sales Tumble," *Financial Times*, October 16, 1995; John Griffiths, "World Car Sales To Rise 1% In 1995, Says Report," *Financial Times*, September 11, 1995.

8. DRI/McGraw-Hill, op. cit. note 1.

9. Ibid.

10. "Revving Up Exports," *Asiaweek*, June 9, 1995.

11. DRI/McGraw-Hill, op. cit. note 1; Angus Foster, "Top Carmakers Converge on Brazil," *Financial Times*, August 11, 1995.

12. DRI/McGraw-Hill, op. cit. note 1; Kevin Done, "Boom in Polish Sales Draws Western

Carmakers," *Financial Times*, April 28, 1995.
13. Gene Linn, "Asia's Huge Potential Beckons U.S. Makers," *Auto Trade & Transportation, Journal of Commerce Special Report*, August 17, 1995.
14. Kieran Cooke, "Asian Growth Fuels Car Sales Boom," *Financial Times*, August 19, 1995.
15. "GM's Plant Site to Be Thailand or the Philippines," *Wall Street Journal*, December 6, 1995; "Ford Opens the Throttle," *Business Week*, September 18, 1995; "Revving Up Exports," op. cit. note 10.
16. AAMA, *World Motor Vehicle Data*, op. cit. note 1; "China's Car Industry: Ich Bin Ein Beijinger," *The Economist*, July 15, 1995.
17. Seth Faison, "China's 'Family Car' Dream Fades," *International Herald Tribune*, July 21, 1995; "Ford Joins the Crowd in China," *Business Week*, September 4, 1995.
18. John Ward Anderson, "Foreign Car Makers Make Drive for India's Middle Class," *Washington Post*, September 17, 1994.
19. DRI/McGraw-Hill, op. cit. note 1; DRI/McGraw-Hill, "Vehicle Markets of the Indian Subcontinent," London, 1995.
20. Cooke, op. cit. note 14.
21. William K. Stevens, "With Energy Tug of War, U.S. Is Missing Its Goals," *New York Times*, November 28, 1995.

POPULATION INCREASE SLIGHTLY DOWN (pages 88–89)

1. U.S. Bureau of the Census, Center for International Research, Suitland, Md., private communication, January 23, 1996.
2. Ibid.; Population Reference Bureau (PRB), *1995 World Population Data Sheet* (Washington, D.C.: 1995).
3. Bureau of the Census, op. cit. note 1.
4. Ibid.
5. Ibid.; United Nations, *World Population Prospects: The 1994 Revision* (New York: 1995).
6. Bureau of the Census, op. cit. note 1; United Nations, op. cit. note 5.
7. United Nations, op. cit. note 5.
8. Toni Nelson, "Russia's Population Sink," *World Watch*, January/February 1996; Michael Specter, "Plunging Life Expectancy Puzzles Russia," *New York Times*, August 2, 1995.
9. Bureau of the Census, op. cit. note 1; Nelson, op. cit. note 8.
10. Nelson, op. cit. note 8.

11. Ibid.
12. Bureau of the Census, op. cit. note 1.
13. Ibid.; United Nations, op. cit. note 5.
14. Bureau of the Census, op. cit. note 1.
15. PRB, *1993 World Population Data Sheet* (Washington, D.C.: 1993); PRB, op. cit. note 2.
16. Jack Freeman, "International Working Groups Report on Specific Actions to Follow up on Agreements," *Earth Times*, May 31–June 14, 1995; C. Alison McIntosh and Jason L. Finkle, "The Cairo Conference on Population and Development: A New Paradigm?" *Population and Development Review*, June 1995; "The New Challenge: Translating Cairo Success into Meaningful Activities," *UN CHRONICLE*, June 1995.
17. George Moffett, "Next Steps After Beijing Laid out by the Numbers," *Christian Science Monitor*, September 6, 1995; Fiona Katauskas, "Women in Development, Women and Development," *SEEDlinks*, August 1995; Luke T. Lee, "Population: The Human Rights Approach," *Colorado Journal of International Environmental Law and Policy*, Vol. 6, No. 2, 1995.

CIGARETTE PRODUCTION HITS NEW HIGH (pages 90–91)

1. U.S. Department of Agriculture (USDA), "World Cigarette Production By Country" (computer printout), Washington, D.C., December 8, 1995.
2. Ibid.; population figures from U.S. Bureau of the Census, Center for International Research, Suitland, Md., private communication, January 23, 1996.
3. USDA, op. cit. note 1; Census Bureau, op. cit. note 2.
4. USDA, op. cit. note 1.
5. Ibid.
6. Ibid.
7. "US, Russian Firms Form Cigarette Venture," *Journal of Commerce*, August 4, 1993.
8. USDA, op. cit. note 1.
9. Ibid.
10. Ibid.
11. Ibid.
12. Ibid.
13. Taxes totalled $3.57 (in Canadian dollars) before the rollback and $1.29 after it; today the tax in Ontario, the most populous province, is $1.36; David Sweanor, Non-Smokers' Rights Association of Canada, Ottawa, private commu-

nication, December 19, 1995.

14. Hiroshi Nakajima, Director-General, World Health Organization, excerpts from an address as printed in *Tobacco Alert* (World Health Organization), July 1995.

15. Ibid.

16. David Brown, "Smoking Boosts Risks for Young Adults, Study Says," *Washington Post*, August 19, 1995.

17. Nakajima, op. cit. note 14.

18. "Wellness Facts," *University of California at Berkeley Wellness Letter*, October 1995.

19. "Smoking in Japan: Anything You Can Do, I Can Do Better," *The Economist*, November 4, 1995.

20. Ibid.

21. Ibid.

22. Ibid.

HIV/AIDS PANDEMIC SPREADING FASTER (pages 92–93)

1. Jonathan Mann and Daniel Tarantola, eds., *AIDS In the World*, Vol. II (New York: Oxford University Press, in press); Daniel Tarantola, Global AIDS Policy Coalition (GAPC), Harvard School of Public Health, Cambridge, Mass., private communication, January 18, 1996; World Health Organization (WHO), "The Current Global Situation of the HIV/AIDS Pandemic," *Weekly Epidemiological Record*, December 15, 1995. All HIV/AIDS data are actually projected estimates, since there is such extreme underreporting of the disease. The text and figures use estimates from GAPC, founded by Jonathan Mann, former head of WHO's Global Programme on AIDS. WHO does not release historical data series, and GAPC is less constrained by official data-reporting channels of national governments that may still be somewhat unwilling to admit how bad the epidemic has gotten in their countries.

2. Mann and Tarantola, op. cit. note 1; Tarantola, op. cit. note 1.

3. Mann and Tarantola, op. cit. note 1; Tarantola, op. cit. note 1.

4. Mann and Tarantola, op. cit. note 1; Tarantola, op. cit. note 1.

5. Mann and Tarantola, op. cit. note 1; Tarantola, op. cit. note 1.

6. Mann and Tarantola, op. cit. note 1; Tarantola, op. cit. note 1.

7. Mann and Tarantola, op. cit. note 1; Tarantola, op. cit. note 1.

8. Mann and Tarantola, op. cit. note 1; United Nations, *World Population Prospects: The 1994 Revision* (New York: 1995).

9. Peter O. Way and Karen A. Stanecki, *The Impact of HIV/AIDS on World Population* (Washington, D.C.: Economics and Statistics Administration, U.S. Bureau of the Census, 1994); Karen A. Stanecki and Peter O. Way, "Review of HIV Spread in Southern Africa," Center for International Research (CIR), U.S. Bureau of the Census, Washington, D.C., 1994; Health Studies Branch, CIR, "Trends and Patterns of HIV/AIDS Infection in Selected Developing Countries," Research Note No. 14, U.S. Bureau of the Census, Washington, D.C., 1994.

10. Mann and Tarantola, op. cit. note 1; Tarantola, op. cit. note 1.

11. Jonathan M. Mann and Daniel J.M. Tarantola, "Preventive Medicine: A Broader Approach to the AIDS Crisis," *Harvard International Review*, Fall 1995.

12. Ibid.

13. Gordon Fairclough, "AIDS: A Gathering Storm," *Far Eastern Economic Review*, September 21, 1995; "AIDS: Counting the Cost," *The Economist*, September 23, 1995; "Growing Awareness: Thais Confront AIDS—and Their Own Prejudices," *Asiaweek*, April 7, 1995.

14. Mann and Tarantola, op. cit. note 11.

15. Ibid.; Emilia Casella, "Africa is Priority for New UN AIDS Chief," *WorldAIDS*, Panos Institute, March 1995; Barbara Crossette, "U.N. Fields Odd Allies As It Wages AIDS Battle," *New York Times*, December 3, 1995.

16. "Kenya, NGOs and World Bank to Battle AIDS at Community Level," *World Bank News*, March 16, 1995.

17. Mann and Tarantola, op. cit. note 11; Jonathan M. Mann, "The Global AIDS Strategy: Public Health, Human Rights and Development," *DEVELOPMENT: The Journal of the Society for International Development*, No. 2, 1995.

18. Mann and Tarantola, op. cit. note 11; "Final Report," Workshop on the Status and Trends of HIV/AIDS Epidemics in Africa, Co-sponsored by the AIDS Control and Prevention (AIDSCAP) Project of Family Health International and the Francois-Xavier Bagnoud Center for Health and Human Rights of the Harvard School of Public Health, December 8-9, 1995, Kampala, Uganda.

19. Mann and Tarantola, op. cit. note 11.

RAPID URBANIZATION CONTINUES (pages 94–95)

1. United Nations, *World Urbanization Prospects: The 1994 Revision* (New York: 1995).
2. Ibid.
3. Ibid.
4. Ibid.
5. Andrew Lees, *Cities Perceived: Urban Society in European and American Thought: 1820–1940* (New York: Columbia University Press, 1985), cited in Lester R. Brown and Jodi L. Jacobson, *The Future of Urbanization: Facing the Ecological and Economic Constraints*, Worldwatch Paper 77 (Washington, D.C.: Worldwatch Institute, May 1987).
6. United Nations, op. cit. note 1.
7. Ibid.
8. Ibid.
9. Jane Jacobs, *The Economy of Cities* (New York: Vintage Books, 1969).
10. U.S. Department of Commerce, Bureau of the Census, *Historical Statistics of the United States: Colonial Times to 1970* (Washington, D.C.: U.S. Government Printing Office, 1975); U.S. Department of Commerce, Bureau of the Census, *Statistical Abstract of the United States 1994* (Washington, D.C.: 1994).
11. Census Bureau, *Historical Statistics*, op. cit. note 10; Census Bureau, *Statistical Abstract*, op. cit. note 10.
12. Nicholas D. Kristoff, "Tokyo's Lights Lure the Young To Forsake Rural Way of Life," *New York Times*, January 2, 1996.
13. Ibid.
14. Murray Hiebert, "Parading for Work: Vietnam's Farmers Seek Better Fortunes in the Cities," *Far Eastern Economic Review*, May 27, 1993; Laurence J.C. Ma and Chusheng Lin, "Development of Towns in China: A Case Study of Guangdong Province," *Population and Development Review*, September 1993.
15. Ma and Lin, op. cit. note 14.
16. Brown and Jacobson, op. cit. note 5.
17. Marcia D. Lowe, *Shaping Cities: The Environmental and Human Dimensions*, Worldwatch Paper 105 (Washington, D.C.: Worldwatch Institute, October 1991).
18. Ibid.

REFUGEES ON THE RISE AGAIN (pages 96–97)

1. U.N. High Commissioner for Refugees (UNHCR), "UNHCR at a Glance," data sheet, November 1995.
2. Historical data from UNHCR, *The State of the World's Refugees 1995* (New York: Oxford University Press, 1995).
3. Ibid.; UNHCR, "Populations of Concern to UNHCR: A Statistical Overview, 1994," Geneva, 1994.
4. The Brookings Institution and the Refugee Policy Group, "Improving Institutional Arrangements for the Internally Displaced," Washington, D.C., October 1995.
5. UNHCR, op. cit. note 1.
6. Ibid.
7. Ibid.
8. Ibid.
9. Hal Kane, *The Hour of Departure: Forces That Create Refugees and Migrants*, Worldwatch Paper 125 (Washington, D.C.: Worldwatch Institute, June 1995).
10. U.S. Committee for Refugees, *World Refugee Survey 1995* (Washington, D.C.: 1995).
11. Ibid.; Brookings Institution and Refugee Policy Group, op. cit. note 4.
12. UNHCR, op. cit. note 1.
13. Ibid.
14. Ibid.
15. Ibid.
16. Ibid.
17. Ibid.
18. Ibid.
19. Ibid.
20. Ibid.

NUCLEAR ARSENALS CONTINUE TO DECLINE (pages 100–01)

1. These numbers include both deployed warheads and those that are in reserve or awaiting dismantlement. Robert S. Norris, Natural Resources Defense Council, Washington, D.C., private communication, January 17, 1996.
2. Peter Gray, "Briefing Book on the Nonproliferation of Nuclear Weapons," Council for a Livable World Education Fund, Washington, D.C., December 1993.
3. Institute for Defense and Disarmament Studies (IDDS), *The Arms Control Reporter 1995*

(Cambridge, Mass.: 1995), section 602.B; 1995 Conference of Parties to Treaty on Non-Proliferation of Nuclear Weapons, "Conference Extends Indefinitely Treaty on Non-Proliferation of Nuclear Weapons," press release, May 11, 1995.

4. Norris, op. cit. note 1.

5. Ibid.

6. Ibid.

7. The White House, Office of the Press Secretary, "Statement by the Press Secretary," press release, October 20, 1995; Steven Erlanger, "After 3-Year Wait, Start II Wins Senate Approval But Now Faces Russian Opposition," *New York Times*, January 27, 1996.

8. Robert S. Norris and William M. Arkin, "U.S. Strategic Nuclear Forces, End of 1995," *Bulletin of the Atomic Scientists*, January/February 1996; Robert S. Norris and William M. Arkin, "Estimated Russian (C.I.S.) Stockpile, September 1995," *Bulletin of the Atomic Scientists*, September/October 1995.

9. Norris and Arkin, 1995, op. cit. note 8.

10. Greenpeace, "The Comprehensive Test Ban Treaty in Jeopardy?" July 1995, as posted in the APC electronic conference igc:ctb.clips on July 26, 1995.

11. Ibid.

12. Comprehensive Test Ban Clearinghouse, "France Says Tests Will End by March 1," December 31, 1995, as posted in the APC electronic conference igc:ctb.clips on January 10, 1996.

13. Ibid.; Stockholm International Peace Research Institute, *SIPRI Yearbook 1995* (New York: Oxford University Press, 1995).

14. Associated Press, "France Sets Off Nuclear Blast," January 27, 1996, and Associated Press, "France Ends Nuclear Tests," January 29, 1996, both as posted in the CompuServe electronic forum AP Online.

15. Comprehensive Test Ban Clearinghouse, "Full-Court Press Needed to Secure Test Ban," December 31, 1995, as posted in the APC electronic conference igc:ctb.clips on January 9, 1996; Rebecca Johnson, "Geneva Update, 1/19/96," as posted in the APC electronic conference igc:alt.activism.nuclear-test.news on January 20, 1996.

16. Tim Weiner, "U.S. Suspects India Prepares to Conduct Nuclear Test," *New York Times*, December 15, 1995; John F. Burns, "India Denies Atom-Test Plan But Then Turns Ambiguous," *New York Times*, December 16, 1995.

17. Michael Krepon, "Indian Nuclear Tests, the CTB, and Disarmament," The Henry L. Stimson Center, Washington, D.C., as posted in the APC electronic conference igc:alt.activism.nuclear-test.news on January 3, 1996.

18. *Disarmament Times*, Nobel Peace Prize Special Issue, January 1996.

19. Stephen Kinzer, "World Court Weighs Legality of Atomic War," *New York Times*, November 20, 1995; Stephen Kinzer, "Refusing to Learn to Love the Bomb: Nations Take Their Case to Court," *New York Times*, January 14, 1996; various postings in the APC electronic conference igc:disarm.worldcr.

20. IDDS, op. cit. note 3, section 455.

21. "Statement by the Prime Minister, the Hon. P.J. Keating MP; Australian Initiative for a Nuclear Weapons-Free World," as posted in the APC electronic conference igc:alt.activism.nuclear-test.news on December 5, 1995.

PEACEKEEPING EXPENDITURES LEVEL OFF (pages 102–03)

1. Luisa Anzola, U.N. Department of Peace-Keeping Operations, New York, private communications, October 23 and December 20, 1995; pre-1986 expenditures calculated from Joseph Preston Baratta, *International Peacekeeping: History and Strengthening* (Washington, D.C.: Center for U.N. Reform Education, 1989), and from U.N. Department of Public Information, *United Nations Peace-keeping* (New York: 1993).

2. U.N. Department of Public Information, "Setting the Record Straight: Some Facts About the United Nations at 50," October 1995, as posted on the APC electronic conference igc:unic.news on October 20, 1995.

3. Ibid.

4. Calculated from Anzola, op. cit. note 1.

5. Barry M. Blechman and J. Matthew Vaccaro, *Training for Peacekeeping: The United Nations' Role*, Report No. 12 (Washington, D.C.: The Henry L. Stimson Center, 1994); Pamela L. Reed, J. Matthew Vaccaro, and William J. Durch, *Handbook on United Nations Peacekeeping*, Handbook No. 3 (Washington, D.C.: The Henry L. Stimson Center, 1995); William J. Durch, Henry L. Stimson Center, Washington, D.C., private communication, January 9, 1996.

6. Blechman and Vaccaro, op. cit. note 5; Reed, Vaccaro, and Durch, op. cit.note 5; Durch, op. cit. note 5.

7. Office of the Secretary-General's Spokesman, United Nations, New York, private communication, December 23, 1995.

8. Ibid.

9. Elaine Sciolino, "Accord Reached to End the War in Bosnia; Clinton Pledges U.S. Troops to Keep Peace," *New York Times*, November 22, 1995.

10. Christopher S. Wren, "U.N. Votes to Make Haste Slowly in Retreat from the Balkans," *New York Times*, December 1, 1995; Associated Press, "UN OKs 5,000 Troops to Croatia," January 15, 1996, as posted in the CompuServe electronic forum AP Online. Although its peacekeeping presence in Bosnia has ended, the U.N. is establishing a police task force to help implement the Dayton agreement; United Nations, Security Council Resolution, New York, December 21, 1995.

11. U.N. Department of Public Information, op. cit. note 2.

12. U.N. Daily Highlights, press release, December 22, 1995.

13. Gareth Evans, *Cooperating for Peace: The Global Agenda for the 1990s and Beyond* (St. Leonards, Australia: Allen and Unwin, 1993).

14. United Nations, "Supplement to an Agenda for Peace: Position Paper of the Secretary-General on the Occasion of the Fiftieth Anniversary of the United Nations," General Assembly document A/50/60 and Security Council document S/1995/1, January 3, 1995; 1995 number of resolutions from United Nations, Security Council, "Security Council Adopts Annual Report to General Assembly," press release, November 13, 1995.

15. U.N. Daily Highlights, press release, September 14, 1995.

16. U.N. Daily Highlights, press release, January 11, 1996.

17. Ibid.

18. U.N. Daily Highlights, op. cit. note 15.

19. U.N. Daily Highlights, press releases August 26, 1994, and October 13, 1995.

20. Michael Renner, *Remaking U.N. Peacekeeping: U.S. Policy and Real Reform* (Washington, D.C.: National Commission for Economic Conversion and Disarmament, 1995).

21. Ibid.

22. United Nations, Security Council, "Security Council Ends UNAMIR Mandate on 8 March 1996, Adjusts Objectives, Responds to Wishes of Rwandan Government," press release, December 12, 1995; Associated Press, "U.N. Mulls Haiti Mandate," January 30, 1996, as posted in the CompuServe electronic forum AP Online.

23. Calculated on basis of mission-by-mission expenditures during 1995 from Anzola, op. cit. note 1, with the addition of projected costs for the new U.N. mission in Eastern Slavonia from United Nations, "Report of the Secretary-General Pursuant to Security Council Resolution 1025 (1995). Addendum," New York, January 15, 1996.

24. Phyllis Bennis, *Calling the Shots: How Washington Dominates Today's UN* (New York: Olive Branch Press, 1996); James C. McKinley Jr., "Growing Ethnic Strife in Burundi Leads to Fears of New Civil War," *New York Times*, January 14, 1996; Barbara Crossette, "U.N., Pressing for Restraint, Delays Its Action on Burundi," *New York Times*, January 30, 1996.

EFFORTS TO CONTROL PESTICIDES EXPAND (pages 108–09)

1. Pesticide Action Network (PAN), "Demise of the Dirty Dozen Chart," San Francisco, various editions; Anne Schonfield et al., "PAN's Dirty Dozen Campaign—The View at Ten Years," *Global Pesticide Campaigner* (PAN, San Francisco), September 1995. Pesticides included in the "Dirty Dozen" were selected on the basis of hazards to human or environmental health, evidence of widespread use and resulting harm, bans in exporting countries, and their value as examples of problems caused by pesticide dependence.

2. PAN, op. cit. note 1.

3. Angus Wright, *The Death of Ramon Gonzalez* (Austin: University of Texas Press, 1990).

4. David Pimentel et al., "Environmental and Economic Costs of Pesticide Use," *BioScience*, November 1992; David Pimentel, Cornell University, Ithaca, N.Y., private communication, February 16, 1996.

5. British Agrochemicals Association, *Annual Review and Handbook 1995* (Peterborough, U.K.: 1995).

6. Arnold Aspelin, "Pesticide Industry Sales and Usage: 1992 and 1993 Market Estimates," U.S. Environmental Protection Agency, Washington, D.C., June 1994.

7. Ibid.

8. Rachel Carson, *Silent Spring* (Boston: Houghton Mifflin Company, 1962).
9. World Health Organization/UNEP, *The Public Health Impact of Pesticides Used in Agriculture* (Geneva: 1990); J. Jeyaratnam, "Acute Pesticide Poisoning: A Major Problem," *World Health Statistics Quarterly*, Vol. 43, No. 3, 1990.
10. Diana Lutz, "No Conception," *The Sciences*, January/February 1996.
11. Ibid.; Sharon Begley with Daniel Glick, "The Estrogen Complex," *Newsweek*, March 21, 1994.
12. Pimentel et al., "Environmental and Economic Costs," op. cit. note 4.
13. Ibid.
14. David Pimentel, "Pest Management, Food Security, and the Environment," Cornell University, Ithaca, N.Y., March 27, 1995.
15. Pimentel et al., "Environmental and Economic Costs," op. cit. note 4.
16. Ibid.
17. Barbara Dinham, *The Pesticide Trail: The Impact of Trade Controls on Reducing Pesticide Hazards in Developing Countries* (London: The Pesticides Trust, 1995).
18. U.N. Food and Agriculture Organization (FAO)/U.N. Environment Programme (UNEP), Joint Programme for the Operation of Prior Informed Consent (PIC), "Circular V," Rome, July 31, 1995.
19. Ibid.
20. Sandra Marquardt, former Greenpeace researcher, Washington, D.C., private communication, February 1, 1996.
21. Ibid.; Dinham, op. cit. note 17.
22. Dinham, op. cit. note 17.
23. FAO, *World Agriculture: Towards 2010* (New York: John Wiley & Sons, 1995).
24. FAO/UNEP, op. cit. note 18.
25. Dinham, op. cit. note 17.
26. Greenpeace International, "Global Ban on Persistent Toxic Chemicals," Briefing paper prepared for UNEP Intergovernmental Conference on Protection of the Marine Environment from Land Based Activities, Washington, D.C., October 23-November 3, 1995.
27. Kurt Kleiner, "World Ban in Sight for Persistent Pollutants," *New Scientist*, November 11, 1995.
28. Greenpeace, op. cit. note 26; Ellen Hickey, "Persistent Organic Pollutants—Time for Action," *Global Pesticide Campaigner* (PAN, San Francisco), December 1995.
29. UNEP, "Summary: Study on International Trade in Widely Prohibited Chemicals," Geneva, 1996. The study involved almost 60 countries, representing about 75 percent of chemical trade worldwide.
30. UNEP, "Interim Report, Study on International Trade in Widely Prohibited Chemicals," Geneva, 1995. The 44 chemicals examined are subject to either the PIC procedure or Council Regulation No.2455/92, adopted by the Council of the European Communities on July 23, 1992, concerning the export and import of certain dangerous chemicals.
31. UNEP, op. cit. note 30; UNEP, op. cit. note 29.
32. Foundation for Advancements in Science and Education, "Exporting Risk: Pesticide Exports from U.S. Ports, 1992-1994," Los Angeles, Calif., Spring 1996. Researchers were only able to identify about 25 percent of the pesticides exported, suggesting that total exports of banned pesticides could be as high as 28,000 tons.
33. Carl Smith, "Countries Accept 'Dirty Dozen' Pesticides from U.S. Shippers Despite National Bans," *Global Pesticide Campaigner* (PAN, San Francisco), September 1995.

ORGANIC FARMING UP SHARPLY
(pages 110–11)

1. Ken Mergentime, "Organic Industry Comes Into Its Own," *In Business*, July/August 1995.
2. European Commission, *Organic Farming* (Luxembourg: Office for Official Publications of the European Communities, 1994).
3. Mergentime, op. cit. note 1.
4. In Germany, for example, organics were 1.5 percent of total food sales in 1993; Ulrich Hamm, "The Market for Organic Products in Germany and Marketing Strategies Today," Association Universitaire pour l'Environnement, *Le Marche des Produits de l'Agriculture Biologique dans l'Union Europeenne*, les actes du colloque, (Brussels: Association Universitaire pour l'Environnement, March 23, 1994.)
5. Mergentime, op. cit. note 1.
6. International Federation of Organic Agricultural Movements, "Basic Standards," Tholey-Theley, Germany, 1994.
7. Ken Mergentime and Monica Emerich, "Organic Sales Jump Over $2 Billion Mark in 1994," *Natural Foods Merchandiser*, June 1995.
8. Robert Steuteville and David Riggle, "Outlook on Sustainable Enterprise," *In Business*, May/June 1995.
9. "Pesticides Used on Cotton," *Pesticide News*,

June 1995.

10. Mergentime, op. cit. note 1.

11. Markets with produce from ibid.; rise in sales from "U.S. Organic Sales Top $2 Billion," *Pesticide Action Network North America Updates Service* (electronic newsletter, San Francisco), July 12, 1995.

12. "U.S. Organic Sales Top $2 Billion," op. cit. note 11.

13. David Barton Bray, "The Permanent Reconstruction of Nature: Grassroots Sustainable Development in Rural Mexico," *Journal of Environment and Development*, Summer 1995.

14. Ibid.

15. Ibid.

16. Martin Khor, "Towards Sustainable Agriculture," Third World Network Features (electronic newsletter), June 21, 1995.

17. "Fetzer Vineyards Goes Organic," press release, Fetzer Vineyards, Hopland, Calif., April 1995; "The Better Way: Big California Growers Turn to Sustainable Agriculture," *The Gene Exchange* (Union of Concerned Scientists), February 1994.

18. Hamm, op. cit. note 4. Dollar figures calculated from an average exchange rate taken from International Monetary Fund, *International Financial Statistics Yearbook 1993* (Washington, D.C.: 1993).

19. Hamm, op. cit. note 4.

20. Gert Lynge Sorensen, "Difficult to Switch to Organic Farming," *Danish Environment*, No. 3, 1995.

21. Ibid.

22. Hamm, op. cit. note 4.

23. Laurie Drinkwater, Rodale Institute, Emmaus, Pa., private communication, June 2, 1995.

24. Mayumi Morizane Saito, Japan Organic Agriculture Association, Tokyo, private communication, January 18, 1996.

25. Ibid.

26. Ibid.

27. Donald C. Slivka et al., "Compost: United States Supply and Potential Demand," *Biomass and Bioenergy*, Vol. 3, Nos. 3–4, 1992.

28. Hamm, op. cit. note 4.

29. Ken Mergentime, New Hope Communications, Boulder, Colo., private communication, December 19, 1995.

ENVIRONMENTAL TAXES SPREAD
(pages 114–15)

1. Table 1 is based on Victoria P. Summers, "Tax Treatment of Pollution Control in the European and Central Asian Economies in Transition and Other Selected Countries," in Charles E. Walker, Mark A. Bloomfield, and Margot Thorning, eds., *Strategies for Improving Environmental Quality and Increasing Economic Growth* (Washington, D.C.: Center for Policy Research, 1995), on Michel Porter, "China Charges for Pollution," *The OECD Observer*, February/March 1995, on Organisation for Economic Co-operation and Development (OECD), *Environmental Taxes in OECD Countries* (Paris: 1995), on OECD, *Managing the Environment: The Role of Economic Instruments* (Paris: 1994), on David O'Connor, "The Use of Economic Instruments in Environmental Management: The East Asian Experience," in OECD, *Applying Economic Instruments to Environmental Policies in OECD and Dynamic Non-member Economies* (Paris: 1994), on Ronald T. McMorran and David C.L. Nellor, "Tax Policy and the Environment: Theory and Practice," IMF Working Paper, International Monetary Fund, Washington, D.C., 1994, on "European Commission Approves Dutch Environmental Tax Rules," *International Environment Reporter*, June 14, 1995, and on "Commission Approves Danish Legislation Containing Most Ambitious Green Tax in EU," *International Environment Reporter*, July 26, 1995.

2. Summers, op. cit. note 1; Porter, op. cit. note 1.

3. Summers, op. cit. note 1; Porter, op. cit. note 1.

4. Summers, op. cit. note 1; Porter, op. cit. note 1.

5. Summers, op. cit. note 1; Porter, op. cit. note 1.

6. Earth Summit Watch, "Four in '94. Two Years After Rio: Assessing National Actions to Implement Agenda 21," Natural Resources Defense Council and Campaign for Action to Protect the Earth, New York, December 1994.

7. Ibid.

8. Ibid.

9. O'Connor, op. cit. note 1.

10. OECD, *Environmental Taxes in OECD Countries*, op. cit. note 1.

11. Ibid.

12. John Moffet and François Bregham, "The User Pay Waste Management Initiative for Recycling Household Waste," in Robert J.P. Gale and Stephan R. Barg, eds., *Green Budget Reform: An International Casebook of Leading Practices*

(London: Earthscan Publications, 1995).

13. OECD, *Environmental Taxes in OECD Countries*, op. cit. note 1. The U.S. tax was instituted primarily to absorb windfall profits created by new regulations that restricted the supply of CFCs; it appears to have been set high enough, however, to actually accelerate the phaseout of CFCs. See J. Andrew Hoerner, "Tax Tools for Climate Protection: The U.S. Ozone-depleting Chemicals Tax," in Gale and Barg, op. cit. note 12.

14. U.S. Office of Management and Budget, *Budget of the United States Government, Fiscal Year 1997* (Washington, D.C.: U.S. Government Printing Office, 1996).

15. Kees Baas, Central Bureau of Statistics, The Hague, Netherlands, private communication and printout, September 19, 1995.

16. Jan Paul van Soest, Centre for Energy Conservation and Environmental Technology, Delft, Netherlands, private communication, October 11, 1995.

17. Figure of $170 billion is a Worldwatch estimate, using market exchange rates and based on OECD, *Environmental Taxes in OECD Countries*, op. cit. note 1.

18. OECD, *Energy Prices and Taxes* (Paris: various editions).

19. Ibid.

20. Ibid.; United Nations, *Energy Statistics Yearbook* (New York: 1995).

21. United Nations, op. cit. note 20.

22. Worldwatch estimate, based on Ministry of the Environment and Natural Resources, "The Swedish Experience: Taxes and Charges in Environmental Policy," Stockholm, 1994, and on OECD, *Revenue Statistics of OECD Countries 1965–1994* (Paris: 1995).

23. Anders Nørskou, Ministry of Finance, Copenhagen, private communications, September 29 and October 3, 1995.

24. Worldwatch estimate, based on Koos van der Vaart, Ministry of Finance, The Hague, Netherlands, private communication, December 18, 1995, and on OECD, op. cit. note 22.

25. Martina Schuster, Federal Ministry of the Environment, Vienna, private communication, October 2, 1995; Odd Froean, Ministry of the Environment, Oslo, Norway, private communication, October 12, 1995; "Economics Minister Says He Supports National CO_2 Tax If Wider Accord Fails," *International Environment Reporter*, June 14, 1995.

PRIVATE FINANCE FLOWS TO THIRD WORLD (pages 116–17)

1. World Bank, *World Debt Tables 1996* (Washington, D.C.: 1996).

2. Ibid.

3. Ibid.

4. Ibid.

5. Ibid.

6. Ibid.

7. Ibid.

8. World Bank, *World Debt Tables 1994–1995* (Washington, D.C.: 1994).

9. Ibid.

10. Ibid.

11. Robin Broad and John Cavanagh, "Don't Neglect the Impoverished South," *Foreign Policy*, Winter 1995–1996.

12. Liz Barratt-Brown, Lando Velasco, and Scott Hajost, "Financial Reform and the Climate Convention," *Eco*, September 2, 1994.

13. Jessica Hamburger, *China's Energy and Environment in the Roaring Nineties: A Policy Primer* (Washington, D.C.: Pacific Northwest Laboratory, 1995).

14. Nigel Sizer and Richard Rice, *Backs to the Wall in Suriname: Forest Policy in a Country in Crisis* (Washington, D.C.: World Resources Institute, 1995).

15. Neelam Mathews and Lyn Harrison, "Soaring Sales to Private Sector," *Windpower Monthly*, September 1994.

16. Nigel Sizer, "Suriname's Fire Sale," *New York Times*, May 14, 1995; Russell Mittermeier, "What Costa Rica Can Teach Suriname," *Wall Street Journal*, September 1, 1995.

17. Hilary F. French, "Rebuilding the World Bank," in Lester R. Brown et al., *State of the World 1994* (New York: W.W. Norton & Company, 1994).

18. See, for instance, Andrea Durbin, Friends of the Earth–U.S., "Discussion Paper on the World Bank Group's Role in Private Sector Lending," October 19, 1995, as posted on Econet at brettonwds.coc.

19. Stephan Schmidheiny and Federico Zorraquín, *Financing Change: The Financial Community, Eco-Efficiency, and Sustainable Development* (Cambridge, Mass.: The MIT Press, 1996).

20. "New $100 Million Fund Created to Promote Environmental Investments," *International Environment Reporter*, October 10, 1990; Anne Goodwin, "Ex-Im Bank Board of Directors Approves Environmental Review Procedures, Guidelines," *International Environment Reporter*,

January 11, 1995.
21. Robert Bryce, "Aid Canceled for Gold Project in Indonesia," *New York Times*, November 2, 1995.
22. "International Backers of Indonesian Mine Should Review Support, NGO Officials Say," *International Environment Reporter*, November 29, 1995.
23. United Nations Centre on Transnational Corporations, *Criteria for Sustainable Development Management* (New York: United Nations, 1991).
24. Harris Gleckman, "Transnational Corporations' Strategic Responses to 'Sustainable Development'," in Helge Ole Bergesen and Georg Parmann, eds., *Green Globe Yearbook* (Oxford: Oxford University Press, 1995).
25. Ibid.
26. Governments of Canada, Mexico, and the United States of America, "The North American Free Trade Agreement," September 6, 1992.
27. Governments of Canada, Mexico, and the United States of America, "North American Agreement on Environmental Cooperation," September 8–14, 1993.
28. Guy de Jonquieres, "Brittan Attempts to Map Out WTO's Agenda," *Financial Times*, October 24, 1995.

INSURANCE INDUSTRY REELS
(pages 118–19)

1. Intergovernmental Panel on Climate Change (IPCC), *The IPCC Assessment of Knowledge Relevant to the Interpretation of Article 2 of the UN Framework Convention on Climate Change: A Synthesis Report* (draft), Geneva, July 31, 1995.
2. Gerhard A. Berz, Munich Reinsurance Company, Munich, Germany, private communication, September 1, 1995.
3. Franklin W. Nutter, Reinsurance Association of America, testimony before Subcommittee on Clean Air and Nuclear Regulation, Committee on Environment and Public Works, U.S. Senate, Washington, D.C., April 14, 1994.
4. G.A. Berz, "Greenhouse Effects on Natural Catastrophes and Insurance," The Geneva Papers on Risk Insurance, July 17, 1992.
5. Thomas R. Karl et al., "Trends in U.S. Climate During the Twentieth Century," *Consequences*, Spring 1995.
6. Doug Cogan, "Bracing for Bigger Storms: Hurricane Andrew May Be a Harbinger of

Trouble for the Insurance Industry if the Globe Warms," *Investor's Environmental Report*, Vol. 3, No. 1, 1993.
7. Friedman cited in ibid.
8. Greenpeace International, *The Climate Time Bomb: Signs of Climate Change from the Greenpeace Database* (Amsterdam: 1994), supplemented by "Update," March 1995.
9. Ibid.
10. Ibid.
11. "Going to Extremes," *Newsweek*, January 22, 1996.
12. Greg Steinmetz, "Andrew's Toll: As Insurance Costs Soar, Higher Rates Loom," *Wall Street Journal*, January 6, 1993.
13. Ibid.
14. Ibid.
15. E.N. Rappaport and R.B. Sheets, "A Meteorological Analysis of Hurricane Andrew," *Lessons of Hurricane Andrew*, Special Publication of the Annual National Hurricane Conference, April 13-16, 1995.
16. Dork L. Sahagian, Frank W. Schwartz, and David K. Jacobs, "Direct Anthropogenic Contributions to Sea Level Rise in the Twentieth Century," *Nature*, January 6, 1994.
17. IPCC, op. cit. note 1.
18. Ibid.
19. H.R. Kaufmann, "Storm Damage Insurance—Quo Vadis?" paper produced by Swiss Re, November 1990.
20. Quoted in Cogan, op. cit. note 6.
21. Berlin insurance meeting description from author's observations, Berlin, March 26, 1995.

FOREST LOSS CONTINUES (pages 122–23)

1. U.N. Food and Agriculture Organization (FAO), *Forest Resources Assessment 1990: Global Synthesis*, Forestry Paper 124 (Rome: 1995). Net forest area is "forests and other wooded lands," which takes into account natural forest loss as well as growth in industrial plantations.
2. Norman Myers, "The World's Forests: Need For a Policy Appraisal," *Science*, May 12, 1995.
3. FAO, op. cit. note 1.
4. Ibid.
5. Myers, op. cit. note 2.
6. FAO, op. cit. note 1.
7. Ibid.
8. Ibid.

9. World Resources Institute (WRI), *World Resources 1994–95* (New York: Oxford University Press, 1994).

10. FAO, *Forest Resources Assessment 1990: Tropical Countries*, Forestry Paper 112 (Rome: 1993).

11. WRI, op. cit. note 9.

12. Nigel Dudley, *Forests in Trouble: A Review of the Status of Temperate Forests Worldwide* (Gland, Switzerland: World Wide Fund for Nature, 1992).

13. Ibid.

14. WRI, op. cit. note 9.

15. Valhalla Society, "Deforestation in Canada," in Canada's Future Forest Alliance, *Brazil of the North* (New Denver, B.C., Canada: 1993); Myers, op. cit. note 2; Anatoly Shvidenko and Sten Nilsson, "What Do We Know About the Siberian Forests?" *Ambio*, November 1994.

16. Nigel Dudley, *Bad Harvest? The Timber Trade and Degradation of the World's Forests*, cited in Scott Sonner, "Group Blames Timber Trade for Deforestation," *Journal of Commerce*, December 29, 1995.

17. "Forest Damage Increases in Europe," *Arborvitae*, September 1995.

18. Ibid.

19. FAO, op. cit. note 1.

20. Dudley, op. cit. note 12.

21. FAO, op. cit. note 1.

22. A. Scott Denning, Inez Y. Fung, and David Randall, "Latitudinal Gradient of Atmospheric CO_2 Exchange with Land Biota," *Nature*, July 20, 1995; P. Ciais et al., "A Large Northern Hemisphere Terrestrial CO_2 Sink Indicated by the 13C/12C Ratio of Atmospheric CO_2," *Science*, August 25, 1995.

23. Denning, Fung, and Randall, op. cit. note 22; Ciais et al., op. cit. note 22.

24. George M. Woodwell and Fred T. Mackenzie, eds., *Biotic Feedbacks in the Global Climatic System* (New York: Oxford University Press, 1995).

25. Narendra Sharma, ed., *Managing the World's Forests: Looking for Balance Between Conservation and Development* (Dubuque, Iowa: Kendall/Hunt Publishing Company, 1992).

26. Ibid.

AQUATIC SPECIES DISAPPEARING (pages 124–25)

1. Alan P. Covich, "Water and Ecosystems," in Peter H. Gleick, ed., *Water in Crisis: A Guide to the World's Fresh Water Resources* (New York: Oxford University Press, 1993).

2. Extinction estimates from Peter B. Moyle and Robert A. Leidy, "Loss of Biodiversity in Aquatic Ecosystems: Evidence from Fish Faunas," in P.L. Fiedler and S.K. Jain, eds., *Conservation Biology: The Theory and Practice of Nature Conservation, Preservation, and Management* (New York: Chapman and Hall, 1992).

3. Table 1 is based on Moyle and Leidy, op. cit. note 2, except Amazon River from Michael Goulding, "Flooded Forests of the Amazon," *Scientific American*, March 1993, Asia from Brian Groombridge, ed., *Global Biodiversity: Status of the Earth's Living Resources* (New York: Chapman and Hall, 1992), North America extinct and imperilled from The Nature Conservancy, *Priorities for Conservation: 1996 Annual Report Card for U.S. Plant and Animal Species* (Arlington, Va.: 1996), Mexico from Salvador Contreras-B. and M. Lourdes Lozano-V., "Water, Endangered Fishes, and Development Perspectives in Arid Lands of Mexico," *Conservation Biology*, June 1994, and Lake Victoria from Les Kaufman, "Catastrophic Changes in Species-Rich Freshwater Ecosystems: The Lessons of Lake Victoria," *BioScience*, December 1992, and from Rosemary Lowe-McConnell, "Fish Faunas of the African Great Lakes: Origins, Diversity and Vulnerability," *Conservation Biology*, September 1993.

4. The Nature Conservancy, op. cit. note 3.

5. Moyle and Leidy, op. cit. note 2.

6. Ibid.

7. Robert R. Miller, James D. Williams, and Jack E. Williams, "Extinctions of North American Fishes During the Past Century," *Fisheries*, November/December 1989.

8. Jack E. Williams et al., "Fishes of North America Endangered, Threatened or of Special Concern: 1989," *Fisheries*, November/December 1989.

9. Mats Dynesius and Christer Nilsson, "Fragmentation and Flow Regulation of River Systems in the Northern Third of the World," *Science*, November 4, 1994.

10. Arthur E. Bogan, "Freshwater Bivalve Extinctions (Mollusca: Unionidae): A Search for Causes," *American Zoology*, Vol. 33, 1993, pp. 599–609.

11. Ibid.

12. Larry Master, "Aquatic Animals: Endangerment Alert," *Nature Conservancy*, March/April 1991.

13. The Nature Conservancy, op. cit. note 3.
14. James D. Williams et al., "Conservation Status of Freshwater Mussels of the United Sates and Canada," *Fisheries*, September 1993.
15. Paul W. Parmalee and Mark H. Hughes, "Freshwater Mussels (Mollusca: Pelecypoda: Unionidae) of Tellico Lake: Twelve Years After Impoundment of the Little Tennessee River," *Annals of the Carnegie Museum*, February 25, 1993.
16. Melanie Stiassney, "An Overview of Freshwater Biodiversity: With Some Lessons from African Fishes," *Fisheries*, in press.
17. Goulding, op. cit. note 3.
18. Stuart L. Pimm et al., "The Future of Biodiversity," *Science*, July 21, 1995.
19. Ibid.
20. Jonathan Coddington, speech at The Living Planet in Crisis: Biodiversity Science and Policy Conference, American Museum of Natural History, New York, March 9–10, 1995.
21. Robert J. Naiman et al., eds., *The Freshwater Imperative: A Research Agenda* (Washington, D.C.: Island Press, 1995).
22. Miller, Williams, and Williams, op. cit. note 7.
23. Dynesius and Nilsson, op. cit. note 9.
24. U.S. Department of Commerce, Bureau of the Census, *Statistical Abstract of the United States, 1990* (Washington, D.C.: U.S. Government Printing Office, 1990), as cited in National Research Council, *Restoration of Aquatic Ecosystems: Science, Technology, and Public Policy* (Washington, D.C.: National Academy Press, 1992); T.E. Dahl, *Wetland Losses in the United States 1780's to 1980's* (Washington, D.C.: Fish and Wildlife Service, U.S. Department of the Interior, 1990).
25. Dahl, op. cit. note 24.

ENVIRONMENTAL TREATIES STRENGTHENED (pages 126–27)

1. Table 1 is based on United Nations Environment Programme, *Register of International Treaties and Other Agreements in the Field of the Environment 1993* (Nairobi: 1993); U.S. International Trade Commission, *International Agreements to Protect the Environment and Wildlife* (Washington, D.C.: 1991); "More than 100 Countries Agree on International Desertification Treaty," *International Environment Reporter*, June 29, 1995; Wilma Wilson, Office of Treaty Affairs, U.S.

Department of State, Washington, D.C., private communication, March 20, 1996; U.N. Department of Public Information, "UN Conference on High Seas Fishing Adopts Legal Agreement," press release, New York, August 4, 1995; "Multilateral Treaties Deposited with the Secretary General of the United Nations, Status as of February 1, 1996," U.N. Treaty Office, New York, February 1, 1996; Patricia Anholdt-Hubber, U.N. Treaty office, New York, private communication, February 23, 1996.
2. U.N. Department of Public Information, op. cit. note 1.
3. Ibid.
4. U.N. Food and Agriculture Organization, *The State of World Fisheries and Aquaculture* (Rome: 1995).
5. Clyde H. Farnsworth, "Canada and Spain Face Off Over Fish Rights," *New York Times*, March 12, 1995.
6. "Summary of the Fifth Substantive Session of the U.N. Conference on Straddling Fish Stocks and Highly Migratory Fish Stocks, 24 July–4 August 1995," *Earth Negotiations Bulletin*, International Institute for Sustainable Development, August 7, 1995.
7. U.N. Department of Public Information, op. cit. note 1.
8. "Countries Adopt Program of Action to Curb Marine Pollution from Land," *International Environment Reporter*, November 15, 1995.
9. Ibid.
10. "Concrete Action on Protocol Deferred; Two-Year Negotiation Process Launched," *International Environment Reporter*, April 19, 1995.
11. Ibid.
12. "Parties to Montreal Protocol Agree to Phase Out Methyl Bromide by 2010," *International Environment Reporter*, December 13, 1995.
13. Ibid.
14. Ibid.
15. "COP-2 Agrees on Biosafety Protocol, Initiative on Marine, Coastal Biodiversity," *International Environment Reporter*, November 29, 1995.
16. Ibid.
17. Ibid.
18. "Ban on Waste Exports Outside OECD Pushed Through Basel Treaty Meeting," *International Environment Reporter*, October 4, 1995.
19. Ibid.
20. Ibid.

INFECTIOUS DISEASES RETURN
(pages 130–31)

1. Report of the Director-General, *The World Health Report 1995: Bridging the Gaps* (Geneva: World Health Organization (WHO), 1995).
2. Ibid.
3. Ibid.
4. Ibid.
5. Ibid.
6. Ibid.
7. Paul John Dolin, Mario C. Raviglione, and Arata Kochi, *A Review of Current Epidemiological Data and Estimation of Future Tuberculosis Incidence and Mortality* (Geneva: WHO, 1993).
8. Chrystia Freeland, "Diphtheria Fear in Former USSR," *Financial Times*, June 20, 1995.
9. "Expanded Programme on Immunization: Diphtheria Epidemic in the Newly Independent States of the former USSR, 1990–1994," *Weekly Epidemiological Record*, May 19, 1995.
10. "Cholera in 1993, Part I," *Weekly Epidemiological Record*, July 15, 1994; James Brooke, "Cholera Kills 1,100 in Peru and Marches On Reaching the Brazilian Border," *New York Times*, April 19, 1991.
11. Report of the Director-General, op. cit. note 1.
12. D.J. Gubler and D.W. Trent, "Emergence of Epidemic Dengue/Dengue Hemorrhagic Fever as a Public Health Problem in the Americas," *Infectious Agents and Disease*, Vol. 2, 1994.
13. Duane J. Gubler, *Virus Information Exchange Newsletter*, No. 8, 1991, reprinted in Thomas P. Monath, "The Challenge: Biotechnology Transfer to Public Health. Examples from Arbovirology," in David H. Walker, ed., *Global Infectious Diseases: Prevention, Control, and Eradication* (New York: Springer-Verlag, 1992).
14. Ibid.
15. Report of the Director-General, op. cit. note 1.
16. Ibid.
17. Nancy Chege, "Access to Safe Water Expands," in Lester R. Brown, Nicholas Lenssen, and Hal Kane, *Vital Signs 1995* (New York: W.W. Norton & Company, 1995); "Water Related Illnesses," *WIT's World Ecology Report*, Fall 1994.
18. Manmade malaria from N.L. Karla, *Status Report on Malaria and Other Health-Related Aspects of the Sardar Sarovar Projects, and Recommendations Regarding Short-Term and Long-Term Remedial Measures*, January 1992, as cited in Bradford F. Morse and Thomas R. Berger, *Sardar Sarovar: The Report of the Independent Review* (Ottawa: Resource Futures International

Inc., 1992).
19. David Brown, "'Wonder Drugs' Losing Healing Aura," *Washington Post*, June 26, 1995.
20. Sharon Kingman, "Resistance a European Problem, Too," *Science*, April 15, 1994.
21. Ibid.
22. "World Malaria Situation in 1992: Middle South Asia, Eastern Asia and Oceania," *Weekly Epidemiological Record*, November 4, 1994; "World Malaria Situation in 1992, Part I: Africa and the Americas," *Weekly Epidemiological Record*, October 21, 1994.
23. Laurie Garrett, *The Coming Plague: Newly Emerging Diseases in a World Out of Balance* (New York: Farrar, Straus, and Giroux, 1994).
24. Figure of 80 percent from Frances Williams, "End to Polio by 2000," *Financial Times*, April 7, 1995; "Polio Eradication: The Finishing Line in Sight," *CVI (Children's Vaccine Initiative) Forum* (Global Programme for Vaccines, WHO), No. 9, June 1995.
25. John Schwartz, "Worm Disease Nearing Extinction," *Washington Post*, December 5, 1995.
26. Report of the Director-General, op. cit. note 1.
27. Ruth L. Berkelman et al., "Infectious Disease Surveillance: A Crumbling Foundation," *Science*, April 15, 1994; National Center for Infectious Diseases, *Addressing Emerging Infectious Disease Threats: A Prevention Strategy for the United States* (Atlanta, Ga.: Centers for Disease Control and Prevention, 1994).

LANDMINES PROLIFERATE (pages 132–33)

1. Robert Semeniuk, Cooperation Canada–Mozambique, "Landmines and Other Observations in Mozambique," as posted in the APC electronic conference igc:disarm.landmin on December 14, 1995.
2. Kenneth Anderson, Director, The Arms Project of Human Rights Watch, Statement before the U.S. Senate Apropriations Committee, Subcommittee on Foreign Operations, Hearing on the Global Landmine Crisis, Washington, D.C., May 13, 1994.
3. United Nations, "UNHCR Calls for International Ban on Land Mines," press release, May 26, 1994.
4. Human Rights Watch/Arms Project and Physicians for Human Rights, *Landmines: A Deadly Legacy* (New York: Human Rights Watch,

1993).

5. United Nations, General Assembly, "Assistance in Mine Clearance. Report of the Secretary-General," New York, September 6, 1994.

6. Saferworld, "Controlling Anti Personnel Mines: The Inhumane Weapons Convention Review Conference and Beyond," London, July 1995.

7. United Nations, op. cit. note 5.

8. Afghanistan from European Parliament, "Report of the Committee on Development and Cooperation on Anti-Personnel Landmines: A Murderous Impediment to Development," Brussels, June 21, 1995.

9. James Grant, Executive Director, UNICEF, and Cyrus Vance and Herbert A. Okun, Statements before the Hearing on the Global Landmine Crisis, Washington, D.C., May 13, 1994.

10. United Nations, op. cit. note 5.

11. Ibid.

12. Ibid.

13. A U.S. employee of the International Rescue Committee became a mine victim in December 1993. In the first two years after the accident, medical treatment for him cost $250,000. Christopher S. Wren, "Everywhere, Weapons that Keep on Killing," *New York Times*, October 8, 1995.

14. European Parliament, op. cit. note 8.

15. Human Rights Watch/Arms Project and Physicians for Human Rights, op. cit. note 4.

16. Ibid.

17. United Nations, op. cit. note 5; John Battersby, "Gingerly Steps Toward Demining the Globe," *Christian Science Monitor*, October 5, 1994.

18. Paul Lewis, "Red Cross to Urge U.N. to Adopt a Complete Ban on Land Mines," *New York Times*, February 28, 1994; Wren, op. cit. note 13.

19. Gregory Quinn, "The Iraq Conflict," in Michael Cranna, ed., *The True Cost of Conflict* (London: Earthscan Publications, 1994).

20. United Nations, "United Nations Secretary-General Calls High-Level International Meeting on Global Land-Mine Crisis," background note, New York, July 5–7, 1995.

21. United Nations, op. cit. note 5.

22. United Nations, "International Meeting on Mine Clearance Ends in Geneva, Recommends Range of Humanitarian Action," press release, Geneva, July 13, 1995.

23. Ibid.

24. United Nations, op. cit. note 5.

25. *CCW News* (Newsletter of the International Campaign to Ban Landmines), No. 6, October 13, 1995, and No. 7, January 15, 1996, as posted in the APC electronic conference igc:disarm.landmin on October 16, 1995, and January 18, 1996.

26. United Nations, General Assembly, "Moratorium on the Export of Anti-Personnel Land-Mines," New York, December 16, 1993; European Parliament, op. cit. note 8.

27. *Landmines Update*, No. 12 (December 1995), as posted in the APC electronic conference igc:disarm.landmin on December 4, 1995; *CCW News*, January 19, 1996, as posted in the APC electronic conference igc:disarm.landmin on January 24, 1996.

28. *Landmines Update*, op. cit. note 27.

29. Associated Press, "U.N. Land Mine Efforts Fail," January 19, 1996, as posted in the CompuServe AP Online electronic conference. The formal name of the Inhumane Weapons Convention is the Convention on Prohibitions or Restrictions on the Use of Certain Conventional Weapons Which May Be Deemed to Be Excessively Injurious or to Have Indiscriminate Effects. Its cumbersome title is matched by the weakness of its provisions.

30. Battersby, op. cit. note 17.

31. United Nations, op. cit. note 5; U.S. General Accounting Office, *Unexploded Ordnance: A Coordinated Approach to Detection and Clearance Is Needed* (Washington, D.C.: 1995).

32. European Parliament, op. cit. note 8.

VIOLENCE STALKS WOMEN WORLDWIDE (pages 134–35)

1. U.N. Development Programme (UNDP), *Human Development Report 1995* (New York: Oxford University Press, 1995).

2. World Bank, *World Development Report 1993* (New York: Oxford University Press, 1993); Lori L. Heise et al., *Violence Against Women: The Hidden Health Burden*, World Bank Discussion Paper No. 255 (Washington, D.C.: World Bank, 1994).

3. World Bank, op. cit. note 2; UNDP, op. cit. note 1.

4. Heise et al., op. cit. note 2.

5. Ibid.

6. Ibid.

7. World Bank, op. cit. note 2; Heise et al., op. cit. note 2.

8. World Bank, op. cit. note 2; Heise et al., op. cit. note 2.

9. Efua Dorkenoo and Scilla Elworthy, "Female Genital Mutilation," in Miranda Davies, ed., *Women and Violence* (London: Zed Books, 1994); World Bank, op. cit. note 2.

10. United Nations, *The World's Women 1995: Trends and Statistics* (New York: 1995).

11. Ibid.

12. Ibid.

13. United Nations, op. cit. note 10.

14. Lori Heise, Kirsten Moore, and Nahid Toubia, *Sexual Coercion and Reproductive Health* (New York: The Population Council, 1995).

15. Heise et al., op. cit. note 2.

16. Ibid.

17. United Nations, op. cit. note 10.

18. European Community, "Report to European Community Foreign Ministers of the Investigative Mission into the Treatment of Muslim Women in the former Yugoslavia," January 1993.

19. Heise et al., op. cit. note 2.

20. World Bank, op. cit. note 2.

21. Ibid.

22. Lori Heise, "Violence Against Women: Global Organizing for Change," in J. Edleson and Z. Eisikovits, eds., *The Future Intervention with Battered Women and Their Families* (Thousand Oaks, Calif.: Sage Publications, 1996).

23. Lori Heise, Health and Development Policy Project, Washington, D.C., private communication, March 5, 1996.

24. Heise, op. cit. note 22.

25. Heise et al., op. cit. note 2; Heise, op. cit. note 22.

26. "Vienna Declaration and Programme of Action," Report of the World Conference on Human Rights, Vienna, June 1993.

27. Heise et al., op. cit. note 2.

VOTERS TURN OUT IN LARGE NUMBERS (pages 136–37)

1. International Foundation for Electoral Systems (IFES), Washington, D.C., various computer printouts.

2. "Akayev Confident in Kyrgyzstan's First Real Presidential Election," *Washington Times*, December 25, 1995.

3. "Rule by Referendum Comes to Kazakhstan," *New York Times*, April 30, 1995.

4. IFES, computer database, Washington, D.C., private communication, January 19, 1996.

5. Ibid.

6. "Voter Apathy Said Strong, ANC, NP," Foreign Broadcast Information Service—Africa, October 31, 1995.

7. Donatella Lorch, "A Joyful but Anxious Vote in Tanzania," *New York Times*, October 29, 1995.

8. "Statement by Electoral Commission Chairman Judge Lewis MaKame," Foreign Broadcast Information Service—Africa, November 24, 1995.

9. IFES, op. cit. note 4.

10. Ibid.

11. Youssef M. Ibrahim, "Huge Turnout Is Reported by Algerians in Election," *New York Times*, November 17, 1995.

12. "Election Sets Up Tussle for Niger Prime Minister," *New York Times*, January 16, 1995.

13. Howard W. French, "Security Forces, But Few Voters, Take to Streets of Ivory Coast," *New York Times*, October 23, 1995.

14. IFES, "Elections Today: News From the International Foundation for Electoral Systems," Washington, D.C., October 1995.

15. James Rupert, "Belarus Voters' Turnout Blocks President's Plan to Rule Alone," *New York Times*, December 1, 1995; IFES, op. cit. note 4.

16. Rupert, op. cit. note 15.

17. Ibid.

18. IFES, op. cit. note 4.

19. Lee Hockstader, "Russian Turnout Heavy Despite Blizzards, Cynicism and Delays," *New York Times*, December 18, 1995.

20. Ibid.

21. IFES, "Elections Today: News From the International Foundation for Electoral Systems," Washington, D.C., May 1995.

22. Bernard Simon, "Canada Faces Battle for Unity," *Financial Times*, November 1, 1995.

23. Douglas Farah, "Haitian Turnout Light in Vote for President," *New York Times*, December 18, 1995; IFES, op. cit. note 4.

24. Farah, op. cit. note 23.

25. Robert D. Kaplan, "Democracy's Trap," *New York Times*, December 24, 1995.

26. Ibid.

27. Ibid.

28. Harald Muller, Director, Frankfurt Peace Research Institute, private communication, February 1991.

29. Amartya Sen, "The Economics of Life and Death," *Scientific American*, May 1993.

THE VITAL SIGNS SERIES

Some topics are included each year in Vital Signs; *others, particularly those in Part Two, are included only in certain years. The following is a list of the topics covered thus far in the series, with the year or years each appeared indicated in parentheses.*

Part One: KEY INDICATORS

FOOD TRENDS
Grain Production (1992–96)
Soybean Harvest (1992–96)
Meat Production (1992–96)
Fish Catch (1992–96)
Grain Stocks (1992–96)
Grain Used for Feed (1993, 1995–96)
Aquaculture (1994, 1996)

AGRICULTURAL RESOURCE TRENDS
Grain Area (1992–93, 1996)
Fertilizer Use (1992–96)
Irrigation (1992, 1994, 1996)
Grain Yield (1994–95)

ENERGY TRENDS
Oil Production (1992–96)
Wind Power (1992–96)
Nuclear Power (1992–96)
Solar Cell Production (1992–96)
Natural Gas (1992, 1994–96)
Energy Efficiency (1992)
Geothermal Power (1993)

Coal Use (1993–96)
Hydroelectric Power (1993)
Carbon Use (1993)
Compact Fluorescent Lamps (1993–96)

ATMOSPHERIC TRENDS
CFC Production (1992–96)
Global Temperature (1992–96)
Carbon Emissions (1992, 1994–96)

ECONOMIC TRENDS
Global Economy (1992–96)
Third World Debt (1992–95)
International Trade (1993–96)
Steel Production (1993, 1996)
Paper Production (1993, 1994)
Advertising Expeditures (1993)
Roundwood Production (1994)
Gold Production (1994)
Television Use (1995)

TRANSPORTATION TRENDS
Bicycle Production (1992–96)
Automobile Production (1992–96)
Air Travel (1993)

ENVIRONMENTAL TRENDS
Pesticide Resistance (1994)
Sulfur and Nitrogen Emissions (1994–96)
Environmental Treaties (1995)
Nuclear Waste (1995)

SOCIAL TRENDS
Population Growth (1992–96)
Cigarette Smoking (1992–96)
Infant Mortality (1992)
Child Mortality (1993)

Refugees (1993–96)
HIV/AIDS Incidence (1994–96)
Immunizations (1994)
Urbanization (1995–96)

MILITARY TRENDS
Military Expenditures (1992)
Nuclear Arsenal (1992, 1994–96)
Arms Trade (1994)
Peace Expenditures (1994–96)
Wars (1995)

Part Two: SPECIAL FEATURES

ENVIRONMENTAL FEATURES
Bird Populations (1992, 1994)
Forest Loss (1992, 1994-96)
Soil Erosion (1992, 1995)
Steel Recycling (1992, 1995)
Nuclear Waste (1992)
Water Scarcity (1993)
Forest Damage from Air Pollution (1993)
Marine Mammal Populations (1993)
Paper Recycling (1994)
Coral Reefs (1994)
Energy Productivity (1994)
Amphibian Populations (1995)
Large Dams (1995)
Water Tables (1995)
Lead in Gasoline (1995)
Aquatic Species (1996)
Environmental Treaties (1996)

AGRICULTURAL FEATURES
Pesticide Control (1996)
Organic Farming (1996)

ECONOMIC FEATURES
Wheat/Oil Exchange Rate (1992, 1993)
Trade in Arms and Grain (1992)

Cigarette Taxes (1993, 1995)
U.S. Seafood Prices (1993)

SOCIAL FEATURES
Income Distribution (1992, 1995)
Maternal Mortality (1992)
Access to Family Planning (1992)
Literacy (1993)
Fertility Rates (1993)
Traffic Accidents (1994)
Life Expectancy (1994)
Women in Politics (1995)
Computer Production and Use (1995)
Breast and Prostate Cancer (1995)
Homelessness (1995)
Hunger (1995)
Access to Safe Water (1995)
Infectious Diseases (1996)
Landmines (1996)
Violence Against Women (1996)
Voter Turnouts (1996)

MILITARY FEATURES
Nuclear Arsenal (1993)
U.N. Peacekeeping (1993)

Now you can import all the tables and graphs from *Vital Signs 1996* and all other Worldwatch publications into your spreadsheet program, presentation software, or word processor with the . . .

1996 WORLDWATCH DATABASE DISK

The Worldwatch Database Disk gives you current data from all Worldwatch publications, including the *State of the World* and *Vital Signs* annual book series, *World Watch* magazine, Worldwatch papers, and Environmental Alert series books.

The disk covers trends from mid-century onward . . . much not readily available from other sources. All data are sourced, and are accurate, comprehensive, and up-to-date. Researchers, professors, reporters, and policy analysts use the disk to—

- Design graphs to illustrate newspaper stories and policy reports
- Prepare overhead projections on trends for policy briefings, board meetings, and corporate presentation.
- Create specific "what if?" scenarios for energy, population, or grain supply
- Overlay one trend onto another, to see how they relate
- Track long-term trends and discern new ones

Order the 1996 Worldwatch Database Disk for just $89 plus $4 shipping and handling. To order by credit card (Mastercard, Visa or American Express), call 1-800-555-2028, or fax to (202) 296-7365. Our e-mail address is wwpub@worldwatch.org. You can also order by sending your check or credit card information to:

WORLDWATCH INSTITUTE
1776 Massachusetts Ave., N.W.
Washington, D.C. 20036